AMERICAN
PRAVDA

MY FIGHT FOR TRUTH
IN THE ERA OF FAKE NEWS

JAMES O'KEEFE

ALL
POINTS
BOOKS

Dedicated to the memory of James E. O'Keefe Sr.

who built things out of nothing,

who was told,

"it can't be done,"

but who did it anyway.

www.allpointsbooks.com

The Library of Congress Cataloging-in-Publication Data
is available upon request.

ISBN 978-1-250-15464-4 (hardcover)
ISBN 978-1-250-15465-1 (ebook)

Our books may be purchased in bulk for promotional, educational, or business use. Please contact your local bookseller or the Macmillan Corporate and Premium Sales Department at 1-800-221-7945, extension 5442, or by email at MacmillanSpecialMarkets@macmillan.com.

First Edition: January 2018

10 9 8 7 6 5 4 3 2 1

AMERICAN
PRAVDA

And Jeffrey Wigand, who's out on a limb, does he go on television and tell the truth? Yes. Is it newsworthy? Yes. Are we going to air it? Of course not. Why? Because he's not telling the truth? No. Because he is telling the truth. That's why we're not going to air it. And the more truth he tells, the worse it gets.

—Al Pacino as *60 Minutes* producer
Lowell Bergman in *The Insider*, 1999

The press has become the greatest power within the Western countries, more powerful than the legislative power, the executive, and the judiciary. And one would then like to ask: by what law has it been elected and to whom is it responsible?

—Aleksandr Solzhenitsyn,
Harvard commencement address, 1978

Contents

Meeting Citizen Trump

r. Trump will see you now," said a secretary, one of several moving around the outer office, each better looking than the last. I was ushered in. The view of Central Park beyond was pretty overwhelming, especially for an everyday guy like me from New Jersey. Trump smiled and stood to greet me.

"That pimp and hooker thing you did, wow!" said Trump. "That was incredible." He turned to Sam Nunberg, the Republican consultant who arranged the meeting, "They shut down ACORN!" I was flattered that he took our work seriously, but he did not agree to this meeting to sing my praises. He was a man with a plan. In 2011, Trump generated a lot of publicity—or, what they call in the business, "earned media"—when he challenged President Obama's birth certificate. Although virtually all of the press was negative, Trump positioned himself in the public eye as the president's equal, someone Obama had to take seriously. When I saw this play out, I could see in Trump a kindred spirit, someone who understood the media establishment and knew how to play it against itself. In 2012, Trump flirted with a presidential run but did not pursue it.

In 2013, Obama still interested him. From what I gathered that day, Trump was not a "birther," never was. He was confident Obama was born in the United States, but he suspected Obama had presented himself as a foreign student on application materials to ease his way into New York's Columbia University, maybe even Harvard too, and perhaps picked up a few scholarships along the way. Trump had reason to believe Obama was capable of this kind of mischief. In May 2012,

Breitbart News unearthed a promotional booklet produced in 1991 by Obama's literary agency at the time, Acton & Dystel. In the booklet, Obama claimed to have been "born in Kenya and raised in Indonesia and Hawaii."[1]

"This was nothing more than a fact checking error by me—an agency assistant at the time," said agent Miriam Goderich in response. "There was never any information given to us by Obama in any of his correspondence or other communications suggesting in any way that he was born in Kenya and not Hawaii."[2] Indeed, Goderich admitted to writing the sentence about Kenya but never stated where she got the idea in the first place. Beyond America's newsrooms, people doubted Goderich's explanation, but those newsrooms aborted the story in the womb. They did that often. In 2013, Obama's Columbia records remained sealed. Trump was hoping my colleagues and I might take an interest in finding out what mysteries those records held.

"Nobody else can get this information. Do you think you could get inside Columbia?" As I explained, that was not exactly our line of work. We were journalists, not private eyes. But Trump does not give up easily. For at least half an hour, even though there were others in the room more important—Citizens United's David Bossie among them—he spoke to me as if Project Veritas were the only thing in the world worth talking about. I have heard the same said of Bill Clinton, but I can vouch for Trump's charisma.

Trump has a thing for magazine covers. Framed covers lined the office walls, and stacks of magazines with his image on them piled up on his desk. Yes, this was a man who knew a thing or two about earned media. Trump would ride that media, good and bad, as far as it could take him, earning by some estimates as much as $5 billion in free publicity during the election.[3] His advisors told him he could not win on earned media, and he proved them wrong. "Media is everything," Andrew Breitbart often reminded me, and Trump would prove him right.

At the end of our discussion, Trump shook my hand, encouraged me to keep up the good work, and half-whispered, "Do Columbia." He then posed for a photo with me in front of a framed copy of a *Playboy* magazine from 1990. I had earlier shown him a *Playboy* from 2011 in which my name was mentioned on the cover: "The Dirty Tricks of James O'Keefe." Trump one-upped me. As he told me, he was "the rare guy whose *picture* had been on the cover." It was that cover we posed in front of.

Trump had Keith Schiller, a tall, tough-looking guy with close-cropped white hair, escort me out. A former NYPD detective and Trump's security director at the time, Schiller would follow Trump to the White House. It was Schiller who got the nod to go to LA and fire FBI honcho James Comey. If you met Schiller, you would understand why Trump sent him. He is pure, understated Alpha. Picture the character Mike in *Breaking Bad*. His instruction this time was to take me to the Trump store and give me however many ties I wanted to take away. Ties were apparently the currency of the realm. On leaving Trump Tower with my booty of ties, it never crossed my mind that one day Trump would be president. I did think, however, he could make one hell of an ally.

As the events of 2016 proved, Trump and I had something fundamental in common, not so much a shared ideology as a shared adversary. At Project Veritas, we take no real position on issues beyond free speech and honest government, and in 2016, let alone in 2013, who even knew what Trump's ideology was. Historian Victor Davis Hanson accurately describes President Trump as "a *reflection* of, not a catalyst for," the widespread anti-statist, anti-globalist resentment that got him elected.[4] The adversary we shared was a powerful one, what might well be called the deep state–media complex. Although the media could exist without the deep state, the deep state could not exist without the media. By exposing the waste, fraud, and abuse of the administrative state, we inevitably disrupt the media's relationship with government and organizations that work with government. Like Trump, Project Veritas is a disruptor. If we have an ideology, it is less "conservative" than anti-statist, anti–status quo.

In their 1988 book *Manufacturing Consent*, Edward Herman and Noam Chomsky anticipated a showdown like the one that played out in the campaign of 2016. By 1988, the dominant mass-media outlets were all large, powerful corporations. Although restricted in some ways by their own ideological blinders, the authors made some useful observations, accurately describing the establishment media "as effective and powerful ideological institutions that carry out a system-supportive propaganda function, by reliance on market forces, internalized assumptions, and self-censorship and without overt coercion."[5] If Chomsky and Herman erred, it was in thinking that the deep state would inevitably skew right. It has not.

In the way of evidence, Donald Trump pulled just 4 percent of the vote in the District of Columbia. In the more affluent neighborhoods—those home to the lobbyists, journalists, contractors, intelligence officers, and high-level bureaucrats who comprise the deep state—Trump fared scarcely better than he had in the poorer ones. In no precinct, not even the most posh, did he secure more than 15 percent of the vote.[6]

Some say that the real difference between the dominant American media and the old Soviet *Pravda* is that the Russian people knew they were being lied to. The fact that *Pravda* is the Russian word for "truth" fooled almost no one. When Russians heard the word *Pravda,* they heard "power." They had little choice but to go along with the lies at least publicly, but privately they rejected them and, very privately, they joked about them.

Pravda was allowed to deceive because no force in the Soviet Union could stop it. The *New York Times* and its media allies and imitators continue to mislead or deceive their audiences for much the same reason. Up until November 2016, no force could stop them either. In the months since, they have done everything in their power to prove that 2016 was a mistake. Indeed, they openly seek to reverse it, and they may yet succeed.

To be sure, there are profound differences between *Pravda* and the major media: the former was denied any freedom; the latter gave theirs away. Famed Russian dissident Aleksandr Solzhenitsyn experienced both. "Nothing is forbidden," he observed of the American media in his provocative 1978 speech at Harvard, "but what is not fashionable will hardly ever find its way into periodicals or books or be heard in colleges." In 1978, fatalist that he was, Solzhenitsyn could not have anticipated how self-censorship for the sake of fashion would harden into statist dogma.

Inevitably, there will be a gap between the way the world is and the way the journalist presents that world. Human nature intrudes. What is not inevitable is that the gap should widen. With the introduction of the internet and new recording technology, the gap between the real and the reported ought to be narrowing. As all parties agree, it is not. The new technologies have democratized news reporting, but the major media, panicked by their loss of control, reject or simply ignore sources that challenge their desired narrative. Having chosen a narrative, they will pound away at it even if it seems to be leading nowhere, believed by few, laughed at by many, as CNN has done with its Russia reporting. If need be, the media and their deep state allies will punish those who thwart their largely shared agenda.

Innocence of Muslims producer Nakoula Basseley Nakoula, now known as Mark Basseley Youssef, can attest to the consequences of countering the deep state narrative. His was the amateurish video that allegedly prompted the assault on the American consulate in Benghazi. Although he was a citizen exercising his First Amendment rights, Obama officials buried Youssef in a Texas prison on a hastily processed parole violation to help sell their lie. The media said nary a word in protest.

In cases like Benghazi, when the major media narrative does not reflect reality, citizens find themselves yelling at their TV sets or giving up on mainstream news altogether. Ultimately, they are forced to choose between what the major media report or what their experience shows them. This is where the new alternative media come into play. These media have been accused of indoctrinating their audience or even deceiving them, but that is not how they succeed.

The alternative media succeed by clarifying and confirming the audience's reality. With the help of alternative journalists, many of them without establishment credentials, citizens can see more of the world more clearly than they ever could before. They have had enough of the major media's misrepresentations, omissions, lies, and journalistic agenda to appreciate the truth when they see it. Importantly too, when they see the truth, the internet gives them the wherewithal to confront the lies. "All that is necessary for the triumph of evil," Edmund Burke reportedly said, "is for good men to do nothing." In the age of the internet, there is no excuse for doing nothing.

I started out as one those citizens yelling at the news, in my case the *New York Times*. As a student at Rutgers University in the early years of this century, I was particularly troubled by the way the *Times* filtered information through the prism of political correctness, a phenomenon that Professor Angelo Codevilla sees as no less than a "war against nature's law and its limits."[7] In nature, I would argue, we receive information by way of our senses. The gift of reason enables us to filter this information through our own experiences and the collective wisdom of our past, which together constitute common sense.

Victor Davis Hanson describes the resulting "truth" as "empirical, hushed and accepted informally by ordinary people from what they see and hear on the ground."[8] The competing truth, Hanson argues, the one "voiced on the news and by the government," is "often abstract and theoretical." Too often the media today ask us to disregard our senses, reject reason, and accept a theoretical construct of events that defies common sense and conforms to a prewritten script. Unfortunately, as I came to see, where the *Times* goes, the other media almost inevitably follow.

To compensate, I started my own newspaper, the *Centurion*. When the PC prism distorted reality, my goal was to straighten it out. Having been born in 1984—prophetic, huh?—I came along just at the time newspapers were losing traction and video was taking hold. It was at Rutgers that I first sensed the power of undercover video. One of my guiding lights, at least in terms of strategy, was Saul Alinsky, celebrated author of *Rules for Radicals*. Troubled by Rutgers speech codes, my pals and I decided to pull an Alinsky on the administrators and force them to "live up to their own book of rules."

"Ancestry" was one of the sensitivities protected by the speech codes. Given my Irish roots, I felt I had as much right to be microaggressed as anyone else on campus. So on St. Patrick's Day 2005, I and my coconspirators arranged a sit-down with the hapless Rutgers dining hall administrator, video discreetly rolling throughout our meeting.

The fellow serving as our "personal advisor" informed the woman that we "had some unpleasant and uncomfortable experiences in the dining halls." What made me uncomfortable, I explained, was that "the dining halls here at Rutgers serve Lucky Charms." I showed the poor woman the box and recounted my personal angst over "the negative stereotypes of Irish Americans" reflected in the leprechaun imagery. How we managed to do this with straight faces I still don't know.

For the flak catchers at Rutgers it was pure lose-lose: either they slight the feelings of a "marginalized" ethnic minority or they ban Lucky Charms from the dining hall. The administrators chose the safer of the two options. They got rid of the Lucky Charms. We posted the video on YouTube and watched the counter go nuts. I saw immediately that video had a viral power that print simply did not have.

This book will document the transformation in the media, in part through my observations of the world at large and in my part through my own struggles, occasionally brutal, with the forces of media and government. As I hope to make clear, the deep state–media complex and its supporters still have not come to grips with this transformation. As a case in point, in early 2017 they helped push *1984* to the top of the bestseller list as therapy, as a way of making sense of Trump's ascension. What they failed to understand was that Orwell was writing about them. "They" are the "Party," the ones who deny that reality is something "objective, external, existing in its own right," the ones who insist others remain equally blind. "The Party told you to reject the evidence of your eyes and ears," observed protagonist Winston Smith. "It was their final, most essential command."[9]

Consider, for instance, the case of my friend David Daleiden. He and his group, Center for Medical Progress, spent more than a year recording undercover video at Planned Parenthood clinics across the country. In perhaps his most shocking video, a young clinician picks through a tray of body parts pulled from a "fetal cadaver"—a heart, a lung, a brain—and discusses the market value of each.[10] Daleiden recorded this during a long unedited segment. The images were so shocking and shifted the public consciousness so much they prompted Hillary Clinton to concede, "I have seen the pictures from them and obviously find them disturbing."[11] Admitted Clinton's campaign chair John Podesta in a leaked email, "The tapes do hurt."[12]

The major media, however, refused to show the videos. Planned Parenthood took advantage of the void and redefined the contents of the videos for those who failed to watch them online. *Since faked criminal videos hit, politicians in 24 states have tried to cut patients' access to Planned Parenthood,* Planned Parenthood tweeted.[13] That was the official party line, and they were sticking to it: Daleiden's videos, like ours, they said, were "faked." Friendly prosecutors in California and Texas saw to it that they were "criminal" as well, arresting Daleiden under various pretenses. Hillary quickly rejected the evidence of her eyes and ears. And the media chose to ignore what millions of ordinary Americans had undeniably seen.

Undercover video has enabled citizens to reopen their eyes and ears. We prove visually—cinema verité—that the statist narratives citizens are fed are often false. Our visuals pressure the media and political class to realign their selectively edited narrative with the inarguable reality we present. Technology is facilitating a sea change in the consciousness of America. We take the filters off. An educated, free people do not need them. We have enough faith in our fellow citizens to believe that once exposed to *veritas* they can make sound decisions for a great, lasting, and moral society.

For their *veritas,* Solzhenitsyn and other Russians turned to the *Samizdat,* real news and authentic literature copied by whatever means available and circulated at no small risk. At Project Veritas, we are a proud part of the American *Samizdat.* We have literally millions of allies sitting in front of computer screens across America fact-checking major media stories and adding new information when they find it. If no force can stop the dominant media, we can at least challenge them. Unlike *Pravda* or the *Times,* our truth is not protected by power. Our truth is *tested* by power on a daily basis. We cannot afford to be wrong.

Defining the Veritas Journalist

The goal of Project Veritas is to show the world as closely as possible the way the world really is. In the twenty-first century, sharing reality is a great way to make enemies, especially if that reality reflects badly on the people in power. From the major media's perspective, our exposure of corruption is often perceived as more of a problem than the corruption itself.

In the not too distant past, however, exposure of bad behavior used to be role of all journalists. As late as the mid-twentieth century, the media landscape was peppered with independent folk heroes who could not be bought or sold. Those reporters, a vanishing breed, would on occasion use whatever means necessary to get at the unvarnished truth, even if it meant using deception to peel back the curtain hiding it. Said veteran urban journalist Ken Auletta, "The journalist's job is to get the story by breaking into their offices, by bribing, by seducing people, by lying, by anything else to break through that palace guard."[1] For a generation or so—perhaps since *and because of* Watergate—everything has changed.

This book will expose the major media's decaying ethics and show that the election was an inflection point in media history, what the managing director of CBS Digital alluded to in saying that the media corporations exhibited "a profound lack of empathy in the service of endless posturing." To lay the foundation for this journey, I hope to show who we are at Project Veritas and what we do. In the process, I will:

- define journalism;
- explain that *real journalism* is America's last saving grace;
- define what is required to do this type of journalism;
- explain that information-gathering should be understood as an activity, not an identity;
- show that Project Veritas has had more direct public policy impact than any comparable entity in the twenty-first century;
- confront specific objections raised against Project Veritas;
- communicate how the media is profoundly guilty of the very sins it lodges against us while sharing few of the virtues;
- detail the techniques in practice;
- reveal the consequences of doing our type of work.

Not everyone has forgotten the spirit of the New Journalism of Tom Wolfe and others, the Pulitzer Prize–winning stings of the *Chicago Sun-Times*, the means-ends analysis of troublemaker Saul Alinsky, and the life-imperiling documentation of *Samizdat* writers like Aleksandr Solzhenitsyn. These are our influences, our guides. We envision our work not as a radical departure from traditional journalism but as a restoration of the same.

What Is Journalism?

"We are what we repeatedly do"; so said Aristotle or at least his interpreters. News-gathering is an act protected by the First Amendment. In that the amendment empowers all citizens to gather news whether they went to J-school or not, it follows that journalism is better seen as an activity rather than as an identity. Establishment journalists, however, cling to their *identity* as journalists. Their friends in government have gone so far as to initiate legislation to protect that status.

Senator Dick Durbin wrote, "We must define a journalist and the constitutional statutory protections those journalists should receive."[2] Senator Charles Schumer introduced a bill that sought to define a "covered journalist" through the Orwellian sounding "Free Flow of Information Act" (S.987).[3] This bill would strip the First Amendment rights of information-gatherers who did not meet Schumer's definition.

The definition runs 270 words long and is loaded with arbitrary bench-marks, tenure requirements, and willfully vague language specifying who exactly is covered. The obvious intent of this bill is to protect the mainstream media cartel and their cronies in government from those of us without credentials, those of us who approach journalism as an *activity*. The deep state does not and cannot trust us.

Actually, anyone with a camera on his or her cell phone can be a journalist. Many times these citizens are more effective because they are closer to the scene of a given event and have less of an agenda than the professionals. When citizen journalism is as organized as it is at Project Veritas, it becomes a threat to the status quo. The estab-lishment demands more accuracy from us than it does from its own credentialed pros. To reinforce their identity, these so-called "pros" dismiss us as "pranksters," "provocateurs," and "hoaxsters." Recently, the *Washington Post* called me a "master of ceremonies" when refer-ring to my anchor role on a video project. No matter. They can call me "SpongeBob SquarePants" if they like. The label does not shape our product, which we take very seriously. So seriously in fact, that we would be willing to go to jail to protect our sources just as any other serious journalist would. Any individual who truthfully informs the public is engaging in the act of journalism.

For a century or more, theorists have been attempting to define the role of the journalist. "There can be no higher law in journalism," said Walter Lippmann, "than to tell the truth and shame the devil."[4] For eth-icist Jeffrey Olen, the journalist's aim was simply to "serve the public's right to know."[5] Investigative reporting, communications expert James Ettema believed, is specifically aimed at exposing matters of importance that "some person or group wants to keep secret."[6] By so doing, the journalist offers the community "an opportunity to test and affirm what is, and what is not, an outrage to the moral order." Ultimately, Ettema argued, the journalist finds success "in unraveling human suffering that hides beneath binds of systemic failures—summoning righteous indignation not merely at the individual tragedy but also at the moral disorder and social breakdowns that the tragedy represents." My friend and mentor Andrew Breitbart described the appropriate attitude of the journalist as "righteous indignation," which was the title of his book.

Ideally, journalists challenge the orthodoxy. If successful, their stories shift what is sometimes called the "Overton Window." While working at the Mackinac Center for Public Policy, Joseph Overton coined the term to describe the range of facts and policies that are viewed as politically acceptable to discuss.[7] Donald Trump pushed that window open wider on the issues of illegal immigration and Islamic terrorism. Although much of the public welcomed the opening, his words inflamed the establishment. Journalists who prod the window open run the same risk. As Ray Bradbury observed in *Fahrenheit 451*, "If you don't want a man unhappy politically, don't give him two sides to a question to worry him; give him one." And that is just what the mainstream media serves up to their audience: one side. The citizen journalist gives them the other.

Why the Veritas Journalist Exists

The mission of Project Veritas is "to investigate and expose institutional waste, fraud, abuse, and other misconduct in order to create a more ethical and transparent society." This is not inherently a political mission. If our objective were to advance a political agenda, as journalists on both sides have admitted doing, we would have to reinforce that agenda time after time with editorial content. We don't. We move on. We do not put words in our subjects' mouths. We cannot create a reality where there is none. If we have any motivation at all, it is to hold the media and administrative state accountable. Not inherently "right wing" or "left wing," we work the opportunities the major media choose to ignore.

No ordinary American advocates for general waste, fraud, and abuse. No politician does either. That does not stop the political class from practicing—indeed perfecting—all of the above. So mired are so many lawmakers and administrators in everyday abuses that the Trumpian word "swamp" seems altogether appropriate to describe the contemporary deep state. For many of the swamp dwellers, the Constitution is not a guide but an obstacle. Without the journalist's external light—and lots of light day after day, night after night—the swamp will not be drained.

The Claremont Institute's Michael Uhlmann describes well how the swamp has come to be. "A newer breed has come to dominate Congress, which now sees its self-interest less in legislating than in delegating legislative authority to departments and agencies," he writes. "Such members console themselves with the thought, which is only sometimes true, that if a particular agency steps on a favored constituency's toes, they can always intervene, while collecting campaign contributions from lobbyists benefiting from that intervention."[8]

Political author Charles Murray sees the swamp as deep and stagnant. "Restoration of limited government is not going to happen by winning presidential elections and getting the right people appointed to the Supreme Court," he writes in *By the People*. Our government, he believes, has slipped into an "advanced state of institutional sclerosis." Our legal system, he adds, has become "lawless" and "systemically corrupt."[9]

Electing Republicans to Congress is no more likely to drain the swamp than electing Democrats. Both parties prefer the muck pretty much as is. It is in most everyone's self-interest to maintain a political apparatus that keeps his or her portfolio growing year after year. Without external pressure, the state will remain deep and swampy. That pressure has to come from citizens. Citizens must create new counterweights to expose the corruption within. For reasons I will explain later, they can no longer count on the mainstream media to help. Charles Murray argues that one solution is civil disobedience. Another solution, our solution, is investigative journalism.

The Project Veritas journalist has a profound faith in the power of a free people to make their own decisions regarding what is best for them and their families and, in the process, to create a great, lasting, and moral society. Public policy solutions become self-evident when the people in a democratic republic have access to unfiltered information.

Our vision stands in stark contrast to the de facto vision of the mainstream media that detest a free people. They would say, "Pay no attention to the man behind the curtain!" They prefer to spoon-feed select information and final conclusions to the public rather than to provide individuals the raw information required to reach conclusions on their own. Instead of "news," their audiences get relentless punditry, editorializing, and politically loaded programming. Post-election, for instance, the focus on Russia and identity politics in particular eroded the canons of journalism and devolved into near mania.

To put pressure on the media and their deep state allies, we shock them with reality—cinema verité. Done well, cinema verité has the capacity to breach what Ettema and Theodore Glasser call "the threshold of outrage."[10] Our medium is video, usually undercover, supplemented and distributed by the people's media, by the internet. We gather the information guerilla-style and distribute it the same way. This allows us to bypass traditional establishment channels and take our product directly to the people. You will see how this plays out in our (exciting!) account of the 2016 election campaign.

The Results

One defining characteristic of a journalist is that he or she gets results. Seymour Hersh single-handedly broke the story of the My Lai massacre. Woodward and Bernstein helped force President Nixon out of office. *Rolling Stone*'s Michael Hastings got Gen. Stanley McChrystal to resign. These results were impressive and lauded. "Great reporters exude a certain kind of electricity," *Rolling Stone*'s Will Dana said of Hastings.[11]

Given the historic respect for results-oriented journalism, I will argue that the media's generalized contempt for the work of citizen journalists, ours in particular, is pure hypocrisy. As much respect as I have for some of these journalists, even a few still in the field, I am unable to identify any journalistic entity in the last ten years whose work has had more immediate impact on more corrupt individuals or organizations than Project Veritas. Today, journalists are rewarded not for challenging the establishment but for reinforcing it.

In 2009, CBS's Katie Couric won the esteemed Cronkite Award for her "extraordinary, persistent and detailed multi-part interviews with Republican vice-presidential candidate Sarah Palin."[12] No, she won the award by badgering Sarah Palin about what newspapers she read. That is how flippant journalism has become in the twenty-first century.

At Project Veritas, we hold—at the risk of being targeted by our government—that skewering the sacred cows (and pigs) that feed off the administrative state is a far more worthy pastime for a journalist.

Our critics can say what they will about Project Veritas, but they cannot deny we get results. In less than ten years, with undercover video as our primary medium, we have been able to accomplish the following:

- Project Veritas video evidence prompted Congress to propose and pass, and President Obama to sign, legislation defunding the corrupt $2 billion community organizing cartel known as ACORN. This came to pass in 2009 while Democrats controlled both Houses of Congress.
- Project Veritas video evidence forced the termination of two top NPR executives, including a CEO, and inspired the House of Representatives to cut NPR funding.
- A Project Veritas video empowered Senator John McCain to grill Department of Homeland Security representatives about border security, referring to our work.
- Project Veritas video evidence forced New Hampshire to change voting laws twice, once in 2012 and again in 2016. The state now requires photo ID and in-state residency to vote.
- Project Veritas video evidence prompted overriding vetoes of legislation by the governor who sought our prosecution in New Hampshire.
- Project Veritas video evidence forced resignations of Medicaid staff in Ohio, Virginia, and Maine and inspired widespread worker retraining in entitlement programs.
- Project Veritas video evidence inspired Texas to open criminal investigations into voter fraud and prompted reactions from the attorney general and governor.
- Project Veritas video evidence inspired Virginia to change voter laws after catching a congressman's son in the act of encouraging fraud.
- Project Veritas video evidence exposed a New York City election board commissioner acknowledging widespread voter fraud,

leading to calls for his resignation by officials who did not want the truth to be told.

- Project Veritas video evidence forced the termination of three Common Core executives.
- Project Veritas video evidence exposing discussion of an illegal PAC (political action committee) prompted a Republican campaign treasurer to resign and the Republican state senate president Mike Ellis to drop out of a senate race.
- Project Veritas video evidence exposed teacher union mischief in several states leading to multiple terminations and investigations. Inspector generals in New York backed up our reports.
- Project Veritas video evidence forced the suspension and termination of four Obamacare navigators and led to defunding of the navigators program in Texas.
- Project Veritas video evidence caused the termination of two high-level Democratic operatives during the 2016 presidential campaign and was credited with shifting the momentum in the campaign. The videos were seen at least 22 million times in October 2016. Both Trump and Hillary Clinton discussed the videos in the final presidential debate.
- Project Veritas video evidence forced the Wisconsin attorney general to reopen a criminal investigation into voter fraud during the 2016 presidential election.
- Project Veritas video evidence enabled the FBI to arrest and convict three DisruptJ20 operatives in a criminal plot to put butyric acid in the ventilation system of the National Press Club.
- Project Veritas video evidence caused CNN major embarrassment by showing its staff ridiculing CNN's own "Russia" coverage. The video prompted the deputy press secretary of the United States to "urge everyone to watch the videos."

The above is just a partial list. The fraud, lies, and criminal behavior we have uncovered have been so outrageous and the legislative consequences so undeniable that the mainstream media have been forced to pay heed, if not respect. In 2017, the *Washington Post* wrote of our DisruptJ20 investigation, "To O'Keefe, who for years has tar-geted liberal groups with undercover stings, the arrest validates his group and its controversial methods."[13] Said ABC's George Stepha-nopoulos of an earlier sting, "An undercover upstart has dealt a major blow to the establishment."[14]

Writing for the *Nation* in a piece posted on the CBS News site, vot-ing rights activist Brentin Mock described the effect of our journalism on the voter fraud debate as "jarring." This compliment was about as left-handed as compliments get, but Mock at least admitted the obvi-ous. "When you hear activists and state senators say we need voter ID laws because of voter fraud, instead of citing data, or even anecdotes, lately they've been citing O'Keefe." Mock referred to a poll in which 64 percent of respondents registered their belief that voter fraud exists, and he attributed that high a number to "people like O'Keefe."[15]

Mock overstates our effectiveness. We did not carve out a new area of citizen interest. We confirmed suspicions. Through their own experience, many Americans had sensed something amiss at the polls. Despite their ample resources, the major media have almost univer-sally refused to investigate this problem. Worse, they have routinely slighted or smeared those reporters who have been documenting voter fraud for decades. Our videos could not be dismissed that easily.

Our more cynical supporters fret that some of these groups we investigate may get defunded but will just form again under some new banner. That may be true, but our objective is not to get groups defunded. Our objective is to expose wrongdoing. I list these successes to show what journalism, as *activity,* can accomplish. The best way for us to address the concern that our results are transitory is to pro-duce more videos, produce them more frequently, and to encourage other citizen journalists to do the same. In the viper pit that is politics, corruption will regenerate like a snakeskin. That does not take away from the fact that our videos help facilitate the legislative and judicial process. As the *Washington Post* likes to tell itself, democracy dies in darkness. We agree. Without the light journalists shine, the legislative process sputters, stalls, even dies. In the words of Irish statesman John Philpot Curran, "The condition upon which God hath given liberty to man is eternal vigilance."[16] That's our job, eternal vigilance. This is the job of all of us, eternal vigilance. The solution to the problem of waste, fraud, and abuse is to press on, eternal vigilance.

How Project Veritas Confronts Its Detractors

Those familiar with our work *only* through the major media may not know of our accomplishments, but there are likely several things they *do* know, most of which are at best marginally true, and some are downright false. Mainstream journalists repeat these charges so consistently that we have taken to playing a sort of BS Media Bingo when we review what they report about our work. We check the appropriate box when each accusation appears: uses deception, selectively edits, degrades public discourse, convicted of a criminal act, sued for invasion of privacy. Keep in mind when reading these criticisms that the media are often as guilty or more guilty of the very charges they level against us.

"Project Veritas uses deception to gain access!"

Perhaps the most fundamental charge we face is that we use undercover video. "The techniques employed by O'Keefe and his associates, [journalists] say, fall far outside journalistic norms," wrote Paul Farhi in the *Washington Post* a day after our videos forced the termination of two high-level operatives in the 2016 Clinton campaign.[17] We hear this all the time, but using deception to get information out of people is hardly a new methodology. As you will see in a subsequent chapter, journalists have been using this technique for more than a century. Indeed, *60 Minutes* built its brand using deception. Just as *60 Minutes* and others have done, we act the part required to cover the subjects of our investigations. Acting the part is a means of obtaining access. With access, we can report the truth about what the subject is saying or doing when the public isn't looking, as well as discovering who else is involved.

As we all know from our own experiences, what public figures say from the podium is often quite the opposite of what they say in private. So, too, for what they do in public versus what they do in private. No revelation there. CNN's Alisyn Camerota once complained of this reality when she remarked about a Project Veritas sting: "Erica Garner was caught on tape not knowing she was being videotaped." In an unwitting defense of Project Veritas, cohost Chris Cuomo replied, "Well, sometimes that's when you're the most honest." Cuomo's words would come back to haunt him, but we will see more about that in our chapter on CNN.

When the police tried to bluff George Zimmerman with the possibility that the fatal shooting of Trayvon Martin had been recorded on camera, he replied, "I prayed to God that someone videotaped it." Those most vulnerable to the honest presentation of video are those of all political stripes whose existence is rooted in hypocrisy and illogic, especially those who have been protected by the major media for so long they have neglected to protect themselves.

Here is the key distinction between the Project Veritas journalist and establishment reporters: while we use deception to gain access, we never deceive our audience. Traditional journalists who simply report what their subject tells them may not deceive the subject, but they often deceive their audience. When they tilt questions to their subject to produce a desired result, they doubly deceive their audience. Then, too, there is the traditional journalist's technique of choosing people to interview that they assume will support their "scripted news."

"Project Veritas 'deceptively' edits footage."

In almost every case, the media find some way *not* to address the conversations caught on camera in the videos. If they cannot attack the facts, they attack the methodology. If they cannot attack the methodology, they attack the premise. If they cannot attack the premise, they attack the journalist. If they cannot attack the journalist, they often write off the evidence as some sort of a nutty conspiracy and ignore it.

In our experience, the media prefer to seize on some tangential detail to circumvent the focal point of these investigations. One criticism, as noted, is that we employ deception. A second is that we deceptively edit the videos we record. Without any evidence, the major media routinely call into question our editing. The first major allegation of deceptive editing came at the beginning of my career during the ACORN investigation. Some will remember that ACORN was a powerful, well-funded community-organizing cartel that engaged in any number of illegal and unethical activities from shaking down businesses to stealing votes. Worse, ACORN did it largely on the public dime. Indeed, there were reportedly billions set aside for ACORN in Barack Obama's 2009 stimulus program.[18]

My partner in the ACORN project, Hannah Giles, had been made aware of the organization's dark heart and signed on to help me expose it. By this time I had already formulated what would become Project Veritas's operating philosophy: *Content is king. Without strong content, nothing else matters.*

I sometimes describe Project Veritas's style as one-third intelligence operation, one-third investigative reporting, and one-third *Borat.* For those who may not remember, *Borat* was a 2006 quasi-documentary starring Sacha Baron Cohen as Borat, a fictitious journalist from Kazakhstan. Borat wanders across America having oddball encounters with people who think he's for real. This movie is better seen than explained, but those who have viewed it will know why I reference it. In the early days of Project Veritas, especially in the ACORN videos, we skewed *Borat.* We have largely moved away from our *Borat* stage, but we embrace our roots proudly.

I first experimented with this style in a sting I had done with the help of formidable pro-life activist Lila Rose, then an eighteen-year-old freshman at UCLA. A little too bold for our own good perhaps, Lila and I took on Planned Parenthood. Lila posed as a fifteen-year-old with me trailing along as her twenty-three-year-old boyfriend. Our goal was to see if the Planned Parenthood office in Los Angeles would offer a fifteen-year-old an illegal abortion and ignore its mandatory reporting duties on a likely statutory rape. The answer was unequivocally "yes."

Our content was strong and undeniable. Without the video, however, Planned Parenthood would have simply denied any such encounter. As we have seen since, its executives now deny even the most undeniable video evidence. "Who are you going to believe, us or your lying eyes?" they might as well have said.

In the *Borat* spirit, I shot some B-roll with me as the rogue boyfriend, edited it all into an MTV-style video, and posted it on YouTube. Planned Parenthood was not at all ready for a guerilla-style assault from young America. Neither were the media. We were supposed to be on their side of the culture war. Dislodged from its safe space, Planned Parenthood overreacted and sent Lila a threatening letter. That letter found its way to Bill O'Reilly. He asked Lila to be on *The O'Reilly Factor* and showed clips from the video on air.[19] Helped by its playful hipness, this video went viral. Just a year out of college with few resources and no useful connections, I found myself on the ground floor of a brand-new medium, looking up and learning as I went.

The ACORN project was a major educational experience. It thrust me fully into the limelight before I was prepared to deal with it. For our establishing shots, I dressed as a garishly over-the-top pimp, and Hannah dressed as a prostitute. We visited six local ACORN offices across the country and asked the operatives if they would help us find housing for our stable of underage Central American sex slaves. In every case but one, they happily obliged us.[20]

The ACORN project had a generous dose of *Borat* about it. My pimp costume and Hannah Giles's casually sexy walk attracted a much broader audience than the average political video could. Always quick with the right metaphor, my friend and mentor Breitbart called our exposé "the Abu Ghraib of the Great Society."[21] It was something everyone could understand and be repelled by. Yes, our video bumper was a bit flashy, but the networks use fancy graphics to grab viewers' attention all the time. The *Daily Show*'s Jon Stewart said about our videos, "It probably cost CNN that much just to turn on their Hologram machine,"[22] and the holograph has no news function beyond creating eye candy for the viewer.

Advising me on the distribution of the resulting videos was Breitbart, a multitasking media marvel. Expecting national ACORN to either deny the content of our first video outright or insist that the corruption at a specific office was an anomaly, he schooled me in the way to release the videos—one at a time. ACORN did exactly as Andrew predicted after the release of our Baltimore video. Once its executives dismissed the video as a one-off, we started dropping the others: Washington, Brooklyn, San Bernardino, Los Angeles. Still not sure what to make of us, the *New York Times* summed up the results of our efforts as follows:

> After the activists' videos came to light and swiftly became fodder for 24-hour cable news coverage, private donations from foundations to Acorn all but evaporated and the federal government quickly distanced itself from the group. The Census Bureau ended its partnership with the organization for this year's census, the Internal Revenue Service dropped Acorn from its Voluntary Income Tax Assistance program, and Congress voted to cut off all grants to the group.[23]

This was not bad for beginners. Given ACORN's powerful alliances, I dare say that many major media outlets have never had this big a score. We had embarrassed ACORN to be sure, but, more problematically for the statists, we embarrassed the dominant media. The media should have exposed this cabal years earlier. Instead, they nurtured it. Their reaction to our efforts ran from uneasy to hostile.

Again, to avoid addressing the conversations caught on camera in the videos, the media charged us with deceptive editing. For our opening sequence, Hannah and I dressed more flamboyantly than we did in our office visits. This was a useful strategy. For instance, the *New York Post* so loved the pimp-prostitute imagery that its editors put us on their front page.

The media, however, rejected much of what we undeniably captured because I dressed as a pimp only in the video bumper. The unedited video, protested *New York* magazine, "shows that [O'Keefe] not only did not dress that way at the ACORN offices, he never even claimed to be a pimp."[24] This was a common refrain. The fact that I openly discussed importing underage sex slaves was, in the media's eyes, negated by the fact that I did not introduce myself as a "pimp." Does pimp protocol require the wearing of a chinchilla-fur coat?

To briefly double back on the charge of our "deceptive editing," the media have cited a press release from then California attorney general Jerry Brown. After a cursory investigation of our charges, Brown wrote, "The evidence illustrates that things are not always as partisan zealots portray them through highly selective editing of reality. Sometimes a fuller truth is found on the cutting room floor."[25]

By referring to us as "partisan zealots," Brown was projecting his own partisanship into what should have been an objective investigation. He did not reference a single specific deceptive edit in his report. Instead, he used the word "edit" as though selective editing was something other than the norm in all video journalism.

Buried in the report was the admission that the ACORN employees were up to no good: "A few ACORN members exhibited terrible judgment and highly inappropriate behavior in videotapes obtained in the investigation." In fact, Jerry Brown admitted in a footnote the real reason why the ACORN employees were cleared of lawbreaking: "Because O'Keefe and Giles's criminal plans were themselves a ruse, one cannot be criminally complicit in those plans."

In other words, because I was only *playing* a pimp in the video, there could not be a criminal conspiracy. But that legal reasoning was deceptively edited out of mainstream media coverage. Mainstream journalists also ignored Brown's admission that the ACORN employees actually said what they appeared to say in our video. Once inside the ACORN offices, we explained exactly what we hoped to accomplish. There were no editing tricks needed to establish the willingness of the ACORN workers to enable our proposed sex trafficking. It was the *content* of our videos that killed ACORN.

President Obama could not deny the *verité* of our visuals. "What I saw on that video was certainly inappropriate and deserves to be investigated," said an embarrassed Obama.[26] Yes, I think instructing a faux pimp on how to shelter his underage, illegal alien sex slaves would seem "inappropriate" to most sane human beings. When we exposed how ACORN worked and what its operatives thought, said, and did, the organization collapsed.

For years, the major media let this group inflict its cultural rot on America with impunity before our raw video shook the zeitgeist. The two of us, goofy as we must have seemed, showed how complacent, ideologically complicit, and downright corrupt American journalism had become. To his credit, the public editor of the *New York Times,* Clark Hoyt, came to our defense. He challenged the widely held media position that the story would "fall apart over the issue of what O'Keefe wore." Said Hoyt, "If O'Keefe did not dress as a pimp, he clearly presented himself as one: a fellow trying to set up a woman—sometimes along with under-age girls—in a house where they would work as prostitutes." In fact, the costume switch was the one and only bit of "deceptive" editing we practiced. Hoyt acknowledged as much. After a thorough review, he argued that the video's "most damning words match the transcripts and the audio, and do not seem out of context."[27]

Let me share one more example of the deceptive-editing accusation. In 2011, we created a website for a fictitious Muslim group and asked for a meeting with NPR brass to discuss a possible donation. As is our custom, we secretly videotaped a meeting with the executives over lunch. I cite this case because all the parties involved were sophisticated people with access to high-power attorneys.

We recorded the executives calling Tea Party members "xenophobic" and "seriously racist" in a conversation that veered from patronizing to scornful.[28] After we posted the videos, the NPR CEO and the NPR Foundation senior vice president were forced to resign. Writing about the sting in the *Washington Post,* establishment Republican Michael Gerson severely criticized our journalism. This wasn't unusual. Ever since I launched Project Veritas, our critics have accused us of selective editing or deceptive editing—or, in Gerson's case, "selective and deceptive" editing.[29]

The three questions I continually raise are:

Why do people keep getting fired or defunded or forced to resign if everyone believes the editing to be deceptive and the story fake?

When was the last time a major media outlet aired any video that had not first been edited?

When have the major media ever posted their raw footage for all to see?

We posted the unedited video online. If NPR brass felt their employees did not say what they appeared to be saying, why accept their resignations? Besides, the executives who quit were people of means. If they felt they had been wronged, they could have sued NPR or Project Veritas or both. They did not.

The *National Review*'s Mona Charen took the time to watch the two hours of raw tape. "Contra Michael Gerson," she wrote, "James O'Keefe's editing of the Ron Shiller NPR video was not 'selective and deceptive.'"[30] What editing is not selective? All articles are written, selectively so. And if we could actually open up reporters' notebooks and their drafts on Microsoft Word, we would find that the information they receive and relay from their sources, especially the anonymous ones, is not always accurate, sometimes not even close; or, for that matter, not even used (aka, selectively edited out completely) because it did not fit their story. So if the major media will not believe any evidence from citizen journalists unless it is on video and unedited, why, I continue to wonder, do they not hold themselves to the same standard? *Using their standard for citizen journalists, why should anyone believe anything the mainstream media produce?*

Charen understood. "Some of what I saw," she wrote, "was even worse than the bits included in the edited version—such as the oleaginous Ms. Liley earnestly comparing American treatment of Muslims with our treatment of Japanese Americans during World War II." Few in the media are willing to do what Charen did: watch two hours of raw tape. They would rather just repeat what others have said before them.

Likewise, few in the media are willing to hold themselves to the same standards they hold us. George Zimmerman sued NBC over a racially inflammatory editing job that cost a few low-level people their careers. Members of the Virginia Citizens Defense League are suing former NBC superstar Katie Couric over a bit of editing so conspicuously deceptive it will likely cost Katie Couric her career. Closer to home, CNN's Alisyn Camerota fronted a selectively edited panel discussion in which one of the participants cited Project Veritas.[31] As with the Couric case, leaked audio from a person in the room showed just how flagrantly CNN cut out the fellow's detailed testimony about vote fraud he was aware of in New Hampshire. More on this later.

"James O'Keefe is a 'convicted criminal.'"

Another accusation thrown at Project Veritas with shocking consistency is that I am a "convicted criminal." In fact, I was convicted on a misdemeanor charge by an incredibly corrupt judicial system in New Orleans. Here is how it went down. In 2010, three of my colleagues and I attempted an ill-planned sting at Senator Mary Landrieu's office in the Hale Boggs federal building. Our goal had been to simply test the truth of Landrieu's claim that callers could not get through to her office to protest the impending Obamacare bill because the lines were busy.

Two of my friends posed as telephone repairmen. They were supposed to get the office workers talking about the telephones. As a casual office visitor, I was to record the conversation. That was the sum of it, but we had not prepared nearly as well as we should have. When our sting fell apart, the Feds fell upon us outside the building as if we were an ISIS cell.

Throughout the day, they moved us from cage to cage in that same building. At day's end, they shackled us and sent us by bus to the St. Bernard's Parish jail. There I got to wear my first and hopefully last orange jumpsuit, perfect for the photo op that would follow the next morning. The media still trot out that photo when it suits their purposes.

Eventually we were charged with a misdemeanor—18 USC § 1036, "Entry by false pretenses to any real property, vessel, or aircraft of the United States or secure area of any airport or seaport." Although we showed our real driver's licenses upon entering the federal building, prosecutors insisted I had committed a crime by telling the Landrieu staffers I was waiting for someone when I really wasn't. (As a matter of fact, I was waiting for my undercover reporter to arrive, so even on that basis there wasn't a "false pretense.") This was pure petty political retaliation. The New Orleans *Times-Picayune* would admit "we were off a little bit" in its characterization of the charges against us but turning a silly misdemeanor into Watergate is more than a "little bit."[32]

In reality, we had offended the deep state, New Orleans branch. Our attorneys advised us not to contest the federal judiciary in New

Orleans. It was a losing cause. Their operatives had already confiscated the exculpatory video I shot and had no intention of surrendering it.

"We don't try cases in the press," US Attorney Jan Mann said at the time about my case. But while she was spinning, her colleague Sal Perricone was anonymously blogging on a *Times-Picayune* website: "Sure [O'Keefe] should be punished. Throw the book at them." Both Mann and Perricone later resigned under pressure after similar mischief was exposed in the "Danziger Bridge" case, which is now taught to US attorneys in ethics classes. In that case, convictions against several police officers were vacated in September 2013 as a result of "grotesque prosecutorial misconduct." The prosecutors had been posting anonymous online comments defaming the accused officers.[33] Had the Danziger case been made public before I pleaded guilty, my case would have been thrown out. In December 2014, we filed a bar complaint against prosecutors, Jim Letten, Jan Mann, Jim Mann, and Sal Perricone, all of whom resigned. Although there was no formal response to our complaints, they became part of the file against the attorneys.

After all was said and done, the federal court document signed by the US attorney stated unequivocally that *there was no evidence or intent to commit any felony.* Our goal, the court conceded, was "to orchestrate a conversation about phone calls to the Senator's staff and capture the conversation on video, not to actually tamper with the phone system, or to commit any other felony."[34]

"O'Keefe was sued for 'invasion of privacy.'"

Still another fact that appears regularly in articles about Project Veritas is that we were once sued for invasion of privacy and settled the case for $100,000. The suit was brought by an individual recorded in one of the California ACORN videos, Juan Carlos Vera. This lawsuit, by the way, relied on unconstitutional two-party consent laws that we are currently fighting in states such as Massachusetts. We settled the suit for $100,000 because it was a far cheaper option than fighting Vera in a California court. The actual court document affirms that the settlement *"is in no way representative of any actual or implied admissions of liability regarding the recorded conversations among Vera, O'Keefe and Giles . . . but is executed solely to avoid costs and risks of potential litigation.*"[35]

If a $100,000 payout brands us as rogue journalists, then what does that say about operations such as ABC News, which recently settled a defamation lawsuit for $1.9 billion with Beef Products Inc.,[36] or NBC News, which famously settled for umpteen millions with General Motors after the faked staging of a fiery test crash?[37] Just in the year 2017, media companies have been attracting lawsuits left and right. The *New York Times* was sued for defamation by former Alaska governor Sarah Palin for reporting that she was linked to an Arizona mass shooting in 2011. The case was dismissed only because Palin could not prove the acknowledged error by the *Times* was malicious.[38] In another case, John Oliver and HBO are being sued by coal company Murray Energy for "false and malicious" coverage.[39] Murray Energy also filed a lawsuit this year against the *New York Times* for libel. But major news companies get to brush these lawsuits aside and are never described, for example, as "the *New York Times,* which has been sued for defamation."

In September 2017, an appeals court sided with University of Virginia fraternity brothers against *Rolling Stone* magazine in the "'Jackie' Rape Dispute."[40] With no video evidence and only a single source, *Rolling Stone* published a defamatory piece alleging that "Jackie" was gang raped during a frat initiation. Although *Rolling Stone* eventually retracted this horrible story, the damage had been done. Unlike with Project Veritas, however, this incident will be considered an aberration, not the norm. That it could even run such a story with so little homework confirms the suspicions of the public that much of the news even from established journals is fake.

"Their work degrades the 'public' discourse."

Still another routine criticism of the work of Project Veritas is that it somehow coarsens the national conversation. In the words of Yael Bromberg, an attorney representing Democracy Partners and Robert Creamer in a lawsuit against me, our videos "degrade public discourse during a time of heightened importance, which is when the public is most in tuned into politics."[41] This of course, is not an argument. It's a worthless characterization made by somebody who doesn't like the effects of our work. The thing about "public discourse" is that it's public. The people ought to decide what's worth discussing, not some litigator looking for a contingency fee. What degrades "public discourse" is trying to silence discussions before they can even begin.

In another ongoing dispute, the League of Conservation Voters is asking the California attorney general to initiate a legal action against us, specifically asking for my criminal prosecution. Its attorneys allege that three people who *might* be associated with Project Veritas *may* have used a hidden camera to record them. In tune with deep state rhetoric, the letter the League sent to the state attorney general lobbying for my criminal prosecution claimed "the actions of [Project Veritas does] nothing to further *legitimate political discourse.*"[42] Someone obviously likes the term "discourse."

In the absence of evidence, the media make stuff up

If the half-truths, endlessly repeated, were not annoying enough, the major media complement them with flat-out falsehoods. In that these journalists at least feign objectivity, when pressured they will often "correct" what they have reported. This happens so often, in fact, that we have a dedicated "Wall of Shame" at the Project Veritas office filled with their retractions.

Our first major sting also netted our first major retraction. Embarrassed by our ACORN revelations, the media retaliated with the most lethal weapon in their arsenal—race. According to the *Washington Post,* we "targeted ACORN for the same reasons that the political right does." Specifically, the *Post* decided that I planned to undermine ACORN's "massive voter registration drives that turn out poor African Americans and Latinos against Republicans."[43] Without a shred of evidence, the Associated Press piled on, attributing thoughts to me that had never crossed my mind. "James O'Keefe, one of the two filmmakers, said he went after ACORN because it registers minorities likely to vote against Republicans."[44]

I had no major media backers, no friends in Washington, no resources beyond my overextended credit cards, and now the AP and the *Washington Post* were trashing me as a racist smear artist on America's front pages. Both the *Post* and the AP issued retractions, but they were halfhearted and went largely unread. "Th[e] article about the community organizing group ACORN incorrectly said that a conservative journalist targeted the organization for hidden-camera videos partly because its voter-registration drives bring Latinos and African Americans to the polls," said the *Post*. "Although ACORN registers people mostly from those groups, the maker of the videos, James E. O'Keefe, did not specifically [*sic*] mention them."[45] For its part, the AP blamed the *Post*.

Embarrassed by our ACORN sting, our journalist friends howled for revenge after our arrest in New Orleans. As soon as we had been arraigned, they were calling the affair the "Louisiana Watergate" or, given our age, "Watergate Jr." The *New York Times* put us on the front page, "4 Arrested in Phone Tampering at Landrieu Office."[46] Our guys did not even have tools with them, let alone know how to tamper with phones. The *Washington Post* thought our arrest worthy of its front page. "ACORN Foe Charged in Alleged Plot to Wiretap Landrieu," screamed the headline.[47]

A day later the *Post*'s Carol Leonnig was forced to correct her headline story, but she did so on page four. Wiretapping? What wiretapping? Now, Leonnig was reporting, "O'Keefe, 25, waited inside the office and used his cellphone to record his two colleagues saying that the senator's phone was not receiving calls."[48] That was our Watergate. But again, who reads corrections?

There is no love from the establishment for those of us without credentials, those of us who approach journalism as an *ethical activity*. The deep state–media complex does not trust citizen journalists. Indeed, those who dwell within that complex cannot afford to trust us. It is not just their jobs they are worried about. It is their power—their power over the flow of money to them, their friends, and their causes; their power over the elected and the appointed; their power over you and me. As a consequence, its agents actively target, harass, and, if need be, use police power and the courts to silence us. If this talk of harassment sounds like a conspiracy theory, the following chapters will convince you that it is not. Harassment is one very real occupational hazard.

Crossing Borders

In 2014, illegal immigration was not a problem, at least not officially. "The border is secure," Senate Majority Leader Harry Reid told reporters in the summer of that year.[1] Reid cited a Democratic senator from New Mexico who assured his colleagues "without any equivocation" that the border was "secure." In the minds of statists and their media allies, the border would stay secure for the next two years. It had to. Democratic victory in 2016 hinged on preserving this illusion.

Hillary Clinton picked up where Reid left off. "I think we've done a really good job securing the border," she said on the campaign trail in 2016. "The immigration from Mexico has dropped considerably. It's just not happening anymore."[2] Hudspeth county sheriff Arvin West knew better. The cartels knew better, and by this time I did too. I knew something else as well. There was a price to pay for proving Reid and Clinton and the media not just wrong, but preposterously wrong.

* * *

Texas border, August 2014

Sheriff West and his deputies in their F–150s escorted me to a god-forsaken spot sixty miles southeast of El Paso. In his Texas bowl hat and deeply lived-in jeans, the man seemed to have stepped right out of Central Casting. Never less than poker-faced, the good sheriff said no more than he had to, and when he did speak it was to the point.

"You're an idiot," West said to me casually in his monotone Tex-Mex drawl as I scanned the border country through a pair of binoculars.

"Why's that?" I answered, not knowing which of a dozen likely responses I might provoke.

"For doing this," he said. The "this" in question was crossing the Rio Grande dressed as Osama bin Laden. "The US government is going to come after you big time." Soon enough, customs agents in airports across North America would prove that the sheriff understood the ways of government much better than I did.

A dry, wry sense of humor made West's Sisyphean border work bearable. When I asked him, for instance, whether the border at this spot was secure, he looked at the nearby fence and answered, "If you think four strands of barbed wire is securing the border, it is secure."[3] For whatever reason, irony seems to thrive in two states like no others: his Texas and my New Jersey. Don't ask me why.

The sheriff did not know my background, but I sensed that somewhere in his heart he sympathized with what I wanted to accomplish. He had just complained that no journalist cared about his ninety-eight-mile stretch of the border, that none ever dared to air the story he desperately wanted to tell. This frustrated him, as he was the kind of sheriff who said his piece when he had a mind to. His was the power of the hardened lawman. Even the federal border patrol agents feared him. In West Texas the local sheriff could *arrest* these federal agents, and they knew West wouldn't hesitate if he had to. He did not think twice about assisting me and asked no one's permission to do it.

As tough as he was, West had a healthy fear of the border country. The positioning of his deputy sheriff said as much. Lean and eagle-eyed, the man stood on top of the truck cab, his denim shirt blowing in the wind, a cigarette dangling from his lip. He held binoculars in his left hand and an AR-15 in his right. He was a guy I wouldn't want to mess with.

West did not carry a rifle. He relied on a .45 revolver strapped to a brown waist belt sheltered by his ample belly. He caught me looking at it—the gun that is, not the belly.

"You know why I carry a .45-caliber handgun?" he asked. I shrugged. He winked, "Because they don't make anything bigger." Of course.

With me was Joe Halderman, an unfiltered, Type A, Emmy Award–winning producer who came to Project Veritas by way of CBS News.

Joe chain-smoked Marlboros that day and paced anxiously between me and the sheriff. Joe had been in spots rougher than this during his career—Iraq, Afghanistan, Lebanon, Somalia, and Bosnia, among others. The danger did not faze him. What did faze him was his fear of not getting the story he wanted in the face of that danger.

While Joe surveyed the scene and fidgeted with his black frame glasses, West took a phone call. He looked concerned. Watching him, we all fell silent.

"He did what?" said West. "Okay, yeah, you got it," he whispered into his cell phone and then turned to me. "If you want to do this you better hurry." That was the sheriff's way of saying, "If you don't do this in the next thirty seconds, you just might get your fool head shot off."

Joe understood exactly what West meant. He pointed at Jerry, our cameraman, and said, "Camera, speed." I grabbed my Osama bin Laden gear and waded thirty or so feet across the Rio Grande into Mexico. I wasted no time. I slipped into my sleeveless Afghani beige dress and turban, donned an Osama mask, and waded back across the Rio Grande, camera rolling. If the cartels were watching us, the Border Patrol was surely not. There was no agent in sight. I literally could have been Osama bin Laden, and no one would have seen me, let alone stopped me.

This was the easy part. Still dressed as Osama, my sneakers squishy with mud, I set out to duplicate the walk of countless illegal crossers, some relatively harmless, some not harmless at all. I doubt West Texas weather is ever pleasant, especially in August, but I lucked out that day. It was cloudy and only ninety degrees. With my GoPro camera on a stick, I trekked through the desert and saw not a soul. I did see two white Border Patrol vehicles, but they were speeding away from me, not toward me. This all felt unreal, almost comical.

When I reached I-10 six miles away, muddied and dehydrated, I imagined how an illegal immigrant must have felt upon reaching that same spot. That highway could take him anywhere. If he were a terrorist, someone would likely be there in a minute to pick him up. As I stood in this otherwise desolate spot, hard by the highway, I thought about my other colleagues in the media. I wanted redemption, but

I knew they would not grant it. The next week we would release a blockbuster video. We would save and store the footage in multiple locations. I had learned the hard way four years earlier, after a New Orleans magistrate ordered our footage destroyed.[4] This time, however, I did not get caught in the act. I had just turned thirty and had gleaned a little wisdom along the way.

With the tape secured and the video produced, we would show Harry Reid for the reflexive liar he was. We would embarrass the White House. We would highlight a problem that desperately cried out for a solution. More than a million people would watch our video on YouTube alone. While the major media were busy preserving statist illusions, we were busy shattering them.

* * *

New York, December 2014

US Customs and Border Protection paid more attention to our work than the media had. Unfortunately, it was the wrong kind of attention. On December 3, 2014, I flew into JFK Airport in New York from overseas. Upon disembarking, I casually followed the crowd to the passport control area and inserted my passport into the device that verifies it. Out of the device came a white document with my picture on it. To my surprise, there was an "X" straight through all my information.

A Customs and Border Protection (CBP) agent gestured in my direction and told me to follow him. We walked for what seemed like a quarter mile through the airport. Upon reaching our destination, he took my passport and the document with the X, escorted me into a small room, and told me to sit. He then put my passport in a desk drawer and walked away. I attempted to make a phone call, but another CBP agent across the room shouted, "No phones allowed in here."[5] I tried to explain that I needed to alert my travel mate to my detention. He wasn't hearing it. "I said put the phone away," he snapped. "Do not make me ask you again."

I was beginning to feel as if I were in a foreign country, not quite the Iran of *Argo,* but on the line of an alternate America run like a DMV.

"Am I being detained?" I asked.

"Where is your passport, sir?" said the agent.

"The other guy took it from me and walked over there and put it in a drawer or something."

"James, I need to see your passport. And give me your bags."

"Sir, can I ask what this is about?"

Sensing some crazy and possibly illegal behavior from these agents, I slid my hand into my pocket and attempted to turn on the video option of my iPhone. He saw me do it.

"If you touch that fucking phone," he barked, "I will have you arrested."

I kick myself looking back on the incident. I wish I had committed the name of this CBP officer to memory. In subsequent detentions, I would not make that mistake again. The agent took my brown duffle bag and asked me quickly if I made any purchases. Before I could answer, he violently yanked on the zipper and proceeded to dump all my gear onto the table. He then rummaged through my clothes, apparently looking for contraband.

On January 5, 2015, Bill Marshall at Judicial Watch filed a Freedom of Information Act (FOIA) request on our behalf with the Department of Homeland Security. We wanted to know why I was detained and harassed. On January 7, Marshall received an email back from CBP claiming its people were "unable to locate or identify any responsive records." It did not surprise Bill that CBP failed to produce any relevant records. What surprised him, shocked him really, was the speed of the rejection. Two days!

"It is very strange, unheard of, really," said Bill, "that CBP would be able to receive a FOIA request, process it, conduct the search for records related to it, and respond to me within two days of my having sent the request." He added quizzically, "That doesn't even account for the time it took my letter to reach them via USPS."

Judicial Watch pursued this inquiry nonetheless, and finally CBP responded with a single-page inspection document too heavily redacted to be of value. What they blacked out, I imagined, was the reason why they were stopping me. Think this is a conspiracy theory? Read on.

* * *

Lake Erie, September 2014

Equal opportunity border crossers, we decided to stage a crossing of the Canadian border as well. A few weeks after Mexico, we rented a small pleasure craft out of Cleveland and cruised the forty-five miles over to Canada. On the return trip, a high-speed Zodiac boat with a man dressed head-to-foot in black ISIS garb followed in our wake. Needless to say, we recorded his journey. We saw no Border Patrol coming or going. A local skipper we spoke to had never seen the Border Patrol on Lake Erie.

According to CBP rules, small-craft operators are supposed to self-report if they cross from Canada into the United States. Our ISIS rep chose not to. Who can blame him? He was carrying a bag of the deadly poison ricin and a sack of Ebola-infected rags—yes, Virginia, fake in both cases. Holding a British passport, as more than a few ISIS fighters do, our man would have had no trouble getting into Canada and, if anything, even less trouble getting to Cleveland.

Still in full terrorist gear, the fellow docked his boat in downtown Cleveland. He then carried his Ebola-soaked rags and his ricin bag right into the heavily visited Rock and Roll Hall of Fame adjacent to the harbor. I hoped we were not putting any ideas into the deranged heads of our ISIS friends—by this time they had already cited our Osama video in internal documents—but we were definitely trying to get the attention of our government.

In the latter case, we seem to have succeeded. Two days after posting our Lake Erie video, Senator John McCain had the chance to question Francis Taylor, then undersecretary for intelligence and analysis at the Department of Homeland Security (DHS), during a hearing of the Senate's Homeland Security Committee about reports of ISIS urging its followers to infiltrate the United States across its southwestern border.

"There have been Twitter, social media exchanges among ISIL adherents across the globe speaking about that as a possibility,"[6] Taylor responded to McCain.

Taylor then boasted, "I'm satisfied that we have the intelligence and the capability at our border that would prevent that activity." McCain wasn't buying it.

"Well you know it's interesting," McCain responded, "because an American reporter named James O'Keefe dressed as Osama bin Laden walked across the border at the Rio Grande River undetected. Does something like that concern you?"

"Actually sir, he was not undetected," said Taylor who was apparently expecting the question. "He was known to the border security agencies who walked . . . saw him . . ."

McCain cut him off. "Then why didn't they stop him when he came across?" When Taylor proved unable to answer, McCain answered for him: "You can't answer it because they weren't there to stop him."

McCain was right. They were not there. Nor was it the fault of the Border Patrol agents that they were not there. Despite its many promises, the Obama administration had failed to make a serious effort to secure the border. "The fact is there are thousands of people who are coming across our border who are undetected and not identified," said McCain, and he was right.

* * *

Port of St. John, US Virgin Islands, April 15, 2015

More of the same. I went snorkeling at an island near St. John where I was staying with my family. Upon returning, we checked in at a little customs shanty. I waited patiently as an agent pounded away at the keyboard of his computer. It seemed to be taking longer than usual. Suddenly out of nowhere, while staring into his screen, he said quietly and with just a hint of menace, "Do you think what you did was funny?"

Without thinking, I said, "No, it's not the slightest bit funny." To me, the fact that terrorists can easily infiltrate the country is not a laughing matter. The agent's response was curious.

"Are you done with that stuff?"[7]

That "stuff" was investigative journalism into the workings of the US government, the same government that reportedly protects our freedom to do that "stuff."

Looking back, when the agent asked, "Are you done with that stuff?" I wish I would have answered, "Done? No, bro, I'm just getting started." But I knew enough not to joke with CBP people, especially when detained by them. It is a strange feeling, being forced to condemn your own actions while being detained by the US government—forced to beg for forgiveness and their mercy. It reminded me of Tocqueville's condemnation of those people who readily sacrifice their will to the government's. "They submit, it is true, to the whims of a clerk," he wrote, "but no sooner is force removed than they are glad to defy the law as a defeated enemy. Thus one finds them ever wavering between servitude and license."[8]

* * *

St. John Airport, US Virgin Islands, April 16, 2015

In order to ease passage to other Caribbean Islands not part of America, the CBP mans a customs station at the St. John's airport. A day after being harassed at the port, I was detained once again. To document the detention, a friend took a photo of me through the window of the detention room.

This time, too, I thought to record the encounter through the iTalk app on my cell phone. It seemed like a good idea until a CBP agent demanded to see my cell phone. I showed it. *No problem,* I thought, at least at first. The iTalk app records in the background. The agent would have to log in to see that the phone was recording.

"Please unlock your cell phone."

Damn! Now what do I do? "Sir, I'm a journalist," I told him, "and I have confidential sources and methods on this iPhone. I cannot in good conscience unlock it."

"Unlock your phone, please."[9]

With that, I tilted the phone up slightly toward me so it was not easy for him to see. With some fancy finger work, I quickly punched the code and then hit "stop record" in one sequence. To the agent, it appeared as if I had entered one long numerical password. Just as I was exiting the iTalk program, he grabbed the phone out of my hand and swiped the screens to see if there were any apps open. That was close.

When I told Bill Marshall at Judicial Watch about my latest encounter, he sent another FOIA request to CBP. He wanted to find out why I was targeted. This time, he got a letter back saying that the "average time to process a FOIA request related to 'travel/border incidents' is a minimum of 12 months." Last time, it took two days.

* * *

Montreal, June 2015

The game kept getting chippier. Two months after the incident in St. John, I took a short trip to Greece. I traveled there in part to get some man-on-the-street interviews regarding the financial crisis and the ensuing riots. On the way home I landed in Montreal and was processed through US Customs at the Montreal airport. Once again, I had a large "X" stamped on my passport document. This was the fifth X in my last five trips. I was leading the league in X's. At the first customs desk, the agent was friendly enough until he entered my name in the database—then his tone changed.

Understanding now the risk of recording on my iPhone, I recorded everything on a voice-activated device that was also a functional USB flash drive. It was an expensive piece of equipment, manufactured by people in the intelligence community. I even put files and pictures on the device in case the authorities inserted it into a computer. To take it apart and find the recording element they would need a serious technician and maybe a search warrant.

The agents made me empty all my pockets on the table. They went through my phone as they typically did and then examined the flash drive closely. Unknown to them, the flash drive was recording the conversation. When they finished looking at it, one of the agents put the drive on top of a counter about seven feet away. Without being obvious, I tried to keep the discussion as close to that device as possible.

After a few routine questions, an agent pulled my name up on the computer, and his eyes lit up. This agent asked if I had ever "passed the border before in disguise."[10] I answered honestly that I had and explained the purpose behind the Osama bin Laden crossing. I asked whether these recurring detentions were a form of retaliation.

"No, we're not retaliating against you," he said, then added. "Why would you say that?"

The guy was being coy. We both knew why. He led me to a private room where four agents took turns interrogating me. A woman agent led the way, probing further into who I was and what I did for a living. When I tried to explain, she interjected, "You're like a shock reporter. You basically go to the extremes to prove a point?"

I had been called a lot of things in my brief career but never a "shock reporter." I suspect she just sort of combined "shock jock" and "reporter" and conjured the term on the spot. I was impressed. According to the agent, "shock reporter" O'Keefe brought on this added scrutiny by at least appearing to break the law in crossing the Rio Grande.

"I broke the law?" I said to her incredulously. "I'm a journalist who is trying to expose something important." I thought I might be reaching her.

"Deep down in your heart," I continued, "when you set the bureaucracy aside, you have to admit the problem needs to be exposed."

Actually, I didn't reach her. Her mind was pretty well shut. The questions kept coming. Wanting to know why, I asked a male agent about the recurring searches. He explained that his bosses "don't want you to pull a fast one on us." They were afraid, he explained, of "getting egg on their face."

This explanation had a logic to it, but it still made little real sense. The CBP mission was to protect the public "from dangerous people and materials," not to keep egg off the faces of the CBP brass. By my lights, I was helping the CBP improve its service. The CBP apparently did not quite see it that way.

The questions grew progressively more intrusive. They asked what my next project was going to be, how I made money, and, bizarrely, which candidate I intended to back.

"Would you really support Trump as a nominee?" one agent asked. I was so unsettled by the question I laughed involuntarily. "I don't really endorse politicians for, you know, anything," I told him honestly.

When I went public with my experience at the hands of the CBP, I caught the attention of at least a few liberal civil libertarians, a vanishing breed. An immigration lawyer writing under the handle "Timaeus" posted a protest of CBP's actions on the decidedly left-leaning *Daily Kos*. She (I'll presume) was writing against the *Daily Kos* grain. Comments about my detention on the site, Timaeus noted, had turned into "a festival of schadenfreude."[11] Trolls have always delighted in my misfortunes. I expected no less.

Lest Timaeus be accused of coddling a "world class rat" like me, she seasoned her defense with insults aplenty. "His Bin Ladin [*sic*] crossing the river stunt was juvenile and highly offensive," wrote Timaeus. "But I think he was exercising his constitutional right to travel along with his First Amendment free speech right to be a complete jackass. I don't think that deserves punishment with a lifetime of travel restraints." As much as I appreciated her left-handed support, I had to ask myself whom exactly I "highly" offended—bin Laden? Terrorists? Mexicans? Liberals? The media? The CBP? The deep state? Who?

The well-known and respected civil libertarian Jonathan Turley was kinder. Turley acknowledged that I was "controversial" and "hated by many on the left." He cited much of my legal history and questioned whether Project Veritas was the "journalistic organization" it purported to be. The picture he posted in the article had me in an orange jumpsuit, all the rage in New Orleans back in the day.

Unlike Timaeus, however, Turley gave our Osama video its due. "The video succeeded in capturing what critics have complained about for years," wrote Turley, "that the border remain [*sic*] wide open and that the Administration is misleading the public on the ease with which potential terrorists could cross into the United States illegally."[12] This was our point exactly.

"Whatever the merits of that video," Turley continued, "it does seem to me to be either a form of journalism or political speech." He confirmed that the video was obviously "very embarrassing," not just for the CBP but for the Obama administration as well. He found my treatment by the CBP "troubling" for any number of reasons. Among them was the unlikelihood that the CBP would detain a reporter from NBC or the *New York Times* for doing something comparable. He suggested there would be much more attention paid had a major media reporter been detained, and he was right.

"When dealing with a critic like O'Keefe," Turley concluded, "the government should be able to show an objective and consistently applied rule. Perhaps they have one, but there has been little coverage of the incident." Truth be told, during the Obama years, there was relatively little major media coverage of any news that embarrassed the White House. What coverage there was tended to be protective.

The comments from Turley and Timaeus encouraged me. The unapologetic CBP harassment forced them to confront an injustice they were not prepared to tolerate. Unfortunately, there were too few people like them.

* * *

Seattle, July 24, 2015

The relative lack of coverage allowed CBP to continue doing what it was doing. In July 2015, soon after the Turley protest, I had to go through customs in Seattle following an Alaskan cruise sponsored by the *National Review*. I knew at this stage of the game that I had to record these encounters, but I had to be prudent. My lawyer informed me that I could not legally video record the CBP agents. He reminded me too that if an agent asked, "Are you recording me?" I had to answer truthfully. USC § 1001 prohibits false statements to a CBP officer.

Whatever anyone asked, I had to be prepared in advance to answer. We use the same technique in our undercover work to avoid lawbreaking. For example, if one of our journalists is offered a ballot during a voter fraud investigation and is asked if he is the person registered, the journalist cannot say "yes." That would be a lie. Instead, we train our journalists to avoid the heart of the question. "You are always behind Enemy Lines" is a much quoted Veritas rule, sometimes even in our own country.

Seattle was déjà vu all over again. "This is the sixth straight time I've been asked to be inspected," I told the CBP agent assigned to me.[13]

"Okay," he responded.

He looked at the screen for a very long time. I could sense his body language tensing as he read the material before him.

"What do you do for a living, sir?"

"I'm a journalist."

"You're a journalist?"

"Yes, sir."

"Is this sort of freelance or are you working for a company?"

"I started my own company—I've got twenty people working for me. We do a lot of reporting, especially on the border." I added the border jab to see if that would provoke a candid admission from him.

"Do you have any cameras?" he said, his poker face intact.

This was the moment of truth, and I was prepared.

"I didn't bring those with me today," I said without lying. I had sent them through in my bags. My audio recording device, however, was recording every word he was saying. I kept that fact to myself.

"How do you turn this off?" he said, taking my iPhone and jacking with it.

"You just hold down the two buttons down the side there," I said. I was so helpful. My mother would have been proud. He read the screen carefully for a few more minutes.

"Did you make the news for the whole, like, southern border stuff?"

"Yeah, I did," I answered matter-of-factly. "We do YouTube videos and expose stuff like that. Is that why they keep stopping me?"

"Uh, no, that's what you said, you said—basically, it's the southern border, so, it's your, it's your—it's a free country," he stuttered. "Do whatever you want. Here you go."

With that he handed me my passport. As I leaned over to accept it, I stole a glance at the computer. Finally, I got to see what all these agents had been looking at when they typed in "James O'Keefe." There, blinking away in some ancient-looking, pre-Windows version of MS-DOS were the words that had been redacted in all the FOIA responses, the words that caused the agents to tense up when they read them, the words that triggered my repeated detentions: "Subject is an amateur reporter engaged in publicity stunts including unlawfully entering the United States dressed like an ISIS terrorist and crossing the Rio Grande dressed like Osama bin Laden."

At that moment, the truth descended upon me like a tongue of fire. The failure of Department of Homeland Security leadership to define me and characterize my work with any accuracy led to the detentions and harassment. Like bureaucrats everywhere, CBP agents are used to checking boxes. I did not quite fit the "journalist" box they were used to. My constitutional rights hinged on that definition. Apparently, an "amateur reporter" was not entitled to the same protections as a traditionally defined "professional."

The CBP agents took their cues from a media establishment jealously guarding its privileges. For instance, Paul Farhi of the *Washington Post* describes my news anchor role on a series of Project Veritas videos as "master of ceremonies."[14] This was his not-so-subtle way of excluding me from the journalistic ranks, and Farhi was no outlier. Major media reporters routinely employed dismissive language to establish the difference between us and them.

It did not surprise me that the Department of Homeland Security called our videos "publicity stunts" in the records that were redacted in the FOIA requests. "Stunt" had become the word of choice in the journalistic establishment to summarize our undercover reporting. When I Google "James O'Keefe" and "stunt" I get 282,000 hits.

On this occasion, I was able to see those FOIA redactions unmasked. And only I would ever see the unredacted truth for myself. I couldn't film it—that would have been unlawful in those circumstances. The culture, the media, and the government were using language as a weapon, a secret weapon at that, as no one, myself included, was able to expose it. "In our time, political speech and writing are largely the defence of the indefensible," wrote Orwell seventy years ago, and since then political speech has not improved a whit.[15]

As I walked out of the CBP station and into the Seattle rain, I dictated the statement on the computer screen from memory and recorded it on my iPhone. We promptly released a video that included audio from the actual encounter. After its release, I got a call from reporter Jerry Markon of the *Washington Post*. Markon, an old-school reporter with an unusual dose of integrity, assured me he could get a comment from the agency since he had reliable sources there. I was dubious, but as he reminded me, "It's different when you're with the *Washington Post*. They'll call me back." *Enjoy resting on your laurels,* Washington Post, I thought. *One day, there will be nothing left to rest on.*

But Markon seemed to be genuinely fair. Jerry got through to CBP and received a statement from the agency. It read, "CBP does not retaliate against applicants for entry into the United States." A lot depends on the way you define "retaliate." What the CBP did not do, Markon noted, was "contest the video's depictions of O'Keefe's encounters with federal officers."[16] The major media may be losing their grip, but the memory of their power still echoes.

If there is a moral here, it is that sunlight remains the best disinfectant. The CBP can redact information on FOIA requests, but once we published the "O'Keefe" warning on social media and the *Post* amplified that message, the game was over. The CBP has not detained me since. As of this writing, the ACLU is representing ten US citizens for "warrantless searches of smartphones, laptops, and other electronic devices at the border." As the ACLU observes, "None of our clients have been accused of any wrongdoing, nor have they been given any valid explanation for why this happened to them."[17] It is a shame that I do not fit the ACLU profile. I could have saved its people a lot of legwork.

Honoring a Tradition—
The History of Journalism and Its Demise

Although you would not know it by listening to our critics, the kind of investigative journalism we do at Project Veritas has a long and proud history. In fact, for more than a century, reporters have been going undercover and telling stories that otherwise would not have been told. For those who are curious, NYU has done an excellent job of creating a historical database of such reporting.[1] The database includes capsule descriptions of scores of undercover efforts, including several done by Project Veritas. As far as I could tell, ours were the only summaries that came with caveats attached, such as the use of the word "alleged" in the discussion of our NPR sting or the damage-control description of the ACORN employees as "earnest" and "low-level."

Perhaps the most celebrated of all undercover jobs took place more than a century ago. Most Americans of a certain age had to read Upton Sinclair's classic 1906 novel *The Jungle,* and with good reason. Sinclair finessed his way into a Chicago meatpacking plant for a month or more, quietly interviewed workers, and reported what he saw and experienced. Although he worked in an era without hidden-camera technology or the means to distribute information quickly, his account proved truthful enough and powerful enough, even in novel form, to inspire major reforms in the food-processing industry. Those reforms included the passage of the Pure Food and Drug Act.

Like Sinclair, we are not in a position to capture a comprehensive look at whatever subject we investigate. But also like Sinclair, we try to capture an honest slice of it, in context, package it to attract attention, and, ideally, make a difference.

Sinclair was one of a class of "muckrakers," a word adapted from John Bunyan's *Pilgrim's Progress* and popularized by President Theodore Roosevelt. "The men with the muck rakes are often indispensable to the well-being of society," said Roosevelt in a 1906 address.[2] He cautioned, however, that muckrakers had to be truthful and judicious if they were to be effective. Our experience has confirmed the same.

These investigative reporters were well known in their time, and a few of them, such as Lincoln Steffens and Ida Tarbell, still have historical currency. At Project Veritas, we have a special place in our hearts for those who went undercover to gather their facts. For me, among the most impressive was Elizabeth Jane Cochran, a young working-class woman who wrote under the name "Nellie Bly." In 1887, still in her early twenties, Nellie left her native Pittsburgh for New York and secured a job with the *New York World*.[3] The *World* was one of the first muckraking newspapers. Under the leadership of Joseph Pulitzer, who bought the paper in 1883, the *World* did the kind of reporting that today would be all but unthinkable, such as exploring welfare abuse on the recipient end.[4]

Soon after her arrival, Nellie accepted an undercover assignment to feign insanity and get herself treated in the fashion of the day. She had little trouble deceiving the doctors into thinking her "undoubtedly insane." It did not take much; unblinking eyes and a feigned breakdown did the trick. Once committed to the city's hospital for the mentally ill—then, as now, Bellevue—she spent ten brutal days on the receiving end of the care reserved for those in her presumed condition. Fortunately, she lived to write about it, first for the *World* and later in a book, *Ten Days in a Mad-House*.

Nellie's firsthand account of the inhumane everyday treatment meted out to the mentally ill caused a sensation. A grand jury was quickly empaneled, and the jurists seconded the recommendations Nellie had made. As a result, the City of New York was forced to invest considerable sums in improving the conditions for the mentally ill, and doctors were forced to tighten their procedures to determine who was and was not "insane."

At the time, Nellie discovered something we would rediscover more than a century later: when you provoke powerful interests, they will push back, ostensibly against your methods but in reality against your findings. Knowing she was in the right and having the public in her corner, Nellie refused to give in to those "expert physicians who are condemning me for my action." She knew why they were upset and embarrassed. She had proven their ability "to take a perfectly sane and healthy woman" and, through their draconian treatment, "make her a mental and physical wreck."[5]

In 1972, the *Chicago Tribune* made a major investment in undercover work. One of its reporters, William Mullen, got himself hired as a clerk at the Chicago Board of Election Commissioners. Mullen spent three months working undercover. In that role he "gathered and compiled evidence of election shenanigans from public records." His work and that of his colleagues resulted in a major exposé of voter fraud by the *Tribune*.[6] A generation or so later, "journalists" would be dismissing voter fraud as fake news and denouncing groups such as Project Veritas that have gone undercover to expose it.

Also in 1972, a twentysomething Geraldo Rivera, working as an investigative reporter for local WABC-TV in New York, caused a similar sensation. Unannounced and uninvited, Rivera and his cameraman toured the children's facilities at Willowbrook State School for the mentally challenged on Staten Island.[7] Although others had written exposés, no printed report had the impact of Rivera's visuals. Thanks to the camera, citizens did not have to take his word for the conditions at Willowbrook. They could see for themselves. What they saw outraged them and led to major reforms at the institution as well as a new federal law, the Civil Rights of Institutionalized Persons Act of 1980. And, as was true for Nellie Bly, the undercover work launched a successful, if somewhat checkered, career.

Rivera was not the first journalist to cause a sensation with a hidden camera. That honor goes to Tom Howard. In 1928, the New York *Daily News* recruited Howard, a Chicagoan, to photograph an execution at Sing Sing Prison just north of the city. Well aware that prison officials would never allow a photographer anywhere near the electric chair, the New York *Daily News* picked Howard specifically for the reason that no one knew him. He strapped a camera to his ankle and wired a triggering mechanism up the inside of his pant leg. As soon as the executioner flipped the switch, Howard pointed his foot at the prisoner, Ruth Snyder, and snapped just the one photo. That the condemned was a woman made the resulting image all the more powerful.[8]

Despite the possibilities inherent in undercover camera work, the medium has never really taken off. There are several reasons why. The more obvious reasons—cost, time, legal concerns—are ones media analysts are willing to discuss. The less obvious ones these same analysts do not discuss—in part because they do not see the problem; in part because they *are* the problem. Looking at the media establishment from our perspective, outside of it, we can see forces at play that these analysts cannot see from within.

For those doing undercover work, the pushback could get intense, especially in the 1970s and afterward. For years, hard-hitting investigations and undercover work, often in the form of "real news" or cinema verité, were staples of newspapers around the country, especially in Chicago. The willingness of Chicago reporters to engage in extended confidence games was legendary, especially at the *Chicago Tribune* where George Bliss and Bill Jones organized the *Tribune*'s task force.

In 1970, investigative reporter Jones won a Pulitzer for exposing the collusion between police and ambulance companies while going undercover as an ambulance driver. In 1972, as mentioned earlier, young *Tribune* reporter Bill Mullen worked undercover in the Chicago Election Board City Hall office and successfully exposed widespread Democratic Party voter fraud. The story so angered the Chicago machine, said Mullen, that "[my editors] told me to get out of town until the mayor cooled off, so I bought a Pan Am 'Round the World' Ticket."[9]

Tribune investigative reporter William Gaines went undercover as a janitor in a Chicago hospital. In addition to mopping the floors and disposing of the garbage, Gaines was recruited to help doctors and nurses in surgery while still in his janitorial garb. He won a Pulitzer for his efforts in 1976. Gaines's MO could have come right out of the Veritas playbook: find out what the target wants and *become that person*.

"It wasn't hard to get a job," said Gaines. "The first guy would find out [the needs of the target]. The second guy would be exactly that."[10]

As Gaines acknowledged, there was no other way to get the information they obtained.

Arguably the most ambitious undercover investigation ever produced by a newspaper took place in Chicago in 1977. That year the *Chicago Sun-Times* purchased a seedy bar and used it to attract the city's equally seedy politicians. Reporters actually ran the bar, the aptly named Mirage Tavern, and they were able to document a series of shady deals orchestrated by their politician customers. Hidden cameras were rolling the entire time. The journalists posed as waitresses and bartenders. They captured payoffs to city inspectors, shakedowns by state liquor inspectors, and tax fraud by accountants that was estimated to cost the state of Illinois some $16 million.[11]

In 1978, the paper ran twenty-five days of stories on the venture. The results were on par with the Veritas ACORN investigation. Fourteen city employees were suspended. The mayor created a new office of inspections. Internal investigation units were set up at the city, state, and federal levels. A local sensation, the series was a finalist for the Pulitzer Prize. It did not win. Without getting too far ahead of myself, I bring up the lack of awards for a reason. An unwillingness to provide establishment kudos for undercover reporting would lead to the demise of arguably the single most effective technique for gathering information.

Seemingly out of nowhere, the Pulitzer committee deemed the investigation unworthy of its highest honors. "The Pulitzer Prize Board decided not to award the *Sun-Times* the prize because the series was based on deception," *Sun-Times* editor Jack Fuller later explained. "The board concluded that truth-telling enterprises should not engage in such tactics." According to Fuller, legendary *Washington Post* editor Ben Bradlee used his clout to deny the *Sun-Times* the prize. "We would not allow reporters to misrepresent themselves in any way," Bradlee told him.[12] Bradlee added, "I don't think we should be the hidden owners of anything."

If there was a watershed moment in the history of investigative journalism, this may have been it. Although the Mirage story was sensational and lethally effective, it was "overshadowed by what the reporters did to get the story," recalled Gaines. There are various theories as to why the Pulitzer Board voted the way it did and to why, subsequently, journalists largely abandoned undercover reporting. I have some theories of my own.

Trophies

For one, publishers rarely measure a series of this scope by the good their journalists do. Largely for future marketing purposes, they measure success by the awards they win, especially the Pulitzers. The board's pointed rejection of the Mirage series surely discouraged other editors from using undercover techniques. After all, why devote enormous resources and money into something that will not stock the trophy case?

The Watergate Factor

The earthshaking Watergate investigation had a negative effect on undercover reporting as well. Journalists, and not just those at the *Post,* started taking themselves way too seriously. Journalism became more decorous, less fun. The smug among them began using phrases like "stunt journalism" or "gimmick journalism" to dismiss people like Nellie Bly or William Gaines or, down the road, James O'Keefe.

The Collapse of Competition

Then, too, the emergence of TV news, local and national, made it very hard for newspapers to remain profitable. By the turn of the twenty-first century, only the largest markets had more than one viable daily newspaper. The lack of competition bred complacency and ideological uniformity.

The "Professionalization" of the Industry and "Narrative" Journalism

Meanwhile, the J-schools were grooming earnest young "professionals." The media no longer recruited ordinary working people like Nellie Bly. Reporters, like the J-schools that groomed them, had increasingly come to reflect the prevailing statist ethos on America's campuses. With the increasing political polarization of society and the deeming of some subjects as untouchable, producers had less and less interest in pursuing the kinds of stories that once made Chicago a Mecca of undercover reporting.

An investigation into voter fraud at the polls, for instance, could produce no useful political result. From the newsroom's perspective, it might even feed into a racial narrative that would ultimately depress the black vote. An investigation into administrative agency abuse, once a staple of intrepid Chicago reporting, might be viewed as blaming victims and hurting people in need. An investigation into the easy movement of sexual predators from one public school district to another might damage the public school establishment, a bulwark of the Democratic Party. Better to stick to priests. In America's newsrooms today, the "narrative" rules.

The Threat of Litigation

What finally buried hidden-camera journalism were legal and economic concerns. I will go into detail on this issue later in the book, but the use of litigation, even when the law was not in the plaintiff's favor, has sobered many a media executive.

Despite the rich history of undercover journalism, both print and visual, the media often treat Project Veritas as though we invented the practice. After our sting of NPR executives in 2011, one that resulted in the rolling of some high-level heads, I agreed to be interviewed by NPR media critic Bob Garfield.

"If your journalistic technique is the lie," Garfield asked with obvious disdain, "why should we believe anything you have to say?"[13]

"Investigative reporters have used, quote, unquote, false pretenses, like *To Catch a Predator,* or ABC's *Primetime Live,*" I answered. "Even Mike Wallace at *60 Minutes* went undercover. You go undercover in order to get to the truth. Now, is it lying? It's a form of guerrilla theater. You're posing as something you're not in order to capture candid conversations from your subject. But I wouldn't characterize it as lying."

The obvious distinction here was that we don't deceive the audience. We deceive the target in order to get the truth to the audience. Tucker Carlson defended the NPR investigation, saying, "I may have aesthetic qualms about it, but the point of journalism is the story. The main question you ask is, is it true?"[14] But Garfield's question wasn't really about the techniques—not in the abstract—nor about the truth.

Underlying Garfield's questioning was politics—the political consequences of the work as well as the assumed political motivations. He asked, "Why believe anything you have to say?" because we dared to investigate organizations that to him were sacred. If we had used deception to infiltrate and unmask KKK members, Garfield would not have dared to question our motives or our methodology. To quote Ben Shapiro, "Facts don't care about your feelings."[15]

As my answer suggested, however, by 2011 undercover video reporting had devolved from exposing real abuse, as the *Sun-Times* did at the Mirage Tavern or as Rivera did at Willowbrook, to catching would-be predators hot on the trail of imaginary girls. Hidden cameras had become a magnet for litigation, and the legal risks had become too great to justify the rewards in either ratings or prestige to challenge powerful interests. A great art form had been all but lost. Fortunately, we were on the scene to help revive it.

Swilling Chardonnay

If the practice of journalism was faltering, preaching about journalism was more fevered than ever. Long before the 1990s, journalists had created their own university programs and a professoriate to staff them.

Prominent among the preachers was Bob Steele, the Nelson Poynter Scholar for Journalism Values at the Poynter Institute. Steele worked in local TV news for ten years before becoming a career academic. In 1995, he codified "a deception/hidden cameras checklist" and handed it down to working journalists as though he had received it from a burning bush. "You Must Fulfill All of the Criteria to Justify Your Actions," he insisted. To understand the establishment flavor of these widely accepted rules, it is useful to share in full the conditions under which Steele would approve the use of hidden cameras:

> When the information obtained is of profound importance. It must be of vital public interest, such as revealing great system failure at the top levels, or it must prevent profound harm to individuals.

> When all other alternatives for obtaining the same information have been exhausted.

> When the journalists involved are willing to disclose the nature of the deception and the reason for it.

> When the harm prevented by the information revealed through deception outweighs any harm caused by the act of deception.

When the individuals involved and their news organization apply excellence, through outstanding craftsmanship as well as the commitment of time and funding needed to pursue the story fully.

When the journalists involved have conducted a meaningful, collaborative, and deliberative decision-making process on the ethical and legal issues.[1]

The Poynter Institute lent its authority to these rules by reposting them in 2002. The internet was mature enough by this time and video technology was advanced enough to render some of these rules obsolete on delivery. By limiting the use of hidden cameras to those at a "news organization" with ample time and funding to pursue stories "fully," Steele disallowed operations like Project Veritas from even thinking about using hidden cameras.

For sure, when Hannah Giles and I brought down ACORN in 2009, funding our sting on credit cards, we were not exactly the kind of "news organization" Steele had in mind. And yet our target, certainly from our perspective, was one of "profound importance," one whose continued operation revealed "great system failure at the top levels." Had we "exhausted" all other alternatives? No, but the media, liberal and conservative, apparently had. In fact, the deep scandal here was why a twenty-five-year-old with a Sony mini-cam was able to do in a few days what the major media had failed to do over decades.

We understood our medium better than Steele ever could. Technology had broadened the citizen journalist's ability to get information everywhere and anywhere. We did not reject journalistic ethics. We simply had to create those ethics anew. Chicago journalists had to do the same. "[Undercover journalism] had its own peculiar system of ethics," said veteran *Chicago Daily News* columnist Robert J. Casey of the city's press, "justifiable only in behalf of the undefinable, somewhat nebulous service to a public that had only halfheartedly asked for it—the discovery, extraction, and presentation of the news."[2]

On one occasion, for instance, a subject of one of our stings suggested that a couple of Veritas reporters go to her hotel room and engage in a friendly *ménage à trois*. This invitation had nothing to do with the public malfeasance we were investigating. It had to do with someone's personal sexual decisions. We took it out of the finished product. We also scrubbed the identity of an NPR reporter in Libya out of a hidden-camera tape in the NPR sting to protect that journalist. As veteran reporter Philip Meyer observed, and I tend to agree, undercover journalism "is honorable when the truth provides a social benefit greater than the embarrassment to those deceived."[3]

And that brings us to the underlying fallacy of Steele's rules. There was no longer any national consensus, if there ever was one, as to what constituted a "social benefit" or a "vital public interest." In the absence of consensus, we have expanded Steele's rules as to what constitutes a vital interest. By 2009, ACORN had more than five hundred thousand members distributed among some twelve hundred neighborhood chapters. The organization appeared to us to be one of profound importance. It had been scamming the American taxpayer, intimidating businesses, and stealing votes for nearly forty years, protected all along by its powerful alliances. Yet, the journalists who honored Steele's rules responded with something close to complete indifference. Writing in the prestigious *Columbia Journalism Review,* Greg Marx dismissed our work because our "focus on ACORN was the product of a worldview that vastly exaggerated that group's practical political importance."[4] Says who? There again is that sentiment that some topics, no matter how important, are untouchable. This sentiment is unconscionable. A simple, walk-in video report proved to be fatal because no sunlight had ever penetrated the ACORN operation.

In 2012 and 2013, when Project Veritas turned to election fraud, we showed the gap once again between what people could see for themselves and what the media were willing to acknowledge. According to the media, voter fraud was almost impossible to pull off and, as a result, rare enough to be inconsequential. What our undercover videos showed was how pathetically easy it was to secure a ballot in someone else's name, living or dead.

In one case, we secured the ballot of the sitting attorney general, Eric Holder. What made this doubly embarrassing for Holder is that he had been chief among those dismissing voter fraud as a problem. "There is no proof that our elections are marred by in-person voter fraud," Holder insisted on one occasion.[5] But now even he had to face a congressional grilling about his own ballot being offered to someone who was not Eric Holder.

Historically, in the rough-and-ready days of broadcast journalism, journalists were workaday people with a nose for a good story. Many did not go to college or even high school. Like Nellie Bly or even Geraldo Rivera, they made their reputations through daring and ingenuity. By the end of the twentieth century, a new caste of journalists controlled the media. In 2011, a Project Veritas undercover reporter caught up with two of these journalists at NYU of all places.

In a large lecture hall, NYU journalism professor Jay Rosen and his guest, Clay Shirky, a new-media guru, told the students just who it was that set the news agenda. "We are all in this room insiders," said Shirky. "We are the most elite news [creators.]" By "we" Shirky meant "us chardonnay-swilling news junkies." Rosen added, "We are the one percent." He wasn't kidding. The two of them related how they and their colleagues promoted the causes they wanted to see advance. "Elites are perfectly comfortable with there being information about how they make their decisions and what their biases are," said Shirky, "as long as that only circulates among other elites."[6]

With little attempt to conceal their biases, Rosen and Shirky let the students know what they were supposed to think about contemporary politics. Having worked with the *New York Times* on projects, Shirky explained how the paper's Republican-free newsroom manipulated the news to promote Obama's candidacy in 2008. This he saw as a good thing. The Republican candidates, after all, were "crazy" and "insane." A good tagline for the *Times*, he suggested, was, "Go ahead and imagine two things: President Rick Perry and no *New York Times.*" He made these comments, all seconded by Rosen, assuming that the students agreed with him. By 2011, the students understood that if they wanted a career in journalism they had better do just that.

Despite its good work creating the undercover database, the Arthur L. Carter Journalism Institute at NYU represents much of what is wrong with the profession. "At New York University, we believe that journalism has a serious public mission, and can make a difference in the world," reads its website. "We want to educate those who agree."

What helps in that education, the would-be student learns, is that NYU is located in New York City, "where power and wealth concentrate, news and culture originate."[7] The confluence of these interests we captured in Professor Rosen's classroom: the chardonnay-swilling 1 percent of Shirky's imagination telling the 99 percent what is news and what is not.

"Values" arbiter Bob Steele wrote his "rules" for these very people. What was of "profound importance" to the 1 percent, as we saw in the 2016 presidential election, was not necessarily of profound importance to the rest of America. The media entirely missed the story of the election because their journalists were too busy sounding out each other over glasses of chardonnay in those citadels—New York, Washington, Hollywood, Silicon Valley—where "power and wealth concentrate."

As to the other 99 percent, the forgotten men and women of America, who really cared? We did. While my passion is to *show* reality, I, like most journalists past and present, have an inherent desire to *improve* reality. The hidden-camera stories we do are the best vehicle to accomplish that, maybe the only vehicle. Visuals can shock the conscience in a way print cannot, and moving images have more power than static ones. Video can outrage the public and quickly change the moral consensus. If Upton Sinclair had access to button cameras in 1906, you can bet he would have used them.

Practicing Magic

If prostitution is the oldest profession, intelligence-gathering is a close second. It seems somehow fitting that in our first major operation, the ACORN infiltration, we managed to combine both, or at least the appearance of both.

It is from the intelligence world that our reporters learn their greatest lessons. We never deceive our audience. We admittedly use deception against our *targets* as a means to obtain access to them. With access, we can report the hidden truth about what the target is thinking or doing when the public isn't looking. After all, this is when people are their most honest and most true.

Many journalists prefer not to know. They prefer not to look beyond the artifice that sustains the institutions they admire, left or right. During the Obama years, in particular, they preferred to report what the administration told them. The White House sensed this weakness and exploited it.

"The average reporter we talk to is 27 years old," White House speechwriter Ben Rhodes told David Samuels of the *New York Times*, "and their only reporting experience consists of being around political campaigns. That's a sea change. They literally know nothing." Ned Price, Rhodes's assistant, explained to Samuels that he would tee up the White House line, "and the next thing I know, lots of these guys are in the dot-com publishing space, and have huge Twitter followings, and they'll be putting this message out on their own."[1] I cannot say I invented the phrase, "This isn't journalism. This is stenography," but it sure as hell fit.

At Project Veritas, we recruit and train reporters from anywhere—except Washington, DC. To get past the steno pool and into the heart of a story, our Veritas reporters become who they need to be. To succeed, they need to be believed. For lessons on how *not* to get burned we have turned to military intelligence.

When people think about gathering intel, they think about Glock handguns, Omega watches, fake rocks with embedded data, fancy disguises, and the sneaky pilfering of documents à la Charlie Sheen's Bud Fox character in *Wall Street*. The temptation for our new recruits is to lose themselves in the *cover*—the disguises, the scripts, the elaborate backstories. The truth is, however, that the better our journalists master the arts of mau-mauing and interpersonal communications, the less the cover matters.

In the movie, *Imperium*, for instance, an undercover rookie is told by his handler that the one tool an intelligence officer really needs is the Dale Carnegie classic *How to Win Friends and Influence People*. There is some truth to that observation. Undercover work is almost all about what the professionals call "cultivation." Cultivation takes empathy, chemistry, charm. It might take a monthlong internship to cultivate a source, but then again it might take a thirty-second elevator ride. The undercover, or "u/c," has to know the time limits and form the operational plan accordingly.

The so-called "Moscow rules" tell us, "Do not look back; you are never completely alone." Assuming they are always under observation, our u/c's have to remind themselves that everything is a test: what they do, what they say, how they behave. It is essential they maintain their composure and their cover. The Uber driver may have a grudge. The waiter may be listening in. The young woman at the bar may be a plant. Until they lock the bedroom door of their own home, undercovers are at risk of exposure.

You would think, then, that the people who work undercover have no integrity, but the opposite is true. It is the liars and con artists who do not do well in this business. We screen them out. We look for people with a clean conscience and a moral compass. They will be tested even when they think they are not. The better they remember this, the less vulnerable they become. In an unjust media world bent on revenge, Project Veritas journalists are every bit a target as the sources they themselves target, perhaps more. And while we "deceive in order not to be deceived," we *never* deceive the public. Unlike intelligence operatives, we usually reveal the undercover techniques we use to get the information. Although sly with our targets, we are an open book to the American people.

That being said, there is much I can*not* say about how Project Veritas conducts its business. There are many investigations, methods, and sources I cannot talk about. And although we are usually very systematic in what we do, especially in our "deep cover" investigations, sometimes we just stumble into stuff.

Yet stumbling at Veritas is not just about luck. We get lucky by always being ready when we discover something or someone interesting. Call it "controlled discovery." As Alinsky noted, "Tactics means doing what you can with what you have."[2] Our journalists prepare for moments of opportunity and strive to keep their cool at all times. They try not to forget an important Veritas rule: *Everything is a test.*

The star of one of our best and most entertaining discoveries was a fellow named Robert Klein, a stocky, fortysomething, New Jersey health teacher with an accent right out of *The Sopranos.* I include his story for several reasons. For one, it is a compact case study of a successful sting, albeit unplanned. And for a second, the story is really funny—unless, of course, you're Robert Klein. Most importantly, education reform should be the civil rights issue of our time. The reason it is not is because public education is a sacred cow, a very nearly untouchable subject. The lack of critical external exposure breeds internal decay.

Our investigations into public education repeatedly find a corrupt and complacent establishment, one that trumpets altruism but in fact resists reform. For many in the establishment, retaining power takes precedence over educating children. A textbook publisher in our Common Core investigation said out loud what many must think: "I hate kids. I'm in it to sell books. Don't even kid yourself for a heartbeat."[3] We covertly filmed the president of the teachers union in Yonkers, New York, saying, "Don't you fucking tell anybody anything" about the supposed sexual abuse of children.[4] These videos produced results. Houghton Mifflin Harcourt fired accounts manager Dianne Barrow.[5] The Yonkers School District brought charges against Yonkers Teacher Federation president Patricia Puleo. Although the charges against Puleo were later dropped, Yonkers Inspector General Brendan McGrath validated the integrity of our reporting.[6] Given our resources, we can only expose the tip of the iceberg, but every time we explore public education, we find more and more iceberg.

Our reporters met Klein in November 2015 at a New Jersey Educational Association (NJEA) meeting at the Borgata Hotel in Atlantic City, the state's gambling Mecca, an all too appropriate setting for the NJEA. Our work began with targeting. We targeted this teachers union for a reason. Its leaders had grown fat and happy by ensuring that the students in the poorest schools remained trapped in the public education system. To them words like "voucher" and "charter" were hate speech.

In 2010, veteran newscaster Bob Bowdon focused on the NJEA in his award-winning documentary *The Cartel*.[7] The NJEA attracted Bowdon in no small part because New Jersey spends more per pupil than any other state and yet has many of the nation's lowest-performing schools. This is a state of affairs with which the NJEA seems much too comfortable. Like its parent organization the National Education Association (NEA), the NJEA uses its ample clout to keep the politicians in line and the students in public schools, no matter how bad.

The NJEA was a target-rich environment for one obvious reason: its cozy political alliance with much of the mainstream bred complacency and corruption. We had documented strains of that corruption and lack of accountability in New Jersey before, most notably the case of the teacher who bragged that a colleague called a student the N-word and never got fired. Governor Chris Christie reacted, and one union official was suspended.

To show that this was not an "isolated incident," we descended on the Borgata. The next step in the sequence was the approach. This was no longer easy. After our 2010 exposure of the NJEA and Governor Christie's endorsement of the same, the NJEA put out a warning to all teachers about Veritas and a veritable fatwah on me. Our reporter on the case was Laura Loomer, a twenty-three-year-old Jewish blonde from Arizona who had been kicked out of her private Catholic university in Florida. Her offense was catching administrators on hidden video approving the sending of aid to ISIS. I first met her at the Breakers Hotel in Palm Beach. After a speech I gave there, she badgered me about coming to work for Veritas. She was so relentless I could not say no. It was obvious she had the right stuff.

If Jefferson did not exactly say "Eternal vigilance is the price of liberty," he should have.[8] It is a great quote. Many of our Founding Fathers sacrificed their fortunes. More than a few sacrificed their lives. Preserving what they gave us will always take some effort. At Project Veritas we are always on the lookout for people willing to make the sacrifice required.

My only fear about Laura at the time was that she might be a mole. I had been stung six years earlier by a young woman who planted herself in my operations and alleged all types of misconduct. As I documented at length in my earlier book *Breakthrough,* the judge served up a great dose of justice when he announced, "I am not able to find that there is probable cause for the harassment complaint for the incidents that occurred between October 2nd of 2011 and November 21, 2011."[9] Anyhow, Laura's drive and intensity were such that I thought it worth the risk to bring her on board. Project Veritas is no place for the timid, and timid Laura is not.

A bit of a loose cannon, Laura has a style of approach distinctly her own. I think of it as "smash and grab." Instead of starting with a specific informational goal, she focuses on the individual and lets her—or usually him—determine the direction. No shrinking violet, Laura extracts information from her target with only a little more subtlety than Detective Mackey on *The Shield*.

Although no longer with Veritas, Laura was known to approach a subject, flash a smile, and say, "So tell me all the fraud you are going to commit." Sometimes, this approach worked. Sometimes it did not, but in either case Laura would know within fifteen minutes if she was going to succeed. If she was not, she would cut her losses and move on to a new mark.

On Laura's first training exercise, she went to a potentially volatile Black Lives Matter event on Staten Island. Fearless, she approached

Erica Snipes-Garner, the daughter of Eric Garner, the massive cigarette salesman whose death during a police takedown was captured on video. "You think Al Sharpton is kind of like a crook in a sense?" she asked Snipes bluntly. "He's about this," Snipes answered as she rubbed her thumb and index finger together. Anyone watching knew what Snipes meant. For Sharpton, it was all about the money. The Project Veritas video went viral quickly, earning a front-page *New York Post* picture and causing the painfully corrupt Sharpton a ton of well-deserved hurt among his base.[10] I was proud of Laura while hoping the sensational coverage wouldn't go to her head.

Sort of like Forrest Gump, Laura seems to show up everywhere something is happening. Not hesitant to finesse her way into VIP campaign events, she managed to take multiple selfies of herself with Hillary Clinton, Huma Abedin, even Bill Clinton. Recently she asked Hillary a series of hostile ambush questions during signings on Hillary's *What Happened* book tour. On one occasion, at the Investigative Reporters and Editors Conference, I expressed a need for a drink, and the next thing I know Laura somehow wormed her way to the head of a two-hundred-person drink line to get me one.

A shrewd observer of human nature, Laura has a particularly keen eye for the dirty old man. At the NJEA convention, she caught Klein staring at her from across the hotel's atrium. In full view, she pulled out her lipstick, applied it sensuously, and licked her lips. Klein was snagged. "He looked interesting," Laura told me later, "like the kind of guy who would sleep with a student and want to brag about it."

Laura walked over and sat next to him. Klein tried to play it cool. He said he was a middle school phys ed and health teacher from Howell Township, an exurb in the middle of the state. He kept staring at her, and Laura asked how he felt about those teachers who had sex with kids as young as middle schoolers. Klein was not about to approve of the practice, but he was more than happy to talk about sex in general.

When it comes to long-con investigations, the objective of every first meeting is to get a second meeting. Laura let Klein plow deeper into the explicit details of preteen sexuality at Howell before she broke off for an imaginary lunch. They exchanged cell numbers, and she knew he would contact her. He had a dirty old man stereotype to live up to.

Sure enough, flirtatious texts appeared in her message box. Klein wanted Laura to come to his room to "hang out." What a surprise! She now had to make what the pros call an "OPSEC"—operational security—decision. She envisioned this as a high-risk, low-reward venture. It would not have shocked her to find Klein dressed in a raincoat, axe in hand, looking all the world like the *American Psycho* himself, Patrick Bateman.

Bold as she was, Laura was not about to ignore a basic Veritas Rule, "Don't work alone. Tell someone else your plans." Given Klein's creepiness, she went one step further. She brought along a young male Veritas journalist, Cori. Of course, this made it much less likely that Klein would try to woo her, but that was not our goal in any case. "Conventioneer Beds Strange Young Woman in Hotel Room" has not been a newsworthy storyline for about three centuries. Laura and Cori both came wired.

Sure enough, Klein proved to be creepy, but in ways that surprised even Laura. On meeting her at the door, he looked a bit undone, his eyes red and watery. Klein excused himself to "change his shirt" and came out of the bathroom sniffing and wiping his nose. She thought she knew why. Klein then launched into a rambling discussion on the etiquette of sharing drugs and on his own safety guidelines.

"I'm a teacher. I'm not driving around with fucking weed in my car," he told them at one point, but "blow"—health teacher talk for cocaine—was another story. At this point, Cori pushed a little too hard: "Shouldn't you be careful with bringing drugs on campus because you're a teacher?" He even sounded like a journalist. When I first watched the tape during a debrief, I cringed just a little.

Klein flipped. He slammed his vodka glass down on a coffee table and charged at Cori, backing him up against the suite's kitchen island. "What, do you guys have fucking wires on?" he said in a seeming state of paranoia. "He's got a wire on," he repeated to Laura. Now he started to poke and grab at Cori looking for a recording device.

Laura felt like she was trapped in a bad gangster movie. Her pulse pounded out of her temples, and the cortisol pumped through her bloodstream. *Oh my God*, she thought, *this guy is going to find our wires and kill Cori.* In the movie *The Departed*, Leo DiCaprio's character offered some advice that would be useful for a Veritas journalist in a jam: "Your heart-rate is jacked, your hand . . . steady." This approach is easier said than done, but it is essential. There is no more stressful moment in the life of any undercover than when the target suspects a rat. In all investigative work, particularly with groups inclined to violence such as Antifa, DisruptJ20, and the Ku Klux Klan (Veritas has ongoing undercover operations in all three), the bad guys *will* become suspicious. That is the way human nature works. As best we can, we prepare our journalists for that eventuality.

Still, there is just so much preparation one can do. Laura and Cori had put themselves in a tight spot with little knowledge of the man they were recording. Given the thinness of their relationship, the best they could counter with under the circumstances was to laugh him off or at least try to.

"No dude," said Cori with a relaxed smile. "Chill." He inched closer to the black marble kitchen island, hoping that Klein would back off. He didn't. He felt Cori's shoulder and pants, then put his arm on the back of Cori's neck as though he were about to snap it. For her part, Laura continued to laugh and say, "No, no he doesn't." She was growing more alarmed and was looking for a way out of the room. Inches away from Cori, Klein stared at him, then slowly turned to Laura, his gangster scowl morphing into a great big goofy smile.

At this point, the health teacher at the taxpayer-funded union conference began to offer the two undercover reporters cocaine. "If you want some [cocaine], you can have some. Dude, if you want some I'll give you a taste, don't be embarrassed. Have some."[11]

Luck, they say, is where preparation meets opportunity. The drugs may have slowed Klein down. Maybe it was alcohol. In any case, he groped both of our reporters everywhere except where they had their cameras. I suppose we did get lucky that day. Still, I prefer to call our good fortune "Veritas magic."

Going Borat

In a brainstorming session after the Klein sting, my former chief of staff, Ken, came up with an idea so perfectly "Borat" we instantly fell in love with it. We would present Klein with an award for his contribution to keeping America drug free. We went Borat here for a specific reason: the more entertaining we can make our journalism, the more eyes we can draw to the problem at hand. From our own experience, Klein is not nearly the outlier you would hope he was.

Getting into the school would not be easy. Understandably, after Sandy Hook, authorities had hardened schools in suburban New York the way they might an American embassy in some Mideast hellhole. To get in the school, we needed an operational plan. For the plan to work, we needed to understand our target's potential motivation to meet with us at the school. Unlike many of our projects, there was no ideological card we could play.

We would have to come up with a strategy that appealed to the self-interest of both Klein and his principal.

This scheme took some planning. First, we created an educational consulting company with the benignly bureaucratic name "New Star Learning" to present the award. Of course, New Star Learning had to have a credible-looking website with my smiling image on it and plenty of boasting about our relationship with the NJEA. From Howell Township's website I pulled the name of the vice principal, Juanita Alvarez—second bananas being an easier mark than the first almost everywhere—and called her using a burner phone.

As expected, I got her voicemail: "My name is Bill Stern. I work with a company called New Star Learning. We're an educational organization, and we're calling because we're interested in reaching out to Robert Klein who is a teacher there. We'd like to present him with a certificate based on some of the work he's done in the physical education program at Howell Township. Thank you very much."[12]

In our line of work, 80 percent of communication transcends the words spoken, even on a phone call. When I called Alvarez, I made sure I sounded like it was just another day at the office—confidence, gentleness, warmth, and a touch of indifference. I had my voicemail set up with a female assistant. "Thank you for calling New Star Learning," said the voice, adding our dopily believable slogan, "where excellence is in education and we put the students first." As Saul Alinsky reminded us, "Whenever possible go outside of the experience of your enemy."[13] The very last thing on Alvarez's mind was that this was some elaborate sting.

Alvarez and I played phone tag for a month. I didn't push it. Only a scammer would, and we were hardly that. No, not us. On April 23, I finally made contact with Alvarez. I reminded myself that the most critical imperative of that first contact was to obtain a second one.

"Hey, there," I said casually, "we're from New Star Learning, and we're an education consulting company. We're trying to give out awards. Robert came across our radar, and we'd love to sit in on his class and present him with an award."

"That's nice!" said an unsuspecting Alvarez.

"What I'd just like to do is send one of our employees to sit in on his class, present him an award, take his photo, and put it on our website for a new section we are developing for instructors throughout the tristate area."

"That's great," she replied.

"It's called the Stay Ahead award," I elaborated. "It is primarily for anti-drug efforts and education throughout the tristate area."

"Okay."

Alvarez was hooked. Now it was just a question of arranging the details. I kept the conversation light and congenial. She had trouble nailing a date, she laughed, "because of spring break and its effects on us." I kept that laugh line in my memory bank. It would be a good place to pick up next time. I expressed an interest in having Klein say a few words at the awards presentation on the importance of staying away from drugs.

"We'd love to get a photo too!" I enthused.

"Um, the only thing with that is," said Alvarez, "we cannot publish student's pictures."

I quickly backtracked. "We wouldn't," I said. "It would just be of him up front."

As in any sales call, the important thing is to never give the target an excuse to back out. Alec Baldwin's Blake character said it best in *Glengarry Glen Ross:* "ABC. A-always, B-be, C-closing. Always be closing. Always be closing!"[14] Veritas reporters learned how to deal with roadblocks, how to find a work-around, how to let targets find a way to say yes, how, ultimately, *to close*.

And close I did: May 20, 2015, eighth grade phys ed, 9:47 a.m. It does not get more specific than that. I put the phone down, calmly exhaled, and looked at the two journalists in the room. "May 20," I smiled. We would hold off on the champagne until we got the video.

Disguise

A prime Veritas Rule is that your manner matters more than your costume. Nevertheless, a disguise is often needed, especially if the agent is me. I chose high-water khaki pants that fit a little too tight, the inevitable blue blazer, a striped blue tie, and shades straddling the top of my highlighted blonde hair. "You look like a middle-class white kid who works in white-collar education," said my director of field operations. "You play the part well." Thanks, Mac, that's part of the game.

In choosing a name, it is generally wise to use your own first name in case one of your partners slips up. My problem was that my name had become a little too well known, at least in NJEA circles. So I adopted the official-sounding "Bill Stern."

Improvise, Adapt, and Overcome

Since it was critical that we record the award ceremony on camera, Luke, the "New Star Learning cameraman," was to come with me. Although Westchester County and Howell Township are in the same metropolitan area, it is easier to calculate the time for a trip to the moon and back than to calculate how long it would take to drive during rush hour from one end of the New York City metro to the other. I miscalculated. I arrived after 9:47 a.m. I was not too anxious. The class lasted forty-five minutes. As long as we got in before it ended we were good, but Luke was nowhere to be found. He was coming from Jersey City, a slightly easier drive. He should have been there. If we did not record this ceremony, it might as well not happen. There could be no do-over.

Everything, I reminded myself, is a test. I kept calling and texting. Nothing. Finally, I received a text from Luke. The Howell Township police had detained him near the school because his long camera bag looked suspiciously like a rifle case. The police guard their schools as if every kid there was named "Barron." Unfortunately, I had not properly briefed Luke on what to say in a situation like this, in part because I never could have predicted the police would mistake the camera bag for a weapon. At that moment I had to make an instant calculation: abort the mission and get out or somehow *improvise, adapt, and overcome.* I chose the latter.

Problem was I did not have a camera. Well, yes I did, sort of. I had left my old iPad in the car. The resolution was weak and the acoustics weaker, but it did have a video option. I jumped out of my car, pretended to talk on my cell, smiled and waved at the friendly officers like a man on a mission.

The school's two large metallic front doors were intimidating. I felt like I was about to give an award to an inmate at Riker's Island, not to a teacher at a *nice* New Jersey middle school. I went to hit the button and give my name. When I noticed that the door was slightly ajar I opened it slowly and positioned myself inside the foyer in front of the next set of doors. Fifteen seconds later, a teacher leaving the building opened those doors. I breezed by her, still "talking" on my cell, "Hey Rhonda, it's Bill Stern. Did you get those reports on Passaic County for the New Star finalists?" I passed the test. I looked sufficiently dorky and official. She ignored me.

I'm in, I thought to myself. *Here we go.* I headed for the main office, armed with nothing but an iPad, a plaque, a mission, and some high-grade chutzpah. Three secretaries stood just inside the office door. They looked at me suspiciously.

"How did you get in heya?" asked the oldest one in a New Jersey accent as thick as the sludge on the Passaic River. "Can I help you?"

"Yes," I smiled warmly. "I'm Bill Stern and I'm here with New Star to present the Stay Ahead award. I had an appointment with Juanita Alvarez."

"Well," she grunted, "you'll have to show an ID and sign in."

Damn! "Bill Stern" did not have one. Fake IDs can get an under-cover reporter into more trouble than no ID. Without skipping a beat, I started improvising about the traffic and asking her advice. The cur-mudgeon warmed up. No two people in New Jersey get from point A to point B the same way, and they are happy to tell you their way is the better way.

"Here, just initial this form and show me your ID," she said, soft-ening up just a little and pushing the open binder toward me. As she turned around and went to grab something, I scanned the room look-ing for an alibi.

"My supervisor was wondering if we can still do this today. Would you mind checking if the vice principal is here?"

She made a quick call.

"She'll be right with you."

I had my glasses on my head, looking comfortable, pen in hand, touching the white paper looking like I was about to sign the sheet.

"Where is your restroom?" I asked.

"Right over theya," she responded. I went into the bathroom, turned on the faucet, and placed a call to my producer and asked him if he had heard from Luke. He had not. I went back to the office to wait. After another minute of stalling, in walked Juanita Alvarez.

"Bill! How are you?" she said, reaching out to shake my hand. "Robert's other class ended but we still have time for you to do the presentation. In fact, it's better because the entire middle school gym classes are assembled in the auditorium."

She looked down at my pen touching the sign in sheet. "Don't worry about that, here just take one of these."

Thank you, Lord! Alvarez gave me a green visitor badge for my jacket and rushed me down the hallway and into the auditorium. I scanned the room. What a hoot! They had actually set up a speaker and microphone in the front of the room. At least a hundred kids sat Indian-style on the floor facing the mic, and there was the star of our video, wandering around looking confused in a godawful pair of check-ered shorts and a hoodie. He had to be wondering what the hell he had done to deserve an award.

"Would you like to use the microphone?" Alvarez asked.

Sure. Why not? The principal was standing behind me. I pulled the iPad from my official bag, switched it on and handed it to him. I wish I could tell you that I was a natural, that I could pull off a scam like this without breaking a sweat, but I'm not, and I can't. I had to will myself through it—heart rate jacked, hand steady. I was sure the police were going to come into that gymnasium at any minute and arrest me in front of these kids.

In the video, I look halfway calm. In the gym, I was halfway catatonic. Steadying my nerves, I glanced over at Klein and walked in front of the mic. I launched right into it, shouting over the microphone, "My name is Bill Stern," I stuttered, my pulse pounding. "We're with New Star Learning, and we're here today to congratulate excellence in teaching, both in physical education and health awareness. And we're here today to congratulate one of your teachers for his excellence in helping you."

"Wooh!" A kid or two whooped, and the rest cheered, enthusiastic and unsuspecting. This plan was *working*. We never meant to sting the kids, but hell, the Klein award would give them something to laugh about at class reunions fifty years down the road. I was easing into my emcee role, as I usually do about thirty seconds after getting on any stage, whether in character or not.

"We are very, very familiar with Mr. Klein and his wonderful work," I continued, now laying it on for posterity. "And one of the things we focus on is drug prevention, drug awareness education." At this point, I started getting comfortable enough to ham it up.

"So today, I'm here to present the New Star Learning Stay Ahead Award 2015 excellence in drug abuse awareness . . . to . . . Mr. Robert Klein from Howell Township Middle School. Everybody give a round of applause."

The kids had beaten me to it. The whole auditorium filled with cheers. Now, the trick was to get Klein to say something absurdly ironic on camera and to get myself out of there without blowing my cover.

"Mr. Klein, congratulations and thank you for setting a great example for the students," I said to Klein as I handed him the award and shook his hand. "From all of us at New Star Education, thank you for being here." In my nervousness, I changed the name of our company from New Star Learning to New Star Education. No one noticed.

"Thank you," Klein muttered, looking more than a little sheepish. I knew he thought this entire thing was bullshit, but he had to pretend it wasn't. Holding the award, he rambled for a minute about the various programs the school ran "to keep you drug free." He then closed with a better line than we could have scripted, "Give yourself a natural high instead of doing drugs."

Oh, the irony! GOTCHA! CONTENT IS KING! Even in that moment, I paused five seconds to celebrate internally.

After some anxious small talk, I walked down the hallway as fast as I could and made my way to the parking lot. Driving down the county road and beyond city limits, I could resist the urge no longer. I called back to the office. "We got it! We got it!" I shouted, my heart now beating crazily out of pride in my team and joy in our accomplishment. This sting itself wasn't going to change the world. Hell, it would not even change much in Howell Township. But we were pioneering, spiking deeper down into that educational iceberg on which reform inevitably wrecks. We were forcing the issue of whether the union would discipline Klein for his outrageous behavior, and if not, we were asking what line would a union rep like Klein have to cross? Veritas magic was challenging the status quo, and no one we stung ever deserved the challenge more than Robert Klein.

Aftermath

On June 15, 2015, our finished video went online. Man, did Robert Klein have some explaining to do. In addition to helpful conservative blogs, the UK's *Daily Mail* was up and running with a big photo spread laying out the whole story.[15] This included coverage of the final part of our finished video in which a union rep advises Laura on how to handle her "friend's" drug problem, specifically by not telling the school about it. The rep was clearly more concerned about the user keeping his job than about the students being corrupted.

On June 16, the New Jersey media weighed in, none in more detail than the *Asbury Park Press,* the largest paper in central New Jersey.

By this time, as reported, Klein had been placed on administrative leave with pay, and he was making good money, $99,620 a year. As is customary in the mainstream media, the reporters distanced themselves with a quick refresher on media criticisms of our work. Other than the adjectives used to describe us, the story was extensive and more or less factual.[16]

By the following day, June 17, the *Press* had decided that our offenses against good order were at least as troubling as Klein's. The headline laid the story out: "Howell Cops Investigating Teacher, Hidden Camera 'Stunt.'"[17] The key word, here, is "stunt." From the ACORN sting on, the media have been dismissing our undercover reporting as stunts. They do journalism. We do stunts. Yes, we do "stunts," but we do stunts to sell our journalism. The print people still have not caught on.

According to Klein's attorney, his client was simply "the unfortunate victim of a provocateur who uses heavily edited videos to distort the truth for website clicks." As the attorney saw it, Klein was just the latest such victim given that Project Veritas has a "history of this outrageous conduct." In fact, the video was only lightly edited for the sake of time. Nothing was taken out of context. The Klein the viewer saw was the Klein that Laura met.

Finally—and the article ends with his comments—the NJEA's Steve Baker reminded *Press* readers of my "past legal troubles," including the arrest in New Orleans six years earlier. "James O'Keefe is not an honest or reliable source. He's a political smear artist and he's well-known for his use of deceptively edited video," said Baker. "I think the reporting should be on who he is, on his story." With the *Asbury Park Press* at least, Baker got his way. The stenographers at the *Press* chose not to challenge his casual slander. I can't blame them. It would make little sense for the *Press* to burn the NJEA, a group with more political clout than any other in suburban New Jersey.

This is why video is so crucial. There was no denying what everyone saw. The authorities can tell themselves that Project Veritas was the problem, and the media can confirm the same, but the real problem was the *veritas*, the cinema verité, the truth of who Robert Klein is. "If we hadn't released that video," I said in my one brief statement to the *Press,* "Mr. Klein would be standing in front of students right now. Is that what the Howell Township police really prefer?"

It was certainly not what the people of Howell Township preferred. On the Facebook page, "Howell Happenings," they let loose.[18] Only a few questioned Veritas's tactics. The great majority, most of them female, ignored the media spin and saw the problem exactly for what it was.

"Paid suspension, thank you NJEA."

"PAID???"

"He should never be allowed in or near a school again. Get rid of paid suspension. He's getting paid to sit on the beach. He's disgusting!!!"

"Seriously?! Paid suspension . . ."

"Any one else in any other job would have been fired immediately, this ass clown gets paid suspension . . . SMFH."

"Paid suspension. . . . Well at least he could buy more coke. . . . These unions are becoming jokes. . . ."

"Paid for what? He should be fired, exposed for being a fraud and punished for being detrimental to children."

"I think the bigger story is 99600 for a middle school gym teacher. . . ."

The story died a quick death. The police could find no reason to charge us. The school refused to talk about Klein's stature, citing privacy issues, and the media had little interest in pursuing a story that made their educator allies look bad. Some months later, Klein quietly resigned and scurried down the memory hole. And that was that.

The reader may be wondering, what's the point of these investigations if the misbehavior continues? To that, I will say two things. For one, school districts nationwide, under union pressure, have so often allowed problem teachers to walk away with their résumés intact that the practice has gotten a name: "pass the trash." It is one thing to read about a problem teacher. It is another thing to see one—or more—in practice. For another, you will see in the pages that follow how we applied the same techniques to a slightly larger target: the Hillary Clinton campaign. It never hurts to practice.

Meeting Candidate Trump

t's Corey with Mr. Trump. Any chance we can talk soon?

I received this text on June 4, 2015. This was eleven days before we released the Klein video and twelve days before Donald Trump announced his candidacy for the presidency. I had no idea who Corey was, but I was game for something Trump. As I mentioned, I had met Trump before. He was a fascinating guy. He told me he was a fan of the ACORN investigation and some of the work we did on college campuses. I sensed from the beginning a potential synergy in our relationship. I had no idea, at that moment, that Trump was going to run for president of the United States.

Absolutely. When works for you?

By the time Corey Lewandowski and I got together, Trump had declared his candidacy. So had Hillary Clinton, and the nature of the game had changed. Now I was less interested in Trump as ally or even donor than I was in the attention he could bring to bear on our video work. What I was hoping, in particular, was that Trump would publicly comment on an exchange we serendipitously recorded at Hillary's campaign launch on June 13.

Always opportunistic, Project Veritas journalist Laura Loomer was standing in line at a Hillary souvenir stand when she struck up a conversation with the women in front of her. As always, Laura's camera was rolling. "I'm Canadian," the woman said when she reached the booth and tried to buy something. Manning the booth were Molly Barker, the Clinton campaign's director of marketing, and Erin Tibe, the campaign's compliance manager. Tibe is a lawyer. At first, Barker and Tibe declined the Canadian's money because the purchase would amount to a donation, and candidates could only accept donations from US citizens or permanent residents. The Canadian then said of her new friend, "Can I give her the money?" Laura, of course, agreed, and Barker approved the end-around. "So Canadians can't buy [merchandise] but Americans can buy it for them?" asked Laura. "Not technically," said Barker. "*You* would just be making the donation."[1]

"Not technically" translates to "not legally." This was not a low-level staffer making an error. This was the campaign's marketing director approving an illegal donation in front of the campaign's chief compliance officer. The donation was small, but the violation was telling. Heading up to the fifth-floor campaign headquarters in Trump Tower, my communications director, Stephen Gordon, and I hoped to persuade then campaign manager Lewandowski to get Trump behind the video.

On entering the headquarters, however, I quickly lowered my expectations. For all of the attention paid to the Trump campaign in the previous few weeks, there wasn't much campaign to pay attention to. The interior walls and flooring were totally unfinished. The "headquarters" smelled strongly of cement and drywall dust, not at all what you would expect just a few floors down from Trump's personal office.

Just three people were wandering around in the cavernous office space. Lewandowski was one of them. A former state trooper from Massachusetts, he swore like a rap star and buzzed around like a madman. While I tried to speak to him, he was juggling two phones and brushing off network callers as if they were telemarketers or Jehovah's Witnesses. "It's CNN," he said when one call came in. He shut it down. "I'm not going to fucking answer them."

Still, for all the shallowness of the operation, Lewandowski remained confident. He pointed to a pile of "Make America Great Again" hats and told me, "We can't keep up with the demand. People love 'em." One thing that struck me even then was the message scrawled on the whiteboard in his office, "Let Trump be Trump." Someone had already figured something out.

Floating in and out of the space was an eye-catching, twentysomething brunette from Greenwich, Connecticut, with the Hollywood name Hope Hicks. When I learned that she used to model for Ralph Lauren I was not a bit surprised. At the time, she was serving as the campaign's press secretary/communications director.

"Hey, Hope, this is the wild man that crossed the Rio Grande as Osama bin Laden," said Lewandowski, cracking open another Monster energy drink and texting CNN producers at the same time.

"Oh, cool," she said, entirely unimpressed.

The third member of the triumvirate just started the day I arrived. A tall, good-looking guy right out of school, he sat at a plastic desk in the middle of an empty space waiting, I presumed, for his first assignment. If Lewandowski was optimistic, young Johnny McEntee was positively ebullient. "Trump is going to be president, dude," McEntee told me, "and I am going with him."

"You pretty confident?" I asked. I know. Success has a thousand fathers and failure is an orphan, and at this point Trump's unlikely rise has become a cliché. But remember that immediately after Trump announced, all but a handful of human beings thought the candidacy was a joke. In that large unfinished room, with the two-by-fours still exposed and the campaign more imagined than real, there were a few chiefs but only one Indian, and this was his very first day. What was striking about the unsophisticated McEntee was that he *knew,* deep in his heart, with *certainty* that Trump was going to win. I could see it on his face.

"One hundred percent will be president," he answered. When McEntee spoke, he sounded like a coach giving a locker room pep talk. He had probably heard a lot of those. He played quarterback at the University of Connecticut and produced an astonishing trick shot video that has been watched more than 7 million times. McEntee had a good nose for the future. As of this writing, he serves as Trump's official "body man" in the White House, a cross between body guard and valet.

I played the Canadian donation video for Lewandowski on my laptop. "Wow," he said. "Let's go see Mr. Trump." When I arrived at Trump's office, he was on the phone to Scotland, discussing one of his two golf courses there. (In my quick research on these courses, I discovered that every article I could find after Trump announced for the presidency was negative. No surprise there.) I am something of a multitasker myself, but the idea of running a worldwide business empire while running for president of the United States seemed just a bit daunting.

Once again, The Donald carved out what seemed to me to be an exorbitant amount of time given all that was going on around him. I remember thinking to myself, *Who I am to get an hour with Donald Trump?* My hope was that he would go public with the video. Lewandowski's original hope was that I would do some oppo research on Jeb Bush and Marco Rubio. I had already nixed that idea, but Lewandowski was gracious enough to retreat to the far side of the room and let me and Stephen pitch his candidate face-to-face.

Trump placed my laptop on a pile of the papers, magazines, invoices, and miscellaneous clutter on his desk and watched the video. He never removed his suit jacket while sitting at his now-famous desk. And contrary to the way he is perceived in public, he listened a lot more than he spoke. And when he did speak, it was mostly to ask another sharp question in a rather earthy and humble style.

"What do you think, Corey?" he asked.

"I'd go with it," said Lewandowski.

When Trump turned back to me, the whole tone of the conversation changed. He was no longer the friendly fan. He was the serious candidate. He asked us how much in earned media we thought he had netted so far, a month or so into the campaign. Stephen and I both estimated about $100 million. He thought that about right. He knew how the game was played. He asked a few more questions and then made his decision.

"Let's wait until after the primaries."

Trump said this with such conviction that I did not feel as if he were blowing me off. I could sense he was planning ahead, keeping the video on reserve until the time was right to go after Hillary. He and his three-person campaign staff were going to win the Republican nomination. That was a given. He certainly believed it. Lewandowski believed it. And John McEntee did not just believe it, he guaranteed it—100 percent.

I would see Trump one more time before the presidential debate in Las Vegas. It was January 2016. We were doing an investigation into

Common Core in New Hampshire, and Trump was to make a speech in nearby Burlington, his one and only visit to Bernie Sanders's Vermont. Hoping to get Lewandowski interested in our Common Core videos, I decided to check the event out.

The rally was a blast. Trump spoke at the jam-packed Flynn Theater. These were the Vermonters, I guessed, who didn't quite feel the Bern. They were, to say the least, energized. Afterward a Trump aide took me backstage. There Trump bodyguard Keith Schiller noticed me and tugged on Trump's sleeve to get his attention. Trump turned.

"Hey, there's O'Keefe," Trump shouted across the room. "They call me the wild man. He's the real wild man. He crossed the Rio Grande as Osama bin Laden."

I guess the Border Patrol brass were not the only ones who noticed.

Recognizing Propaganda

These early meetings with Trump convinced me he understood the media better than working journalists. I could appreciate that. I have been a student of the media since my Rutgers days, maybe before.

When I started at Rutgers, it had been almost sixty years since F. A. Hayek, an Austrian-British economist, wrote the political classic, *The Road to Serfdom.* His analysis works better for contemporary America than George Orwell's does, I believe, for one simple reason: we have not yet arrived at *1984.* We are, however, well on "the road to" that unholy destination.

In a section aptly titled, "The End of Truth," Hayek describes the mind-set of the aspiring totalitarian: "The whole apparatus for spreading knowledge—the schools and the press, radio and motion picture— will be used to spread those views which, whether true or false, will strengthen the belief in the rightness of the decisions taken by the authority; and all information that might cause doubt or hesitation will be withheld."[1]

If Hayek spoke against such comprehensive propaganda, others spoke on its behalf, none more influentially than Edward Bernays. Like Hayek, Bernays was born in Austria but moved to the United States as a boy. In his 1928 classic *Propaganda,* Bernays argued that even literate citizens are incapable of making their own decisions in that they are guided by "herd instincts and mere prejudice."[2] Bernays, who is Sigmund Freud's nephew, made the case for an "invisible government," one that would filter and explain complicated data in such a way that people would come to the conclusions the elite wanted them to.

The forces behind this invisible government—what we call the "deep state"—know better than to share this worldview with the public. It wars with the self-image Americans have of being a free people capable of making their own decisions. At Project Veritas, we believe that as long as they have the raw information made available to them, Americans can and will make good decisions. In fact, this idea is incorporated in the Veritas Vision Statement.

Sometimes, the elite's real feelings just slip out. In February 2017, the cohosts of MSNBC's *Morning Joe* TV show, Mika Brzezinski and Joe Scarborough, were expressing their frustration that President Trump was not allowing the major media to filter and explain what he was thinking. Instead, he was appealing directly to the American people. This troubled both of them, Brzezinski most notably.

"He is trying to undermine the media and trying to make up his own facts," she told Scarborough. "And it could be that while unemployment and the economy worsens, he could have undermined the messaging so much that he can actually control exactly what people think. And that, that is our job."[3] This kind of gaffe is common enough in the political-media complex that it has its own name, a "Kinsley gaffe," in honor of journalist Michael Kinsley, who first identified the phenomenon.

Aware that she had inadvertently said out loud what she was thinking, Brzezinski tried to control the damage via Twitter, the very medium she and others criticized the president for using. Today I said it's the media's job to keep President Trump from making up his own facts, tweeted Brzezinski, NOT that it's our job to control what people think.[4] In an era before the internet, before citizens could review what broadcasters actually said, Brzezinski might have gotten away with denying the obvious. In 2017, people saw the denial for what it was: another textbook example of how the major media operate in their war against a threat like Donald Trump.

The investigative journalist working for the public interest is the propagandist's natural enemy. The media, as communications guru Elihu Katz famously noted, can "construct reality and impose their construction on defenseless minds."[5] The independent journalist can deconstruct that "reality" and give citizens the information needed to make up their own minds.

On the one end of the journalist spectrum are the propagandists. For a politician, shading the truth comes with the job description. Journalists who do the same betray their craft. For the statist, Hayek reminded us, "*Every* activity must derive its justification from a conscious social purpose."[6] Journalists who yoke themselves to that "purpose" become, in effect, propagandists. They tend to avoid reporting that might subvert the social agenda of the cultural elites and, by default, allow waste, fraud, and abuse to fester in politically protected organizations.

When the COO of Facebook, Sheryl Sandberg, emailed Clinton campaign chair John Podesta that she "wants Hillary to win badly" and that "I am still here to help as I can," she conceded that the social purpose of her powerful media enterprise was the same as Team Hillary's.[7] When the managing director of politics for CBS digital, Will Rahn, said of his media colleagues, "We were all tacitly or explicitly #WithHer,"[8] he acknowledged that the network's primary purpose in 2016 was not to report the facts but to elect Hillary Clinton. Journalists did not have to "lie" to be with her. They simply had to suppress stories that worked against her interest and elevate those that worked on her behalf. The fact that essentially all of them were pulling in the same direction represented a collective giant step on the road to serfdom. As it turned out, our stories at Project Veritas did not work on "her" behalf. In fact, our stories threatened the propagandists' control of the narrative, and, as expected, they retaliated.

Authoritarians prefer that ordinary citizens, especially citizen journalists, not speak up or speak out. They fear, as Hayek warned, that unfiltered information "might produce results which cannot be foreseen and for which the plan does not provide. It might produce something new, undreamt of in the philosophy of the planner."[9]

We will not be silenced. At the heart of our mission, as mentioned, is *veritas,* the Latin word for "truth" and one of the three generally recognized "transcendentals," the other two being goodness and beauty. These correspond respectively with science (the true), religion (the good), and the arts (the beautiful). In a state drifting leftward, as Hayek observed, authorities begin to question any activity within these fields if done for their own sake and "without ulterior purpose." Truth, however, is not something that can be bent or broken. Truth is the way things are, not the way journalists wish they were.

One of the twentieth century's great heroes, and mine as well, Aleksandr Solzhenitsyn, spoke to this issue in his memorable 1978 Harvard commencement address. "Harvard's motto is *veritas*," he reminded the graduates. "Many of you have already found out, and others will find out in the course of their lives, that truth eludes us if we do not concentrate our attention totally on its pursuit."[10] Solzhenitsyn's knowledge came firsthand. The *Gulag Archipelago* author witnessed the workings of a totalitarian state up close, including from the inside of a prison camp.

What discouraged Solzhenitsyn, who had been living in the United States for several years, was the media's indifference to truth and their unwillingness to pursue it. "One gradually discovers a common trend of preferences within the Western press as a whole," he said. "It is a fashion; there are generally accepted patterns of judgment; there may be common corporate interests, the sum effect being not competition but unification."[11] As he saw it, the media were squandering their freedom.

For a journalist, the overriding goal should not be to serve some transitory purpose but to pursue the truth, as Solzhenitsyn said, "totally." Yes, we would all like to better the human condition, but to accomplish that we have to understand our present circumstances, and we can only achieve understanding through truth.

The postmodernists make this pursuit difficult. If Solzhenitsyn believed that truth was rooted "in man's sense of responsibility to God," the postmodernist rejects such absolutes out of hand. To the postmodernist, Solzhenitsyn's ordered moral universe would seem quaint if not downright bigoted. As David Ernst argued in an insightful article on Trump and the postmodernists, the latter operate "according to just one moral imperative: discredit anything that other people presume to stand for goodness, because the belief that anything is superior to anything else inevitably results in prejudice, interpersonal strife, and inequality."[12]

The postmodernist thinks nothing of dismissing or denying real information in order to help craft a political identity or form an agenda. If all truth is relative and personal, why not advance a "truth" that enhances power and facilitates social control? Fueling that advance is the postmodernist's most potent energy source, political correctness. We dismiss the postmodern embrace of this phenomenon at our own risk. This is identity politics waged as war against the truth, against fact, against reason, ironically even against science.

As Hayek observed fifty years before anyone worried about climate change, "A pseudo-scientific theory becomes part of the official creed which to a greater or lesser degree directs everybody's action."[13] Accepted orthodoxy on a wide range of subjects—the true, the good, and the beautiful—are all, said Hayek, "necessarily based on particular views about facts which are then elaborated into scientific theories in order to justify a preconceived opinion."

More than a few pundits have observed that we are now past the point where citizens can agree on facts. The filter of political correctness makes serious conversations about jobs and economics impossible when one camp is employing the filter and the other is not. As to why any sane person would rely on such willful distortion, Ernst traces the answer to the oldest of human impulses, the need to acknowledge and punish sin, real or imagined. The more fault I find in thee, the holier I am than thou, the more power I should have over you and yours. The irony, of course, is rich. The postmodernists begin by tearing down a value system crafted and refined over the millennia and end up replacing it with a jerry-rigged monstrosity that is altogether more punitive.

The postmodern state does not have to flex its muscles. It need only whisper in the public's ear. The fear of being shamed is far greater on the right than the fear of being arrested or censured. Elected Republicans in particular cringe at the thought of being called out by the press. The media have long insisted that Republicans are heartless. Today, they insist Republicans are also homophobic, sexist, racist, classist, Islamophobic, xenophobic, transphobic, even "anti-science."

Anxious about being branded, surrounded in capital cities by press propagandists eager to do the branding, congressional Republicans would rather do nothing than risk a scarlet letter.

Report on fraud at the polls, and you want to bring back Jim Crow. Report on insecurity at the border, and you want to break up families. Report on refugee fraud, and you don't care if dead babies wash up on beaches. Report on abuses inside the teachers unions, and you oppose civil rights and public education. Too often elected officials avoid public shame, no matter how unfounded, by abandoning common sense or withdrawing from the arena altogether. If these examples sound "partisan," it is only because they fall outside the boundaries of an Overton window framed by a nearly monolithic media in their support of a shared, if ever shifting, "social purpose."

No sooner do citizens yield to some new and artificial norm than the statists create a new norm with which to shame them. Who, for instance, could have predicted just three years ago that Bruce Springsteen would boycott the State of North Carolina "to show solidarity for those freedom fighters"? Without intending, Springsteen made Hayek's case that the totalitarian-minded deform the language of virtue to serve their own ends. Here, Springsteen, the "Boss," coopts a term once used to describe those fighting and dying to oppose tyranny to describe those lobbying with impunity for extra bathrooms. Progressives have been degrading the language for years in their push for marriage *equality*, economic *freedom*, social *justice*, and, of course, *choice*.

In the 2016 NFL season, the larger social purpose shifted dramatically when some NFL players openly began to sit or kneel during the national anthem, an unthinkable gesture just a year or two earlier. During the 2017 season, President Trump wished out loud that the players would be fired.[14] Writing for the *Sporting News*, Michael McCarthy observed that the networks used their production capabilities at the televised NFL games "as a golden opportunity to demonstrate unity among players, coaches, and owners—and opposition to Trump's comments." To accomplish this, they instructed their cameramen to avoid crowd shots lest they show protesting fans. "By covering one of the most significant days in NFL history with rose-colored glasses," reported McCarthy, "the networks cheated viewers. We got an incomplete picture of what really happened in stadiums on Sunday and Monday."[15] Unfortunately for the networks, citizens with cell phone cameras were capturing the truth, and many of their videos went viral. In the internet age, content that runs against the monolithic grain will almost inevitably appear "partisan." Whether the networks can bend the majority of football fans to their will remains to be seen.

"The most effective way of making everybody serve the single system of ends toward which the social plan is directed is to make everybody believe in those ends," said Hayek.[16] Those who could not be lulled into throwing off, say, the Judeo-Christian concept of marriage or the will to defend the nation against Islamic terrorism or respect for the flag could be shamed into doing it. These new norms do not emerge organically through trial and error over long periods of time as is true of more traditional norms. No, they are manufactured in the nation's political and media centers and used as weapons to subdue the nation's reluctant citizens. In the midst of these centers, only slightly more real than the outlandish "Capital" of *The Hunger Games,* even good citizens lose their way.

"In spite of the abundance of information, or maybe because of it," said Solzhenitsyn forty years ago, "the West has difficulties in understanding reality such as it is."[17] In our own humble way at Project Veritas, we strive to improve that understanding.

Meeting Alan Schulkin

A month after meeting the prize-winning phys ed teacher Robert Klein at an Atlantic City teachers convention, Project Veritas journalist Laura Loomer found a little more Veritas magic upon meeting Alan Schulkin at a United Federation of Teachers holiday party in New York City.

Like Klein, Schulkin is one of those frumpy middle-aged guys who cannot resist sharing his soul with a twenty-three-year-old blonde. Always opportunistic, Laura got a break here. She got a break by being ready to pursue a new angle when one presented itself—again, controlled discovery. Schulkin wasn't a teacher or an administrator. He was the Manhattan Democratic representative on the city's Board of Elections. Introducing herself as a political consultant, Laura wasted no time getting to the heart of the issue once she realized what Schulkin did for a living.

As Laura was aware, fraudulent voting had been one of our more consistent targets over the last several years. Although we had not finalized anything, we were well along in our plans to investigate election fraud of all sorts in the 2016 election. As tempting as it was to release the video Laura captured right away, I thought it would work better with what would prove to be our "Rigging the Election" series, so we held it until October 10, 2016, just four weeks before the presidential election.

"You think they should have voter ID in New York?" Laura asked Schulkin.[1]

"Yeah, they should ask for your ID," said Schulkin. "You go into a building, you have to show them your ID. I think there is a lot of voter fraud." He elaborated, "People don't realize, certain neighborhoods in particular they bus people around to vote." When Laura asked which neighborhoods, Schulkin affirmed her suggestion about black and Hispanic neighborhoods, adding, "and Chinese too."

Laura prodded the commissioner about Muslims wearing burkas. "They detonate bombs in the public schools, which we are using. That could disrupt the whole election," Schulkin responded, now hypothetically. "Your vote doesn't even count, because they can go in there with a burka and you don't know if they are a voter." Nor did Schulkin have much faith in Mayor Bill de Blasio's ID program.

"He gave out ID cards, de Blasio," said Schulkin. "That's in lieu of a driver's license, but you can use it for anything. But they didn't vet people to see who they really are. Anybody can go in there and say, 'I am Joe Smith, I want an ID card.'"

This was powerful stuff, coming as it did from a Democratic election commissioner in New York who had obviously grown weary of the corruption he was supposed to ignore. "It's absurd. There is a lot of fraud. Not just voter fraud, all kinds of fraud," he sighed. "This is why I get more conservative as I get older." If this commissioner was eager enough to share this information with a stranger at a Christmas party, imagine the info politicians have shared with friendly journalists they trusted enough to keep their mouths shut.

When we released the finished video in October 2016, the reaction was predictable. The *New York Post* and other conservative media reported the story. The liberal New York *Daily News* attacked it, and the *New York Times* ignored it. Completely. In the political back-and-forth that followed, the *Times* never once saw fit to mention Schulkin's name.

Schulkin proved surprisingly resolute. He told the *Post* that Laura, bless her heart, "was like a nuisance," one that he just tried to "placate." Waffling a little, he allowed that he "should have said 'potential fraud' instead of 'fraud,'" but he held his ground that strong voter ID laws were needed to curb fraud.[2]

Not surprisingly, in his weekly "Ask the Mayor" segment on WNYC three days later, de Blasio demanded that Schulkin resign. "That's crazy," de Blasio said of Schulkin's assertions. "What he said was entirely inappropriate and unfair and absolutely the reverse of what someone should be saying on the Board of Elections. He should really step down."[3]

As de Blasio saw things, the commissioner's role was less to ensure an honest election than to generate turnout. "He's supposed to be guaranteeing maximum voter participation and his statements and his values obviously indicate he's not trying to do that," railed de Blasio. "And to attack one of the things that has empowered people to participate which is IDNYC and to attack it falsely proves that he's just not up for the role."

In the Orwellian world of Democratic politics, an official gets taken to the woodshed not for lying, but for telling the truth, not for corrupting the electoral process, but for protecting it. To his credit, Schulkin refused to resign, saying the mayor didn't "control" the board. Unfortunately, he underestimated the mayor's reach.

When the terms of the five Democratic commissioners expired on December 31, the terms of the other four were renewed. Schulkin's was not, at least not immediately.[4] The reason, the *Daily News* insinuated in the opening sentence of an article on Schulkin's seeming demise, was his having been "caught on tape making *wild* claims about voter fraud."[5] Now you would expect de Blasio to call Schulkin's assertions "crazy." He's got a hide to protect. But for the *Daily News* to dismiss Schulkin's claims as "wild" without a lick of investigation subverts the profession. And the *Daily News* is hardly unique in this regard. When alerted to the possibility of voter fraud, we often hear the media saying, "Where's the proof?" I hear myself saying in response, "Look, damn it! That's your job." Happily, Schulkin somehow managed to keep his job. I hate to see people getting fired for being honest.

Former *Wall Street Journal* editorialist John Fund has taken voter fraud more seriously than most in the media. In 2012, he and former Federal Election Commission (FEC) member Hans von Spakovsky published *Who's Counting? How Fraudsters and Bureaucrats Put Your Vote at Risk*. Said the authors, and this I can verify from experience, "The campaign to deny the existence of voter fraud knows no bounds."[6] They cite one example after another of elected officials and unelected pundits dismissing concern about voter fraud as paranoid and probably racist to boot.

The fraud deniers have a lot to explain. Despite the unwillingness of the media and many local prosecutors to investigate, any number of actionable cases have surfaced in recent years. In 2011, for instance, a former city clerk in Troy, New York, pleaded guilty to corrupting an absentee ballot and turned in four of his colleagues guilty for the same. "Faking absentee ballots was a commonplace," one of the defendants told authorities.[7] In West Virginia, a former sheriff was convicted of producing more than one hundred fraudulent ballots. In Texas, the state attorney general has convicted more than fifty of his fellow citizens of voter fraud.[8] The list is a long one, but you could drape the front of the *New York Times* with it and reporters would still find a way not to see.

The *New York Times* did not used to be so blind. In March 2001, for example, *Times* reporter Drummond Ayres led a story on voter fraud with this causal observation: "When it comes to American cities with a notorious history of election fraud, St. Louis can hold its own. Its political past is replete with instances in which people no longer alive got to vote, not to mention people who never lived."[9] Had Ayres written a sentence like that in 2016, his editors would have dispatched him to sensitivity camp. In the fifteen years that followed, the fraud did not go away, but honest reporting on fraud certainly did. Like most other major media, the *Times* had come to align its mission with the deep state's. With a Hillary Clinton victory in 2016, that alignment would be complete. *Pravda* would rule, and *truth* would suffer the consequences.

Channeling Chicago

It doesn't matter what the friggin' legal and ethics people say, we need to win this motherfucker.

—Scott Foval, People for the American Way

I'm not suggesting we wait around. We need to start this shit right away.

—Bob Creamer, Democracy Partners[1]

The story that follows would prove to be the biggest in the history of Project Veritas. Yes, ACORN had been huge and without doubt put Veritas and me on the map. But the Democracy Partners investigation brought us a level of exposure and influence we dared not even hope for when we started the project. It has also allowed me to expand our operations from a handful of associates into something like an investigative army.

Political analysts say WikiLeaks, the Russians, and James Comey all played a role in getting Donald Trump elected the forty-fifth President of the United States of America. Those paying attention give a fair share of credit to Project Veritas. Were we as partisan as the *New York Times*? Not even close. Again, introducing information that a monolithic media establishment denies the American people makes us appear "partisan," but that establishment indicted itself through its relentless suppression of contrary information.

Candidate Trump mentioned our investigation in the third and final presidential debate. On her campaign plane shortly after the first Democracy Partners story went viral, Hillary Clinton tensed up when asked by Fox News about our work. Of course, she dismissed us, but what else could she do? However reluctantly, every major news media platform from the *New York Times* to CBS to my old nemesis NPR had our stories front and center just weeks before the election. Some believe the campaign momentum really shifted on October 17, the day we released the first video in our "Rigging the Election" series. At least 5 million people were given a powerful incentive not to vote for the party that was corrupting the democratic process.

The breakthrough came in a small neighborhood bar in Milwaukee many months before the election. It resulted from a conversation between a Project Veritas journalist wearing a hidden camera and a political operative mouthing off. Few people had ever heard of Scott Foval before that encounter, but he was a key Democratic player, one of the top guys in Wisconsin. Soon enough he would become an internet sensation.

We had sent one of our most seasoned political journalists to Wisconsin a week before its primary in early April 2016. We assigned him the nom de guerre "Steve Packard." A filmmaker from the San Francisco area, Steve came to my attention many years earlier after we released the first ACORN videos. In fact, he volunteered to shoot some background footage for the videos to follow.

As an undercover journalist, Steve has many virtues. First and foremost, he is smart. He knows the lingo of the left and all their little passions. Pushing thirty now, Steve looks like you'd expect a Californian filmmaker to look, cool and blondish, but he has the ability to "blend" almost anywhere. Before Wisconsin 2016, he had done investigations on voter fraud, common core, the Veterans Administration, and many more. When circumstances demanded, he could all but disappear into the woodwork.

We initially deployed Steve to Milwaukee to investigate suspicions of voter bribery. We had gotten wind of this from on-the-ground sources in previous elections. It was Steve's ninth deployment to Wisconsin in five years, his most traveled state and far and away his most successful investigative venue.

The first night after Steve checked into his hotel, he touched base with us over the phone. "I always get something when I'm out here," he told us. Seven days later, on the evening of the primary, he thought he might return home empty-handed, but then he ran into Foval, a gift who would keep on giving.

Steve had begun the week by volunteering at a community organization with the upbeat name YES—Youth Empowered in the Struggle. YES represented the youth division of a social justice operation called Voces de la Frontera. Steve and his new colleagues were trained to canvass neighborhoods for liberal politicians running in the primary, local and state.

In between activities, Steve saw a guy standing in the main Voces office futzing with his iPad. The fellow noticed Steve and said in a familiar tone, "Oh, hey man." He apparently thought he had met Steve before. Considering Steve's veteran status among the Wisconsin left, he may have, but Steve did not recognize Foval at this meeting. Their subsequent meeting later in the week would prove crucial.

Moments later Steve met Christine Neumann-Ortiz, a popular player in Milwaukee politics. He then accompanied a group into the bitter cold of inner-city Milwaukee to canvass. Although not quite at the level of, say, manning the line at a Chicago packinghouse, undercover work at Project Veritas can be unpleasant.

Steve's priority was to find out which groups were doing the "knock-and-drag." This was a practice as old as Chicago. It entailed driving through poor neighborhoods on Election Day and recruiting potential voters using whatever lures were necessary. The intel on previous elections was that knock-and-draggers were giving *dragees* twenty-five-dollar payments and miscellaneous swag in exchange for their votes.

On midterm Election Day in 2014, Steve had followed mysterious black vans around the city for hours hoping to record an exchange. One of his sources saw the vans being parked behind the Carpenters Union building after the polls closed. There, dozens of blue bags were unloaded from the trunks and deposited into pods large enough to hatch a new Democrat. That same night, the source followed one of these vans from the Carpenters Union all the way into Chicago. Neither the source nor Steve could be sure what was going on, but whatever it was, it appeared to be well organized. His sources had witnessed these strange machinations every election day for years. From our experience, the "Chicago way" of doing politics had pretty much become the "Democratic way."

Over time Wisconsin became ground zero for Democratic anxiety. The very existence of union-thwarting Republican governor Scott Walker had driven the left nuts. Elected in 2010, Walker had unnerved the Democrats in 2011 by successfully passing legislation to limit the collective bargaining rights of state workers. The Democrats and their union allies promptly moved to recall Walker. In the January 2012 recall election Walker won by a bigger margin than he had in 2010, and he won again in 2014.

In the tumultuous year of 2011, Steve was on the ground in Wisconsin when fourteen Democratic state legislators fled the Capitol to deny a quorum for Walker's budget repair bill. Where did they go? Where else? Chicago, the city where the dead go to vote. It was also the city where several generations of activists, including Barack Obama, learned the tactics of manipulation, intimidation, and fraud that have served the Democratic Party so well. In time, thanks to Steve's effort, we would meet another community organizer from those same Chicago swamps who worked closely with Obama's White House and was just a speed dial away from Hillary Clinton. He would have a lot to say.

Throughout primary week, Steve played the role of a young Democratic organizer. He knocked on hundreds of doors to make sure voters turned out for the presidential primary. If you had seen Steve in action, you would want to be his agent. The man can act. He infiltrated over half a dozen leftist groups, each one leading to another: YES, Voces, Occupy Wisconsin, Citizen Action, MICAH, SOPHIA, the local campaigns, and finally, on primary day, Wisconsin Jobs Now.

To this point, at least to the degree that anyone let Steve see, none of the canvassers had done anything illegal. Frustrated by his lack of useful video, Steve called us on primary day, April 5. He wanted to share his concerns and brainstorm some possible avenues of attack. We encourage our journalists to be innovative, and Steve was certainly that. During our conversation, he proposed an eleventh-hour gambit that popped into his head while we were speaking. It would prove enormously fruitful.

Although Wisconsin had made voting more accessible by extending the voting period, it recently passed one of those "racist" photo ID laws. Steve had read, or at least thought he had, that an employer-issued ID would work at the polls if it could be reinforced with a verification of residence such as a pay stub or utility bill. Steve conjured up a *re-enfranchisement* plan, one that offset the expected voter loss in the black community from the enforcement of the photo ID law. As Steve explained the rationale, the scheme would make sure that these precincts produced the number of votes Democrats counted on before the passage of the voter ID law—social justice with a wrinkle.

The compensatory votes would come largely from those with the most to lose in a Trump presidency—undocumented immigrants. Here is how it worked: A philanthropist friend of Steve's would create a shell company that would hire scores of phony workers. The company would provide these "employees" with photo IDs and put their Wisconsin addresses on the stubs of their bogus paychecks. To secure those addresses, canvassers like Steve would compile a list of the abandoned apartments and houses they came across. The new employees would be activists, legal or otherwise, bused in to vote as needed.

This "surrogate voting" scheme might sound outlandish to the reader, but I sensed its potential to capture the hearts of the more imaginative Democratic operatives. I authorized Steve to run with it, and he did. Looking for the people most likely to appreciate the scheme, he worked his contacts to get in with Wisconsin Jobs Now. His contact there was an activist named Terri Williams. Among other words of wisdom, she casually acknowledged the reality of "knock-and-drag"—using that very phrase.

During that primary day, Steve rode around with the knock-and-drag crew in an Escalade. When he had the opportunity, he ran the surrogate voting scheme by a few of the crew and, although intrigued, they weren't biting. After the polls closed, crew members invited Steve to join them at Garfield's 502, a jazz and blues bar. As part of their training, our journalists learn that it is important to create friendly relationships with targets in order to be invited to more casual events. In settings like these, their new friends are more likely to open up, unaware, of course, that the conversation is being recorded on a button camera.

The first person Steve ran into was the guy he had seen back at the office early in the week. Here as there, the fellow was hunched over his iPad. He looked up and greeted Steve, introducing himself as Scott Foval, the deputy political director for People for the American Way, an organization founded by television producer Norman Lear in the 1980s as a challenge to the Moral Majority. John Podesta's brother Tony was the founding president. Over the years, PFAW morphed into an activist anti-conservative action group. George Soros is a major donor, no surprise there.

Our journalist introduced himself as "Steve Packard," a consultant for the "Breakthrough Development Group," an all-purpose Potemkin company we had set up on the web some time back and had been nurturing ever since. Foval looked like a thousand other guys you might meet on the campaign trail, somewhat shapeless, lightly bearded, bespectacled. If he had been to the gym in the last decade, it wasn't obvious. He liked to talk, and Steve was prepared to listen and listen some more. That, my friends, is the essence of undercover reporting. Get in place, have a story, win friends and influence people. With Scott Foval, Steve didn't have to do much talking.

Foval was a classic political operative of the genus Democrat—cocky, boastful, and more than a little squirrely. He and his new pal Steve commiserated about past Wisconsin elections. To push the conversation along, Steve went on an elaborate rant about voter ID, insisting that if "we" Democrats kept abiding by rules the Republicans made up, "we" were guaranteed to lose.

"I agree with you that we do have to start pulling out all the stops," Foval affirmed. That said, he was wary about bringing in outside help.[2] "There's too much connective tissue down there," he said.

"Down where?" Steve asked.

"Between the corridor between Chicago and here. It's a pretty easy thing for Republicans to say, 'Well they're busing people in!'"

Foval now angrily addressed himself to some imaginary Republican, "Well you know what? We've been busing people in to deal with you fuckin' assholes for fifty years and we're not going to stop now.

We're just going to find a different way to do it." Given Democrats' indignant denials that any such thing was going on, or ever had gone on, this was bombshell testimony.

When Steve asked him more specifically what local Democrats had been doing for the last, say, twenty years, Foval served up an insider's history of the organized left.

"So what happened was," he explained, "there was a decision in the DNC to physically separate the operations of the labor unions. And that basically came under Bill Clinton. And I was at the DNC when it happened." By "operations," we presumed Foval meant the full range of electoral support, legal and otherwise, for which unions were historically responsible. As Foval explained later, he was particularly keen on their head-busting skills.

He continued, "It was a real bloodbath. Anybody who had union affiliation within the DNC felt pressure to do something, and at the time this was when blue dogs were trying to take over." Foval saw himself as part of the anti–blue dog, pro-union coalition. "It was a real sad situation," he elaborated, "because [the unions] had always been there for us, but then Clinton just enacted the first big round of fights." As a result, according to Foval at least, America lost a lot of jobs, and the Democratic Party lost a lot of union support.

"It literally took the last twenty years for them to even sit at the table together again," Foval told Steve. Given the "bitterness," many union people, "the ones who got fucked over back then," found their way to the Sanders camp. Explained Foval, "They're like, 'I will go this far, but I will not go this far for Hillary Clinton. Fuck Hillary Clinton.'"

Foval threw in some more inside baseball: "And then, of course, there's the misogyny thing there too. So that combo of things is pretty hard to overcome. And here in particular there was a real, I would say, the unions in Chicago could have done a lot more to come up and support us back in '10, but they stayed down there, most of them. There was a decision by the National Labor Council to not send a huge army of people here for activism because it would've actually added to Walker's narrative that these powerful labor bosses were running Wisconsin. And that was, I think, a mistake."

Steve was getting an education. With a hidden camera rolling, Steve asked Foval if it was possible to conceal the fact that the Chicago people were coming in to interfere in the election.

"Well that's the thing," said Foval. "You can't keep that quiet when the license plates are in the parking lot at the hotels all over town. That's just the way it is."

Steve believed that Foval was getting sufficiently worked up that it might be time for him to spell out his surrogate voting scheme, the one that had popped into his head earlier in the day. When Steve started to explain the idea, Foval took it and ran with it.

"You do it under the foreclosed properties," he said, "and they don't get it until afterwards? Wow that's dirty, I like it."

Steve was in.

"You take that data, and you flip it out, and you give it to people, and you have people go vote in it—that's brilliant. I love it." Foval loved it so much he proceeded with a tutorial not only on how to get away with it but also on how to execute the scam on a grander scale.

"You can prove conspiracy if there's a bus. If there are cars? It's much harder to prove. . . . If there's enough money, you have people drive their POVs. Or, you have them drive rentals."

I had to look up POVs. That means personally owned vehicles. I guess when you are in the business of circumventing the law, you develop your own acronyms.

"With Wisconsin license plates!" Steve added.

"Absolutely. Well, you can't have them with Wisconsin license plates because rentals here, most of them don't have Wisconsin license plates. But there's this thing called Used Car Auction. The titles belong to some unknown company—company cars. Cars come from one company. The paychecks come from another. There's no bus involved. So you can't prove that it's en masse. So it doesn't tip people off."

This guy had apparently been around the block. He had tales to tell. He was our own human slot machine vomiting out a mint's worth of pure coinage. Steve couldn't believe it. Foval paused at one point and asked rhetorically, "The question is, when you get caught by a reporter, does that matter?" Excellent question. Foval would learn the answer just about six months later.

Foval kept spitting out those silver dollars. "So what you do," he said, "is you implement the plan on a much bigger scale. You implement a massive change in state legislatures and in Congress. So you aim higher in your goals, and you implement it across every Republican-held state."

But then came the real jackpot. Without naming names, Steve also told Foval about his imaginary philanthropist friend and client. Foval was on top of this. "I know pretty closely who's advising your client on that. I work with that same person. There is somebody who hatches these ideas to people like him on an ongoing basis."

Now, bear in mind, there was no client. Steve made him and the whole scheme up earlier that morning. But apparently there was someone in the Democratic hierarchy who actually conceived schemes like the one Steve imagined. He definitely wanted to meet this guy.

"Who is he?" Steve asked. This is when we learned about Democracy Partners, the firm headed by Bob Creamer, a guy very high up in that hierarchy.

"So Bob Creamer comes up with a lot of these ideas. I work with Bob Creamer one-to-one all the time. I'm the white hat. Democracy Partners is kind of a dark hat. I will probably end up being a partner there at some point because our philosophy is actually the same."

Foval had nothing but praise for Creamer. "Bob Creamer is diabolical," gushed Foval, "and I love him for it. I have learned so much from that man over the last twenty years, I can't even tell you. And he calls me to be his firefighter a lot of the time because there are people who in our movement will not do what it takes to get shit done."

Obliging in ways we would not even anticipate, Foval laid out the organizational chart for us in a subsequent meeting with Steve. "The campaign pays DNC," he told Steve. "DNC pays Democracy Partners. Democracy Partners pays the Foval Group. The Foval Group goes and executes the shit on the ground."

Like *Pulp Fiction*'s Winston Wolfe, Foval was the guy who solved problems. "I'm the one they send when everything has gone to shit," he bragged. "And so he spends a lot of time on the phone with my boss asking me to go places that I don't wish to go. If I were not working for PFAW [People for the American Way] my pattern would be much more recognizable than in other places around the country. Every time you saw a national candidate, like either Cruz or Trump in Milwaukee, you'd be bombarded with Chicago antics."

"In what way?" asked Steve, curious to know what exactly "Chicago antics" entailed. "What's an example?"

Foval continued, "So one of the things we do is we stage very authentic grassroots protests right in their faces at their events. We infiltrate. And then we get it on tape. We train our people, and I work with a network of groups. We train them up on how to get themselves into a situation on tape, on camera, that we can use later."

"So I probably know your work."

"I know you do. Everybody does."

This activity was called "bird-dogging," a word with which we were about to become very familiar. Foval was letting us in on a very dark dirty secret about the campaign activities of the Democrats and Hillary Clinton, a secret about which very few people knew.

"You remember the Iowa State Fair thing where Scott Walker grabbed the sign out of the dude's hand, and then the dude kind of gets roughed up right in front of the stage right there on camera?" Foval asked Steve.

"That was all us," he continued. "The guy that got roughed up is my counterpart who works for Bob. We not only lent ourselves, we planted multiple people in that front area around him and in the back to make sure there wasn't just an action that happened up front. There was also a reaction that happened out back. So the cameras, when they saw it, saw double angles of stuff like, they saw what happened up front, and they saw the reaction of people out back."

Foval was boasting to our journalist that Democratic operatives were paying people to incite violence at Trump rallies and other Republican events. When we watched and listened to the undercover recording back at our office we were stunned. No one had reported anything about this. It was a shocking story, one that we needed to corroborate and ultimately expose. Foval wasn't through yet.

"What I call it is 'conflict engagement.' Conflict engagement in the lines at Trump rallies," he told Steve, unwittingly killing his career. "We're starting anarchy here. And [the mystery donor] needs to understand that we're starting anarchy."

Foval added, "I'm saying we have mentally ill people that we pay to do shit. Make no mistake. Over the last twenty years, I've paid off a few homeless guys to do some crazy stuff, and I've also taken them for dinner, and I've also made sure they had a hotel and a shower, and I put them in a program. Like, I've done that. But the reality is, a lot of people, especially, our union guys, a lot of union guys, they'll do whateeeevvverrr you want. They're rock 'n' roll."

Steve got back to his hotel around 1:00 a.m. totally pumped. He stayed up until 6:00 transcribing the footage. He had hit Triple 7s, all with flames, the jackpot. He could hardly believe what he was typing.

As fortuitous as it may have seemed, that meeting followed long months of planning and action. More than a year before the 2016 presidential election, the senior staff and several Project Veritas journalists met to brainstorm. The Clinton Foundation was a target we had contemplated for a long time. To sharpen our focus, we connected with Peter Schweizer, the award-winning investigative journalist who had written the controversial bestseller *Clinton Cash*. We hoped to capture on video what Schweizer had documented. With his help we had gamed out several scenarios to penetrate and investigate the Clinton Foundation.

The concept was fairly straightforward: we would have one of our people pose as a potentially major foreign donor to the foundation and also to the Center for American Progress. CAP is a liberal think tank and advocacy organization founded by John Podesta. The ultimate Washington insider, Podesta served as Bill Clinton's chief of staff and as counselor to Barack Obama. In 2015, he emerged as chairman of Hillary Clinton's presidential campaign.

Our plan was to approach both the Clinton Foundation and the Center for American Progress to see if either operation was willing to trade political access and favors in exchange for big donations. The hard part, we figured, would not be trading favors. The hard part would be getting our foot in the door.

We had a seriously good volunteer lined up to play the part of our high-dollar money man. In real life, "Michael Carlson" was a wealthy orthopedic surgeon from Atlanta. Better still, he hailed from England and had a posh British accent. As we conceived the plan, "Michael" would claim to represent several wealthy potential foreign investors. At the same time, we purchased three offshore companies. These would cast a believably ambiguous shade over our business practices and serve as a discreet conduit of funds if and when we decided to actually make a donation. We also created a number of shadow company websites and built an ironclad cover for Mr. Carlson that included a UK cell phone and a web address.

For all of our planning, we had little success. Given the election-year scrutiny, let alone a likely FBI investigation, the Clinton Foundation had tightened its controls and access. It soon became clear to us that the word had gone out to foundation staffers to be extremely careful. There would be no taking candy from strangers in 2016.

Working Our Way In

I t was about this same time we were setting up our offshore companies that "Steve Packard" was discovering the wonderfully self-destructive Scott Foval in Milwaukee.

Without intending to have his family secrets broadcast—and thus the beauty of the hidden camera—Foval explained how voter fraud was not the myth the left claims it to be. We knew that. Over the years, Project Veritas has done numerous stories exposing voter fraud. Foval confirmed what we knew. Better still, he alerted us to the provocation of violence at Trump rallies and tipped his hand about his mentor, Bob Creamer of Democracy Partners, the "dark hat."

Creamer is a long-time political organizer and strategist, and a well-connected one at that. He is married to Chicago-area congresswoman Jan Schakowsky and is very close to both the Obamas and the Clintons. According to visitor logs, Creamer made more than 340 trips to the White House during the Obama years, many of those meetings with the president in attendance.

Democracy Partners has advised just about every major player on the left side of the political arena, among them, the DNC, Nancy Pelosi, Wendy Davis, Jan Schakowsky, Cory Booker, Elizabeth Warren, Chuck Schumer, Howard Dean, *Daily Kos*, MoveOn.org, Media Matters, the NAACP, Planned Parenthood, the Brady Campaign, AFL-CIO, SEIU, the Bulgarian Association for Fair Elections, the Committee for Ukrainian Voters, the Democratic Party of Slovakia, as well as clients in Gaza, Hungary, Israel, Moldova, Nigeria, and Romania.

We would learn soon enough that Creamer had been contracted by the Democratic National Committee and Hillary Clinton's campaign to "assist" in the election. It would take some time, a $20,000 donation, and a ton of work before we would begin to understand what that "assistance" entailed. Eventually we discovered Creamer was personally advising Hillary Clinton, through his own admission. By October 2016, Foval had realized his dream and was working directly for Creamer. Before the campaign was through, that dream would turn nightmarish for both of them.

Shortly after Steve's first meeting with Foval, we began to craft an alias for our new rich Democrat. The character we created was to be named "Charles Roth III." One of our more seasoned and experienced undercover journalists was to play the role. The fellow was perfect for this investigation. A well-educated, well-spoken man in his fifties, he can talk to anyone, from a longshoreman on a dock to an heiress on a yacht. He works for us without pay. As I have discovered, the best undercover journalists are the ones whose motives are other than financial. In this case, neither "Charles Roth" nor our British overseas investor needed any money. They both did well in their careers, one as an engineer and the other as a doctor. We only paid expenses. True, "Charles Roth III" does fly first class, but how else would a guy like Roth fly? That perk helped protect his cover. A few weeks after their first meeting, Steve sent Foval an appropriately unctuous email:

Scott,
(Just to refresh we had drinks at Garfield's 502 on election night.)
Dude I owe you a huge debt of gratitude. In our Monday conference call I relayed all your advice (taking full credit—hope you don't mind) on the "surrogate voters" project. I was predicting my senior colleagues were already ahead of us on thinking of those potential fires and coming up with ways around them, so it was a risk in the event I came off as patronizing but it turns out they hadn't thought of ANY of it—the rental cars vs. buses, school surveillance cams, expanding to MI and IN, etc. So thanks to you, I—a junior consultant with two years experience at the firm—am getting mad respect at the office. Shit, I might even be asked to

help handle the account, which would expedite a promotion over-
night. So thank you thank you thank you.

Steve explained that he would love to talk to Creamer. "We seem
to have similar sensibilities and ways of thinking," he wrote and
signed off: "Best, Steve Packard, Breakthrough Development Group,
323.457.5462 breakthroughdevgroup.com."

We decided that Roth III would be a wealthy but reclusive North-
ern California real estate millionaire. In the way of backstory, Roth's
father emigrated from Hungary and made a fortune doing development
deals in and around San Francisco. Many of these deals displaced the
poor and minorities. As he grew older and wiser, this wealthy immigrant came to regret his actions and became a philanthropist, quietly
helping liberal causes.

His son, Charles III, followed in the old man's footsteps even more
aggressively. He became an active donor to liberal causes and candidates, but of late had grown frustrated by the lack of results. Given
the way his father displaced the poor, Charles III was particularly sensitive to the disenfranchisement of minorities by Republican voting
laws. Convinced as he was "that both voter ID laws as well as a Donald
Trump presidency are the death knell of the progressive movement,"
Roth III was prepared to circumvent the laws that would lead to the
lost votes.

Understandably, Foval wanted to talk to Roth on the phone before
he set up the meeting with Creamer. This was most likely a test to
make sure our donor was the real deal. So in May 2016, Roth called
Foval and pushed him to set up a meeting with Creamer. Before meeting, Creamer also wanted to talk with Roth on the phone. That call
went well and led to discussion about a meeting. Creamer suggested
either Washington or Chicago, but Roth pushed for Washington.
Washington, you see, is a more legally friendly environment for one-
person consent recordings than Chicago. Needless to say, Roth did not
mention this.

The meeting took time to arrange, but in July Roth met Creamer
in the lobby of a posh Washington Hotel. Roth recorded the conversation up close, but another one of our people recorded the meeting

from across the room. The meeting lasted more than an hour, with Roth leading the way through the conversation. Roth promised money if he could be assured of *real* action in return. He wanted Creamer to spell out what form this action might take.

Creamer was cautious. He had good reason to be, having served six months in federal prison for check floating in the previous decade. As Foval later told Steve, Creamer was wary of the surrogate voter scheme, but if others were willing to execute the scheme, well, that was another thing.

Despite Creamer's caution, the meeting with Roth went very well. Before the end of it Creamer was calling Roth "brother." The two men agreed to meet soon, the next time over dinner and fine wine. The hook was set. About a week after the meeting, we sent Creamer a case of Pinot Noir from Oregon where our journalist—and Roth, of course—was living at the time.

Over the phone, Roth told Creamer he had a niece who was interested in politics and wanted to volunteer. He asked if Creamer knew of an operation that could use her services. That he did. Creamer got back to Roth immediately and suggested that Roth's niece could help out at the Republican National Convention in Cleveland. That seemed to me like a perfect place to get one's feet wet.

Going Deep

We immediately asked one of our best young journalists if she were willing to be Roth's "niece." It was a role that Allison Maass, aka "Pizza Girl," was literally born to play. Allison is young, pretty, soft spoken, and has the killer instincts of a mafia hitman. Her nickname comes from her diet consisting of carbs, candy, and pizza.

Graduating a year early from college, Allison is mature beyond her years. She is stoic, focused, and organized. I am still impressed by the places she was willing to go, the roles she was willing to play, and the obstacles she was able to overcome. When Creamer called Allison to see if she were willing to go to Cleveland, she was eager and ready. By volunteering to go, she would influence not only the future of Project Veritas but also the outcome of the 2016 election.

We spotted Allison just a year earlier fighting the good fight at the University of Minnesota, located in a state that did not necessarily welcome her brand of fight. The publication she edited, the *Minnesota Republic*, like all other publications at that university, got its funding through an entity called the Student Service Fees Committee (SSFC). When Allison's publication requested funding in 2015, the SSFC decided to review past issues and settled on a 2011 issue to feed its collective sense of outrage. The cover showed an Islamic terrorist, or a facsimile thereof, burning a copy of Allison's publication and saying in both English and Arabic, "The Minnesota Republic: Terrorists Hate It." In the future, the SSFC promised to monitor the publication "to ensure that any material that is produced with student fee funds does not compromise the cultural harmony of the campus."[1]

Instead of rolling over as expected, Allison fought back publicly. The Drudge Report picked up her story. One of our people spotted it, and we invited Allison to come interview with us at Project Veritas. We appreciated her commitment to the First Amendment, just about the only political litmus test we have here at PV, and we certainly liked her spunk.

During her first summer as a full-time Project Veritas employee, Allison traveled around Iowa attending campaign events for Hillary Clinton. One day she was on the way to meet a Clinton campaign organizer for coffee when I called her from the office. A *Time* magazine reporter had phoned us to see what we knew about a young, blonde woman trying to infiltrate the Clinton campaign in Iowa. I was convinced he was talking about Allison, but I was not about to admit it. Still, I figured, if *Time* knew, the Clinton campaign surely knew. I needed to give Allison the heads up before she strolled into the lion's den unknowing.

We instructed Allison to continue on to the office and act as if nothing was out of the ordinary. When she arrived moments later, a whole crew of campaign workers was waiting for her. One of them, the woman she was supposed to meet, Sara Sterner, promptly took her outside to have a conversation.

"I got news from my boss that you are not allowed in any Hillary for Iowa offices or events anymore because they had reports that you've been to other places trying to fool staff and stuff like that," said Sterner almost apologetically. "So unfortunately you're not allowed in any of the offices anymore."[2]

"Me?" said Allison innocently.

"Yeah there are reports from other events like in Cedar Rapids and stuff. Yeah, so . . ."

"I have no idea what that is," added Allison, keeping her cool, but there was no way to talk herself out of this.

"Thank you," said Sterner, wrapping up the conversation. "Sorry about that."

This had to be nerve rattling, but Allison stayed in character the entire time. She played ignorant of the charges and indignant that they were made. Still, despite her best efforts, Allison was banned from the Iowa campaign. I am sure these Clinton staffers congratulated themselves for their shrewdness, but in that notoriously fragmented campaign, no one apparently kept their eyes on Allison. She would strike again, the next time much deeper into the campaign and very nearly to the White House.

Wiser for the experience, Allison undertook a project on her own. Still just twenty-one, she looked the part of a college student, and she certainly remembered how to play one. The role she chose for herself was "snowflake." What offended this particular snowflake, Allison decided, was the United States Constitution. Before she was through she captured on video university administrators shredding a copy of the Constitution to placate her and others freely denouncing the Constitution and the country it helps guide.

Allison had proved she was ready for the next step. It was a big one. She was to be part of our team going deep into the Hillary Clinton campaign. Getting her in the front door was surprisingly easy. Our make-believe major donor Charles Roth III paved the way with Bob Creamer for his niece, "Angela Brandt," to walk right in the front door.

Upon arrival at the Republican National Convention in Cleveland, Angela Brandt connected with Creamer's colleague Zulema Rodriguez. "Zully" was clearly one of the top ground organizers for the Democrats in Cleveland. The idea was to upstage and embarrass the Republicans at their Cleveland convention any way they could. Rodriguez told our journalist that this was no random effort. Everything was being coordinated at the national level.

"I just had a call with the campaign [Hillary for America] and the DNC. Every day at one o'clock," Rodriguez volunteered.[3]

"Do you work for the campaign?" asked Allison/Angela.

"I don't work for the actual campaign," said Rodriguez. "I work with Bob Creamer. We're doing a contract with the DNC. I did the Las Vegas caucus with the campaign."

Rodriguez told Angela about some of the "involvement" she'd had. "So B and I did the Chicago Trump event where we shut down like all the, yeah. . . ." Rodriguez was boasting that she and her colleagues were part of the violent demonstrations in March 2016 that forced Trump to cancel a large political rally in Chicago due to security concerns.

This was a big deal when it happened. According to the *New York Times*, "A large group opposing Mr. Trump merrily taunted the people entering the stadium with shouts of 'Donald Trump has got to go' and signs caricaturing Mr. Trump as a fascist with a Hitler mustache."[4] Par for the course, the media and Trump's Republican opposition put the onus on the Trump camp for the disruption and subsequent cancellation. Senators Marco Rubio and Ted Cruz and Governor John Kasich held Trump responsible "for the tenor of his rallies." Said Cruz of Trump, "He affirmatively encourages violence."[5]

The major media reported the Chicago event as a spontaneous protest. We were learning that these protests were no more "spontaneous" than those outside the Benghazi consulate four years earlier. The hand of Bob Creamer seemed to be touching a lot of things. Rodriguez was corroborating the story we had first heard from Foval.

"Oh and then we also did the Arizona one where we shut the highway down," Rodriguez boasted to Angela. That was March 18, just a week after Chicago, when anti-Trump protesters shut down a major highway just outside of Phoenix in an attempt to stop Trump supporters from attending a campaign rally. This too got widespread press coverage and fueled the impression that Trump was inspiring disorder. The media inevitably covered the protesters sympathetically, far more so than they had the lawful and orderly Tea Party protests during Obama's first term.

"Is it hard to do that?" Angela asked, referring to the highway shutdown.

"I mean I've done it before," said Rodriguez casually.

"So you know and you're really good at it. Cool."

"You have to slow down the traffic," Rodriguez explained. "And then I insisted on us being layers deep. So when the cops towed the first rows of cars there was still, people was still there. . . . So they kept having to tow cars. And they thought this first row and then it was like the second row didn't move and the third row didn't move."

"That's awesome," said Angela, thinking on her feet. "I guess I never think like who started that. It's just a group of people but there has to be someone planning."

"I always have a diversion," said Rodriguez.

"That's so funny. Did you plan the diversion too?"

"Yeah."

"That's smart."

"Yeah always. Always got to have it."

Listening to the tape confirmed our suspicions. Again, we had actual testimony from the organizer of a "spontaneous" anti-Trump protest. Here she was admitting to our journalist that she helped plan major disruptions in Arizona and Illinois, the one leading to a well-publicized cancellation of a Trump event. And Rodriguez was no rogue operator. She worked for Creamer. He had a contract with the DNC and the Hillary Clinton campaign. The news stories we had all read about anti-Trump protests got just about everything wrong. And almost no one outside our office understood this.

Angela did her job well. Her goal was to gain not only information but also the confidence of her new friends, most notably Rodriquez. She would need a good reference to get her deeper into Democracy Partners' operation. Playing her role to its ultimate end, Angela actually joined in the protest at the Cleveland convention.

My role in this investigation was new for me. I was used to being on the front lines, wearing a hidden camera. But for better or for worse, I was now being recognized too often. Although I occasionally did fieldwork using makeup and disguises, my "pimp" days were likely numbered. During the Democracy Partners campaign, I planned strategy, directed operations, and advised the journalists in the field. This work lacked the thrill of working undercover, but Project Veritas had evolved. As eager as I was to be one of the troops on the ground, my team kept reminding me that I was now the CO. Fortunately, we had built a solid team of journalists, production people, and managers.

After the Republican convention in mid-July, we went several weeks without hearing from Creamer. In due time, we had Charles

Roth III email Creamer and ask for another DC meeting. Creamer agreed, and this time he came with a proposal in hand as to how Roth might invest his money. None of his ideas were, on the face of things, illegal. The meeting lasted two hours, and it went well enough that Creamer felt comfortable inviting Roth's niece to come work for him as an intern.

The following day, Creamer had Roth meet with him and Brad Woodhouse, the president of Americans United for Change (AUFC), at Woodhouse's office. At that time, Foval served under Woodhouse as national field director. In the meeting, Woodhouse was happy to talk about a subject that Creamer had raised the day before, "Donald Ducks." Roth recorded everything.

According to Woodhouse, the Democrats had an operative dress as a duck and show up at Trump and Pence rallies. At each rally, the duck called on Trump to release his tax returns. Since Trump refused to release the returns, the Democrats said he was "ducking."

"The key here is to have the visual, the costume and sign," said Woodhouse. "We got so much shit for that [media] blast. Reporters thought it was silly, and reporters still think it's silly. We are not talking to reporters. We are talking to voters."[6]

"And they love it," added Creamer.

"I tell you," said Roth. "That's a pretty clever idea, though, the duck."

Creamer weighed in, "Originally, we were going to do Uncle Sam, 'I want you to release your tax returns.' I agree it's not as good. It's a lot easier to execute."

Creamer then added the kicker: "In the end it was the candidate, Hillary Clinton, the future president of the United States, who wanted ducks on the ground. So by god we would get ducks on the ground."

"Oh she, so it's her. Wow!" said Roth.

"Don't repeat that to anybody," Creamer cautioned.

Of course not, Bob. Not a soul, other than the 10 million or so on YouTube, Facebook, and Twitter. It was yet another great revelation and further proof of how connected Creamer and his shenanigans were to the Hillary Clinton campaign. Clinton and the DNC wanted their Donald to "duck" his taxes at Trump and Pence events. The direct involvement of the Clinton campaign and the DNC with Americans

United for Change in this scheme smacked of illegally coordinated campaign expenditures.

Federal campaign law experts told us specifically, "The ducks on the ground are likely 'public communications' for purposes of the law. It's political activity opposing Trump paid for by Americans United for Change funds but controlled by Clinton/her campaign."

This was a violation of the law. Representatives of the Clinton campaign participated in daily conference calls with Creamer, AUFC managers, and their operatives. They were talking about where to send the duck and the "duck's message." The Democratic National Committee participated as well. This is not hearsay. Our people witnessed these calls. Donna Brazile, head of the DNC, would say in her tell-all, *Hacks,* "I watched O'Keefe's video with a sinking heart, knowing this was something we could not fight back against, not really."

Scott Foval told Steve about the duck campaign: "We have to clear this with DNC, with Democratic National Committee. We have to clear which message we're going to be targeting at which event, but they can insert into multiple events, now, through the end of the election on a continual, on a daily basis, but basically do a chase." This chase, by the way, went "all the way across the country."

Foval and Creamer told our people that the DNC didn't just help place Donald Duck at protests; they were *in charge* of the duck. For all their indiscretion, these guys really wanted to keep this a secret. They were undone by the cleverness of our journalists and the age-old tendency of most behind-the-scenes consultants to brag about their successes. Here is Creamer explaining how the whole process worked:

> Oh, the duck. The duck has to be an Americans United for Change entity. This has to do only with the problem between Donna Brazile and ABC, which is owned by Disney, because there was a trademark issue. That's why. It's really silly. We originally launched this duck because Hillary Clinton wants the duck. In any case, so she really wanted this duck figure doing this stuff, so that was fine. So we put all these ducks out there and got a lot of coverage. And Trump taxes. And then ABC/Disney went crazy because our original slogan was "Donald ducks his taxes," releasing his tax

returns. They said it was a trademark issue. It's not, but anyway, Donna Brazile had a connection with them, and she didn't want to get sued. So we switched the ownership of the duck to Americans United for Change, and now our signs say Trump ducks releasing his tax returns. And we haven't had any more trouble.

We beat the *Wall Street Journal* to this story. In a matter-of-fact article that got little traction, the *Journal* reported on September 8 that the DNC had cut ties with the duck.[7] Formally, this was true, but behind the scenes the DNC and the Hillary Clinton campaign were still running the show and breaking federal campaign coordination laws in the process. Angela would later have this confirmed by Jenna Price, an assistant press secretary at the DNC.[8]

"We kind of divvy up responsibilities. So sometimes it will be, like, campaign owned. So sometimes you will see that they advised something, or they are taking credit for things," Price told Angela. "So, like, we aren't taking credit for the duck anymore. That's like, random ally groups. But it's still something that we're involved in."

Price explained her strategy: "We just have to be careful about these things, and the way we talk about them, and who knows about certain things; but you guys are [careful]. I trust that it will all be fine." It was not going to be fine.

By this time, Angela had accepted her internship at Democracy Partners and ingratiated herself with her new coworkers. This was a closely run thing. Angela started interning at Democracy Partners on September 21, 2016, just seven weeks before the election. The office where she worked sits in the heart of the Washington power complex, no more than a couple blocks from the White House. There it offers, or claims to, "cutting edge strategies for progressive values."[9]

Angela's first day at the office was an anxious one. Before entering the building, she looked in to see if she would have to pass through a metal detector, a common screening tool in post–September 11 Washington. There was none. That was good. She was wearing a wire.

There was, however, a security desk with a sign saying, "Visitors must sign in." That was not so good. Angela had no "Angela Brandt" identification beyond a fake college ID. She decided to brazen it out.

Dressed smartly in heels, black slacks, and a button-up blouse with black buttons—all the better to conceal a button camera—she walked crisply past the security guard and smiled as if she had walked past him a thousand times before. No one stopped her. She was in.

Unlike many people in his position, Creamer did not hit on his female staff at least as far as Angela could tell. He was patient. He seemed more a mentor than a letch. He introduced her to the staff and made her feel welcome. As nice a guy as he seemed, Creamer had already served a prison sentence for illegally floating checks. According to *USA Today,* he "was accused of swindling nine financial institutions of at least $2.3 million while he ran a public interest group in the 1990s."[10] And now he made his living plotting dirty tricks to use against Donald Trump. That is what Angela had come to capture. She would follow a useful Veritas rule: *In the digital era, tape is cheap. In fact, there is no literal "tape," so keep recording all the time, as long as it is legal to do so.*

Legal it was, every minute. People find it easy to talk to Angela. Creamer was no exception. At the end of the workday, he liked to unwind and tell stories out of school. She knew she was getting good stuff. Her one anxiety now, the one anxiety all of us at Project Veritas have felt at some point, was the fear of equipment failure, the fear that pearls were being dropped and she was missing them.

The life of an undercover journalist is, I repeat, not an easy one. Angela would work throughout the day and return after work alone to her Airbnb, there to review her footage and communicate with the office. Staying in character was hard enough during the workday. She did not want to jeopardize her mission by partying at night. Other journalists have lost their jobs at Project Veritas for doing that. A chance encounter with someone from her past could blow everything. In the morning she would take the Metro into the office, living the life not of a well-paid professional reporter but of an intern scraping by. Her daily movements had to reflect her assigned role. She was literally living out her character in America's capital city much as Americans overseas did in Moscow during the Cold War.

Angela disciplined herself to be the person Creamer thought she was. He liked that person well enough to take her with him when he visited the Democratic National Committee headquarters, a few blocks south of the Capitol. The last time operatives got caught stealthily entering the DNC headquarters, those headquarters were in the Watergate complex. Remember that kerfuffle? Having no interest in bringing comparable hell down on ourselves or the nation, we reminded all of our staff of a timeless Veritas rule: *If busted, keep your mouth shut and get the hell out of Dodge.* By this point, we trusted Angela to do just that.

Never having been to the DNC offices, Angela did not know whether she would have to pass through a metal detector. This was not a question she could ask her colleagues in advance. So she prepared an evasive maneuver just in case. If she were compelled to go through screening, she would fake a phone call from her father, step outside to take it, and discreetly place her wire in her purse. That was the plan. She hoped she did not have use it.

As she and Creamer approached the building, he, always the gentleman, opened the door for Angela. Her heart almost leapt out of her chest when she saw the metal detector, but she caught a break. The security guard saw Creamer enter behind her and waved them both on by. "It's a lot of luck," Angela would tell me, "a lot of maneuvering, knowing how to manipulate situations." This was a reporter after my own heart.

At the DNC, as at Democracy Partners, Angela did a whole lot of nothing—counting anti-Trump signs and looking for news items about Democracy Partners' disruptive "Donald Duck" campaign—but she did her "nothing" steadily and conscientiously. Everything she did, she did for a purpose. She needed to be in the midst of the action, her camera always recording. As a fly on the wall, she was able to sit in on planning calls every day during which the DNC, the Hillary campaign, and other consultants like Creamer planned protests and events surrounding Trump rallies. She never knew when she would capture something worth sharing, even if it were just the Trump signs or a guy in a duck costume. By working her way into the target's nerve center and staying vigilant, Angela was able to gather immeasurably more information than she could have from the outside looking in. And unlike the Watergate burglars, she did it legally.

One day, Creamer explained to his wide-eyed intern how things worked. "At one o'clock we have our regular call," he told her. "It's our rapid response call. It's about bracketing." Creamer did not hesitate to tell Angela how "bracketing" worked.

"It's kind of a term of ours," he said, now in his professorial mode. "Wherever Trump and Pence are going to be, we have events. And we have a whole team across the country that does that. Both consultants [like Foval] and people from the Democratic Party, and people from the Democratic apparatus, and people from the campaign, the Clinton campaign." As to Creamer's role, it was "to manage all of that." That was the reason, he explained, for the daily phone calls, "seven days a week until the election."

Angela absorbed everything. In fact, she succeeded in establishing her cover almost too well. One Monday Creamer casually asked her what she was doing the next night, Tuesday. If free, he wondered if she might want to go with him to the White House for a roundtable discussion on the refugee crisis.

The White House! OMG! Angela's first thought was, *Fuck, yeah!* What intern would not jump at the chance to attend an after-hours event at the White House? If that intern were actually an undercover journalist investigating Democratic dirty tricks, this would be the invitation of a lifetime. Instinctively, Angela smiled and nodded her head.

Almost instantly, however, her training kicked in. All of our reporters had learned they could not enter a federal building with a fake ID, let alone the White House. Angela knew all about our New Orleans misadventure. Needless to say, I drilled this story deep into our reporters' heads. With Democrats still in control of the media and the deep state, we could not afford mistakes. "Don't give them the opportunity to punish us," I told our people. Angela learned the lesson well. Within seconds of being invited, her thought process switched from *How do I get into the White House?* to *How do I get out of this invitation?* It would not be easy.

"Okay," Angela told Creamer. "Let me just check my schedule."

"Great," said Creamer. "Just send me your basic information—date of birth, social security number, city you were born in—you were born in the U.S., right?"

"Yes, of course," Angela laughed.

"Okay, send me that info ASAP," said Creamer as he walked down the hallway and disappeared into his office.

"Sure thing," said Angela, knowing that she could not. She also knew she needed guidance, and she wasn't about to make a call from her office. With no time to squander, she headed across the street to Starbucks and sealed herself off in the ladies' room. From there she called the Project Veritas office to review her options. Unable to reach my production supervisor Joe Halderman or me, she sent us an encrypted message explaining her dilemma. She then went back to her office and tried to stall for time. If pressed, she would say, "I have plans." That wasn't going to work. Creamer had just sent her an email: "Send me info for meeting ASAP." In the meantime, I had sent her an email telling her to call us immediately.

Angela rushed back to the stall in the Starbucks ladies' room. This time, she got ahold of Joe. The best option, they decided, was to play sick. Back at the office, Angela made a show of trashing a half-eaten breakfast sandwich—couldn't get it down. She walked back to Creamer's office and found him on the phone. She knocked and entered.

"Sorry," she whispered, "should I come back?"

Creamer put his hand over the speaker. "You need to send me that info."

"I will," Angela said earnestly, "but I'm very sorry. I think I got food poisoning, and I need to leave."

"You're sick," said Creamer sympathetically. "Don't worry about it. Go home."

Angela walked out of the office holding her breath and headed back to the Airbnb. She knew she would have to call in sick the next day as well. That was the day of the White House meeting. Getting sick on Monday established a more credible cover for missing Tuesday. The problem was she had to camp out in her Airbnb. She could not risk running into a coworker. It was a lonely two days, but the mission was still a go. Angela would be back on Wednesday to help save the nation. The relationship Uncle Charles had developed with Creamer was paying off in sound-bites.

Pulling Back the Curtain

One phrase that Angela heard over and over was "bird-dogging." On one occasion, Angela asked Bob Creamer to define the term for her.

"You're trying to actually confront people," Creamer answered. "It's hard with Trump. It's very hard."

"Why?"

"Because the Secret Service and the way the structure is."

"Oh, okay."

"If you're doing Pence it's a little easier," said Creamer. "The thing that makes the best television is of course the target, angry people. That's great TV. Now, Trump you don't . . . maybe you want to get people to do something in advance to cause problems for him and . . . I guess these guys are the Dreamers. They're just pros at this."

The "Dreamers"! Bingo!

"What do you mean by Dreamers?" Angela asked innocently.

"Dreamers are the category of people brought here as children, as immigrants," said Creamer.

Creamer did not mention that the Dreamers were brought here illegally as children. About a dozen years earlier, Democrats nationwide made the quiet decision to welcome illegal immigrants. This major turnabout went unreported. As late as 1995, Congresswoman Barbara Jordan, a black civil rights icon, reflected the Democratic position when she said, "Credibility in immigration policy can be summed up in one sentence: those who should get in, get in; those who should be kept out, are kept out; and those who should not be here will be required to leave."[1] Twenty years later, a Republican who expressed the same sentiment would be branded a racist.

Instead of deporting illegals, Democrats now focused on exploiting them, particularly their children. Obama elevated the children and young adults to "Dreamer" status, as in the American dream, and granted them a reprieve from deportation. As their first milestone on the path to citizenship, some Dreamers were serving as dirty tricksters for the Democratic Party.

"So there's like a specific group of Dreamers?" asked Angela.

"Well there are organizations out there. And this guy Cesar Vargas is probably one of the . . ."

"So, those are the guys that are the best at bird-dogging?" asked Angela.

"Well," answered Creamer, "this crew is spectacular at it."

When we checked the Podesta emails on WikiLeaks, we found references to the term "bird-dogging" to and from the major players in the Clinton campaign, campaign manager Robby Mook included.[2]

This is where Cesar Vargas came into play. It was the first time we had heard the name. I kind of liked it, "Cesar Vargas." The name had sort of a cinematic ring, like, say, "Keyser Söze," the mysterious prince of darkness from the film *The Usual Suspects.* Ultimately we would get Vargas on tape too, and he had a thing or two to tell us about the ways to pull off voter fraud.

"So the DNC doesn't bring these people in?" Angela asked of the bird-doggers.

"Somebody that does that kind of stuff," said Creamer, "you don't want them to be operatives of the DNC or of the campaigns."

"Why?"

"Because it's just not good optics."

Creamer believed the opposition or possibly the media would claim that the bird-doggers worked for the campaign. He believed bird-doggers would have "a lot more legitimacy" if they actually belonged to some Dreamer organization. I had asked Angela to get specific on this issue with Creamer and lock him down on the involvement of Hillary Clinton in all of these activities. The ever-curious Angela played her role perfectly.

"So Hillary is aware of all the work that you guys do, I hope?" she asked.

"Oh yeah," said Creamer. "Yes. The campaign is fully in it."

"And then they tell Hillary what's going on?"

"I mean," Creamer clarified. "Hillary knows through the chain of command what's going on."

Angela was given access to one of Creamer's colleagues, an operative who called himself "Aaron Black." He described himself as "deputy rapid response director for the DNC for all things Trump on the ground." A fortyish charter member of the Occupy Wall Street movement, the scruffily bearded Black specified that he directed the supposedly spontaneous protests at Trump and Pence events. His real name, we learned later, was Aaron Minter. I guess we were not the only ones using aliases.

"No one is really supposed to know about me," he told Angela.[3] He took at least partial credit for shutting down the Chicago Trump rally in March. "That was us," he boasted before qualifying his boast. "It was more [Creamer] than me, but none of this is supposed to come back to us."

Black's reasoning was straightforward. "We want [the agitation] coming from people. We don't want it to come from the party. So if we do a protest, and it's a DNC protest, right away the press is going to say 'partisan.'"

In this campaign, the media were easily fooled because they wanted to be fooled. They chose to know no more than they had to. Black obliged them.

"If I'm in there coordinating all the troops on the ground and sort of playing the field general, but [the activists] are the ones talking to the cameras, then it's actually people," said Black. "But if we send out press advisories with 'DNC' on them and 'Clinton campaign,' [the protest] doesn't have that same effect."

The undercover camera had recorded evidence that the demonstrations were orchestrated. The party's goal was to get news coverage suggesting they were spontaneous, a sign of the strong grassroots opposition to Trump. This was classic Soviet-style "agitprop," consciously created agitation resulting in useful propaganda. As usual, the American Pravda enabled the agitprop by accepting the fiction as real. It was not. We had worked our way deep into the dark side of the Emerald City and now knew from Creamer's own admission that the proverbial man behind the curtain was a woman.

Counting Down

Operatives Bob Creamer and Scott Foval were keen on our mysterious money man, Charles Roth III. They believed Roth was willing to pay for the mischief they hoped to continue right up until the election. The irony was beyond rich. They could all but smell the money Roth promised and convinced us in their eagerness that our investment would pay dividends.

While Charles's niece, Angela Brandt, was gathering information in Washington, Charles's friend, Steve Packard, was continuing his conversations with Scott Foval. On one memorable occasion in Wisconsin, Foval explained the dynamics of provoking chaos.

"If you're there and you're protesting and you do these actions, you will be attacked at Trump rallies," he explained. "That's what we know."

"So that's part of the process?" asked Steve.

"The whole point of it," Foval answered. "We know Trump's people will freak the fuck out. His security team will freak out. And his supporters will lose their shit."

Foval continued, "We are the primary mechanism as a team. Democracy Partners is the tip of the spear on that stuff." He wasn't through yet. He carried on as though he were a double agent and we were paying him by the word.

"We have a clip deliverable that we have to deliver every day for our group of clients who are involved in this project," said Foval. He mentioned several clients, including the Alliance for Retired Americans, which is part of the AFL-CIO. I suspect these retired Americans do not have a clue what their leadership is doing in their name.

Foval continued, "And then there's the DNC and the campaigns and Priorities [Priorities USA, Hillary's super PAC]. Priorities are a big part of this too. The campaigns and DNC cannot go near Priorities, but I guaran-damn-tee you that the people who run the super PACs all talk to each other, and we and a few other people are the hubs of that communication."

"So you're kind of like intermediaries between the super PACs and the DNC," said Steve. "The DNC, they can't talk to each other?"

"We're consultants, so we're not the official," responded Foval. "So those conversations can be had between consultants who are working for different parties. That's why there's Bob, who is the primary there, and I'm a sub to him, and I'm also a primary to AUFC separately."

"So there's like a Morse code between the DNC and the super PACs?"

"It's less of a Morse code than it is a text conversation that never ends. It's like that. It's kind of like an ongoing Pony Express."

"Okay, so I mean that's . . ."

"It's not as efficient as it could be but that's because the law doesn't allow it to [be]. The thing that we have to watch is making sure there is a double blind between the actual campaign and the actual DNC and what we're doing. There's a double blind there. So they can plausibly deny that they knew anything about it."

Foval shifted from strategic considerations to tactical ones. Good undercover that he is, Steve was all ears.

"There's a script of engagement," Foval told him. "Sometimes the crazies bite, and sometimes the crazies don't bite." He elaborated, "They're starting conversations in the line. Right? They're not starting confrontations in the rally. Because once they're inside the rally they're under Secret Service's control. The media will cover it no matter where it happens. The key is initiating the conflict by having leading conversations with people who are naturally psychotic. I mean, honestly, it is not hard to get some of these assholes to pop off. It is a matter of showing up, to want to get into the rally in 'Planned Parenthood' T-shirts or

'Trump is a Nazi,' you know. You can message to draw them out, and draw them to punch you."

Foval's contemptuous view of Trump supporters as "psychotic" seems to be endemic on the left. He went on to boast about the extent of his network of operatives. We had no reason to disbelieve him then and still don't.

"So here, you have a schedule of events. We update this on an ongoing rolling basis every morning. These are all the Trump and Pence appearances. Tomorrow, for instance, we are turning out five hundred people in front of the Trump International in DC. We have to have people prepared to go wherever these events are, which means we have to have a central kind of agitator training. Now, we have a built-in group of people in New York who do this. We have a built-in group of people in DC who do this. We have a group of people in Vegas. We have a group of people in Colorado. We have a group of people in Minneapolis."

When we heard this audio at our Project Veritas offices we quickly arranged for another one of our journalists, "Tyler," to attend the planned protest at the Trump International on the following day. It was there that he ran into Aaron Black, Creamer's attack dog. Black wanted to talk about Donald Ducks as well.

"I wish I could tell you whose idea [the duck] was," said Black.

"That would be funny," said Tyler.

"It would shock you."

"Shock me? I'm sure nothing in American government can shock me anymore."

"Well, it wouldn't shock you," teased Black, "but it would definitely be front-page news." Black was careful not to say who came up with the idea of Donald Ducks, but Bob Creamer had already confided to Charles Roth that the duck was Hillary's brainchild.

Remember Shirley Teter? She was the sixty-nine-year-old sufferer of COPD, chronic obstructive pulmonary disease. According to numerous news stories at the time, she was "assaulted" at a September 2016 Trump rally in North Carolina by a Trump supporter named Richard Campbell. The media ran with her story for days with headlines such as this one from local station WLOS, "69-Year-Old Woman Allegedly Punched in Face by Trump Supporter outside NC Rally."[1]

In one of his subsequent conversations with Steve, Foval took credit for this particular bit of agitprop. "She was one of our activists, who had been trained up to bird-dog," Foval said of Teter. "So the term 'bird-dogging,' you put people in the line, at the front, which means that they have to get there at six in the morning because they have to get in front at the rally. So that when Trump comes down the rope line, they're the one asking him the question in front of the reporter, because they're pre-placed there."

Undercover reporting can get at the truth in ways that conventional reporting simply cannot. We unraveled the Shirley Teter saga before the election. Only months after the election was this retraction added by WLOS, "Buncombe County court documents show the charge was dismissed through prosecutorial discretion, after consultation with the victim and review of the case. A lawyer for Richard Campbell tells News 13 that Mr. Campbell did not do anything illegal or offensive and the victim's allegations were a hoax."[2]

Foval shared with Steve not only his strategies but also his prejudices.

"So, I have to be really honest," he told Steve on one occasion. "Iowa is a difficult case because it's a fifty-fifty state, and honestly, half the state is racist as fuck." This may come as news to Iowans, but not to Democrat activists. They know racism when they see it.

As we counted down to November, Foval and Creamer started to get aggressive when it came to the donation they expected from Roth. "I can't stress with you guys how badly they need that money," Foval told Steve.

Roth's credibility got an unexpected boost from an unlikely source, Nancy Pelosi's daughter, Christine, herself a Democratic strategist. As Foval related to Steve, he happened to tell Christine about Charles Roth. Pelosi claimed to know Charles and told Foval that Roth's "boyfriend" had donated to her mother's campaigns.

"His boyfriend? I didn't know Charles was gay," Foval reportedly said to Pelosi.

"Oh yeah, really gay."

Okay, here's the irony. Our "Charles Roth" is, in real life, gay. How useful a coincidence was it that Nancy Pelosi had a major gay donor named "Charles Roth" with a boyfriend? This had to boost Foval's confidence that our Charles Roth was a heavy hitter.

We were not privy to the conversation, but I can imagine Foval going back to Creamer and sharing the Pelosi news about Roth, and Creamer saying, "Yea, I knew Roth was gay." To strengthen his backstory, Roth had already told Creamer in some elaborate detail about his boyfriend in Portland. God does work in strange and mysterious ways.

Always Be Closing

To keep our investigation going, we made the tough decision to donate $20,000 from the Project Veritas bank account to Robert Creamer's effort. We had determined that the potential benefits of this investigation outweighed the cost.

"First thing, like I said, thank you for the proposal," Roth told Creamer upon receiving a proposed plan of action. "And I'd like to get the $20,000 across to you. The second call I'm going to make here is to my money guy, and he's going to get in touch with you and auto wire the funds to you."[1]

"Okay," said Creamer, "we are running out of time as you know. So we need to do it quick."

"Also," Roth elaborated, "there was [sic] some ideas that have been relayed to me from Steve that Scott [Foval] mentioned to him about Trump events, and I would like to talk about those events as well."

"Now, Trump events are fine," Creamer responded. "I mean, frankly, I spend most of my time overseeing the Trump event rallies. I mean that's what I do for the Clinton campaign. So that's interesting as well."

From our offshore company in Belize, through a bank wire, we sent $20,000 to Americans United for Change per instructions from Creamer. Creamer was prompt in providing the necessary information. After the money changed hands, we pressed Foval and Creamer to introduce us to their vote harvester. The donation certainly greased the wheels.

"It's this guy, Cesar Vargas is his name. So Bob is really good friends with him and talked to him this afternoon," Foval told Steve. We learned Vargas was a New York lawyer, the cofounder of the Dream Action Coalition, and a "Dreamer" himself. Only in the Democratic Party could an illegal alien achieve such heights without disguising his illegality. Vargas apparently had known Creamer for years.[2]

After much back-and-forth with Foval, Steve was able to schedule a meeting with Vargas in New York City. Hoping to learn what, if any, fraudulent activities Vargas was orchestrating, Steve made it clear he was there to discuss voter fraud. He told Vargas that his benefactor, Charles Roth, was prepared to invest thousands to buy some votes. Steve also explained his surrogate voter plan to Vargas.

The idea, said Steve, was "getting a bunch of people on a bus, taking them around the country. They legally can vote. So they can vote. At the same time, they're also getting work permits under a different name, and, again, voting again on behalf of people who cannot vote."[3]

Vargas thought it too late in the 2016 cycle to pull off the surrogate plan. The future held more promise. "We can definitely work on that," said Vargas of the 2018 midterms. From his perspective, a lot depended on who got elected.

"If it's Donald Trump," said Vargas, "[the surrogate plan] even makes more sense. The issue will be more credible, and it'll give us more opportunity to jump in there." If Clinton were elected, "and the voter ID laws are losing, and we have much more opportunity to vote, and we have immigration reform, it's not going to be as significant, right?" In other words, with Hillary as president, there would be an adequate supply of illegal immigrants and no ID laws to stop them from voting.

"If we cross that bridge," said Steve, "can I tell him that you're the one who's going to help us do that?"

"Yeah, absolutely," said Vargas. "I mean, count me in."

"And I assume you don't go tell these conversations to anybody because this is technically illegal," asked Steve.

"No, no," said Vargas, "absolutely, absolutely." Not surprisingly, Vargas claims that our footage was heavily edited and that at no time did he agree to take part in voter fraud.

Steve had done outstanding work with Foval and Vargas and indirectly with Creamer. We had one more job for him—to close the deal with Foval. The closer we got to the election, the tougher the assignment got and the tougher a taskmaster I became.

Sometimes, I think, I can be a real pain in the ass. I don't mean to be, but I have more experience doing undercover journalism than anyone just about anywhere. There is no textbook to which I can refer my staff, no field manual. And as thoroughly as we prepare our people, we constantly face situations in which there is not a firm and fast precedent.

Skilled as they are, our journalists do not always have the sense of urgency I might want them to have. They do not always say what I would want them to say. I have to remind myself they and I are exploring a brave new reportorial world. So much of what we do is improvisational that we rarely have the opportunity to talk strategy on the spot.

As a general understanding, we try to get information out of the person with whom we are speaking without giving away the game. In this one particular case, we were trying to extract a key bit of data from the usually garrulous Scott Foval. Back in Wisconsin, he had told Steve about his conversation with Creamer in regard to Steve's surrogate voter plan. The first "he" in the passage that follows refers to our imaginary donor, Charles Roth. "Bob" is Creamer. Here is what we recorded Scott Foval saying:

> Bob came back to me and asked me, "What is he [Roth] talking about?" I told him what we were talking about. He said, "I'm not gonna touch that with a ten-foot pole." Now I go, "Nor should you, nor should *you*." He goes, "Good, glad we're on the same page there. However, other people can make things happen you don't need to know about."[4]

Other people. Those were the magic words, the key to the next level of information. Guys in Foval's line of work routinely speak in code. Their language is not easy to interpret. Creamer appeared to be telling Foval that such a project was doable, but that he, Creamer, had to keep his distance from it. That said, there were "other people" in the operation willing to execute Roth's surrogate-voter scheme if the money was right.

Steve did not believe Foval and Creamer were merely stringing Roth along. While Foval may have been reckless with his words, he was prudent with his time. He would not have met with Steve and his colleague unless he thought he could get more money out of Roth by coming up with a plan. The best way to sort through these possibilities was to discover who these "other people" were. We suspected one of them to be international man of mystery Cesar Vargas.

On October 7, the phone rang in my office. It was Scott Foval calling for Steve. We were expecting the call. I yelled for Freddy, our production manager. He came in with a lav mic and a camera. Steve took the call. He and I huddled over the speakerphone on the coffee table.

"How did things go with Cesar?" Foval asked.[5]

"I really liked him," Steve said. "So I really sold him, pushed him to Roth." Then Steve talked about Roth and what he would like to invest in. He was trying to find out about these "other people" without being direct about it.

"Are there any other folks who are willing to do that stuff?" he asked, "stuff" being the surrogate voter plan.

"It's too late to do anything but the field stuff now," said Foval. "That's the bottom line. We need to move. It's too late."

"Scott," said Steve, "there are folks out there who are into the civil disobedience strategies . . . like Cesar."

I wanted to tell Steve, "Get to the point about the other people, now." Even though I was only feet away, I had no good way to communicate my thoughts without distracting him. I was hoping not to do that.

"I'm more than happy to have those conversations, but we need to take care of Voces today," said Foval, referring to Voces de la Frontera, a radical protest group. "You need to understand that. Civil disobedience? Voces has been doing that for the last seven years, since Obama has been elected. They are friends with Cesar. That's part of the deal. They are the only people speaking the Spanish language in Wisconsin. It would provide a 7 percent swing."

If Hillary Clinton thought Wisconsin was already in her win column, Foval knew better. Here he was basically admitting that Voces had been engaged in civil disobedience for a long time and in a variety of ways. It was clear Foval wanted Roth's money put into the Wisconsin operation and was trying to close Steve to get it. At the same time, Steve was trying to close Foval to get the information we needed about the "other people."

When undercover, our journalists are trained to never give targets a chance to say no. On the other hand, as W. C. Fields might have put it, "You can't cheat an innocent man." In this case, we knew Foval wasn't innocent. We needed to draw him out. Give him what he wanted in order to keep driving toward the prize. I put the phone on mute.

"Explain to them the civil disobedience about voting," I whispered to Steve hurriedly. "Ask him what he meant by that. I will take care of the payment today. Tell me more about that."

In print, my words sound as if I were writing a telegram. At the time, I think they made sense. I took the phone off mute.

"In terms of voting," Steve stumbled, "in terms of enfranchising . . ."

I quickly wrote on my MacBook in cap locks, WE NEED SUGGESTIONS ON OTHER PEOPLE, and tapped on the screen almost loud enough to be heard on Foval's end.

"Steve, read the line," I mouthed, "read the line, damn it." I pointed to the massive font on my laptop. I could see the frustration in Steve's face. He had a subject who was being evasive and a boss who was being overbearing. But we had to get Scott Foval to admit to us over encrypted messaging who specifically could help us commit voter fraud. In order to do that, we had to get him on record.

DID YOU GET MY WICKR MESSAGE? I typed. DO YOU HAVE WICKR? WHAT'S YOUR USERNAME?

Wickr is an instant messaging app that allows users to exchange encrypted messages that expire when either party wants them to. Foval had already admitted that Cesar Vargas was involved in civil disobedience. We needed to pursue that line of inquiry. But Foval was interested in the here and now and in Wisconsin.

"Tell him the rubber meets the road, man," said Foval referring to Roth. "If he really wants to do it, he needs to get his hands dirty."

Steve meandered as Foval explained that the campaign's focus was GOTV—get out the vote. On my knees now, bowing up and down like a manic imam, I pleaded with Steve to get to the point. I thought, *All you have to do is read the lines I am pointing to with my fingers!* I could not understand why he wasn't.

I told you I could be a pain in the ass.

Another of our journalists was curled up on the couch covering her face. She could not bear to see Steve flounder or me silently scream at him. She had developed a close kinship with Steve in the field. She wanted to escape the moment.

"James, we can't get them to say things," she whispered to me.

Yes and no, I thought. Our problem now was that we were not sticking to the script. We were not executing the way we needed to.

"Civil disobedience doesn't elect people," said Foval as if he were dispensing some axiom for the ages.

Yes, it does, I thought, *if that disobedience takes the form of voter fraud.*

"I really don't feel comfortable with Wickr," added Foval.

Ah, the irony, sucker, I thought. *You are being recorded right now.*

"I don't trust Wickr," he continued.

What? I wanted to laugh. *Are you worried* Russians *will hack you on Wickr?*

"I'd prefer you just text me on my 202 number. This call is encrypted," said Foval. He was growing wary, not for fear of being entrapped into a fraud rap but out of frustration with Steve's ability to deliver more money now. We could hear audible sighs coming from Foval's end of the line.

"Look, Steve, here's how you handle this. You call him up and you tell him to make the donation. As a senior consultant friend of yours, it's time to tell your client he needs to do the right thing. I know he's volatile but you need to handle him. You. Need. To. Handle. Him." The "him," of course, was Roth.

I was at least satisfied that we were not blowing our cover. Scott just wanted the money.

Come on Steve, I thought, *get to the damn point.*

Steve was stuttering, in part, I suspect, because I kept gesturing at the phone trying to get him to put it on mute. I needed to give him advice, but he kept speaking in circles, clarifying things that didn't need to be clarified. I went to grab the phone from him, but he backed away.

"I'm writing everything down so I can give him one final *cri de coeur* . . . so . . . I can sell him on this," said Steve.

Cri de coeur, I thought. *What the hell is that?*

"So he . . . from what I . . . I really pushed Creamer, sold him, to my donor . . . and Roth is . . . he's really fix . . . [laugh] . . . He seems to forget . . . fixations, about, about, the time limits of fraud before this election, saving for the midterms. Voces needs this right now, so I, I, told him he is a good ally for what Voces needs to do the thing for the midterm. So can Voces do my re-enfranchisement thing?"

Steve sounded as if he just had a stroke. I was losing patience. I needed to meet a few objectives: make an offer for money, clarify the nature of the civil disobedience, and get suggestions on the *others* Foval may know. I typed out the message in big caps, got on my hands and knees like a dog, and pounded the computer screen so hard the image splattered into rainbows. In retrospect, I imagine I might have been making Steve a little nervous. You think?

WE NEED OTHER SUGGESTIONS ON PEOPLE. IS THERE ANYBODY ELSE? I typed in caps large enough to be read from space.

TELL HIM YOU'LL WRITE THE DAMN CHECK. I WILL TAKE CARE OF VOCES. TELL ME MORE ABOUT WHAT THEY ARE CURRENTLY DOING ON CIVIL DISOBEDIENCE VOTING. VARGAS SAID THEY ARE DOING IT. WHAT ABOUT THE CIVIL DISOBEDIENCE AND I'LL GIVE YOU THE MONEY.

Maybe it was because I was now using multicolored fonts to get his attention, maybe it was because he just wanted to get me off his friggin' back, but Steve snapped out of whatever stupor he was in.

"I told him he is a good ally, possibly for, . . . so he wanted me to ask if you have any other suggestions so I can connect him with people?

"Honestly, Steve." Foval was losing patience. We waited anxiously to see if Foval would back out of the fraud he had insinuated just moments earlier. But his impatience proved to be strategic. He was trying to close the deal with a donor.

"He needs to step up and do the right thing for Voces," said Foval.

Steve, say you'll write the check, I mouthed.

On the question of voter fraud, Foval seemed to be putting us off. "We can have another conversation after the election's over," he said. But then, just when we least expected it, Foval dropped a bombshell, "He is doing that stuff, but he's doing it in New York." Bingo! Cesar Vargas was doing his "stuff" in New York. At its least incriminating, that "stuff" was orchestrated civil disobedience by noncitizens.

Banned from Twitter

With our Democracy Partners work largely in the can, we decided to check out Russ Feingold's campaign for US Senate in Wisconsin. Scott Foval's claims of voter fraud in the state made Wisconsin worth our attention.

We infiltrated on a couple of fronts, or at least tried to. Fresh from her success in Washington, Allison drove her white pickup to Madison, hoping to find a place in a Feingold campaign field office. Using her real first name and a slight variant on her last, she told the organizers she had done phone banking in her native Minnesota for Democratic governor Mark Dayton and Senator Al Franken.

As we later learned, the campaign was wary enough by now to vet Allison and could find no record of her name as spelled. Scouting around, staffers realized she was the same young woman who attempted to infiltrate the Clinton campaign in Iowa a year earlier. When Allison reported for work on Tuesday, August 16, they were likely recording her. The following quote appeared verbatim in *Time* magazine: "I really like, like, women's health, the environment, that's something that I'm passionate about." She also talked about workers' rights, adding, "People in Wisconsin have to fight for stuff like that, but Scott Walker has made it just so hard for them."

On August 17, Sarah Lindstrom, volunteer coordinator, called Allison in for a meeting, saying, "We have a fun project for you."[1] On this occasion Allison was recording the Feingold people. Lindstrom turned the interview over to Josh Orton, a senior policy advisor, and his research director. Orton took the lead. He explained that the campaign was interested in finding people who could be put on special projects, not just on phone banking. He wanted to talk to Allison about one such project. Although her interrogators strained to seem normal, Allison found the interview "weird" from the beginning, and she was right.

After claiming one of the staff went to the University of Minnesota, he asked Allison outright, "Did you work with the College Republicans?"

"No," she answered honestly.

Orton inquired about her name, her intentions, about whether she worked for the conservative organization Campus Reform. "Is that you?"

"I don't know what you guys are trying to do," Allison answered, knowing her days were numbered. "If there is a problem with me being here I can leave."

"I'm just sort of curious what you were hoping to get from coming in here and misrepresenting yourself," Orton persisted, "because signing under a false name on a nondisclosure it seems like you've maybe put yourself in some legal trouble here. So I'm just sort of curious what your intent was from coming here."

"Yeah," said Allison, "I'm not going to be answering any questions. If you want me to leave I'll leave. If you want me to stay I'll stay."

"Can you tell us if you're working for anyone in particular?"

"Not really going to answer any questions," Allison answered, keeping her cool.

"Are you recording us?"

"Not really going to answer any questions."

"Okay," said Orton, "then we are going to ask you to leave and unfortunately prohibit you from coming back to the campaign."

"Okay, sounds good. Thank you," said Allison, who promptly got up and left. Creepier than need be, the research director followed Angela to her truck. Angela's Madison days were over.

So proud were the "Russ for Wisconsin" people of their detective work, they immediately went to the media. The same day on which they burned Allison, *Time* ran a surprisingly detailed story headlined, "Democratic Senate Campaign Catches Conservative Infiltrator."[2] It was so sufficiently detailed, in fact, that reporter Zeke Miller had to have been in touch with the Feingold campaign before Orton talked to Allison.

Miller even reached out to Project Veritas before running the article. Our spokesman Stephen Gordon was appropriately evasive. "Regarding the person you named below, Project Veritas will neither provide nor confirm the identity of any of our undercover journalists, real or imagined," Miller quoted Gordon as saying, and that is how the article closed. *It must be nice*, I thought, *to have* Time *on your speed dial*.

Unbeknownst to Miller or Orton, on the very same evening the Russ for Wisconsin people were doing their end zone dance in Madison, I was infiltrating a posh Russ for Wisconsin fund-raiser in Silicon Valley. This one was fun. Wearing a wig and glasses, I looked like a young Elton John or an older Justin Bieber, nerdy enough in any case to look like I belonged.

No fool, Feingold understood that you don't get elected senator in Wisconsin advocating gun control. "What I do is I go with the majority view of the people of the state, which is very common sense," he told his audience. Still, when asked by my colleague what Hillary Clinton would do about the Second Amendment, Feingold said without hesitation, "Well, there might be an executive order."

Feingold's straddling did not play all that well with his would-be donors. One of them, Leah Russin, told me, "He wants to be elected. He is from Wisconsin. I wanted him to be stronger. Nobody needs a frickin' handgun."[3] Even host Amy Rao was less than pleased with Feingold's ambivalence.

* * *

On October 12, we released our next video installment. This one focused on Wylie Mao. One of our journalists had caught up with Mao, a Hillary campaign field organizer, at a West Palm Beach bar. The topic of conversation was sexual misconduct within the Clinton campaign, sex being much in the news with the release a few days earlier of the infamous *Access Hollywood* tape that captured Donald Trump talking dirty. According to Billy Bush, the NBC host with whom Trump was speaking, neither he nor Trump knew they were being recorded. Releasing it anonymously was arguably illegal. The media seemed okay with that, but they have qualms with our tapes, which are all legally one-party consent.[4]

"I think the bar of acceptable conduct in this campaign is pretty low," Mao told our journalist with a laugh. "To be fired, I would have to grab Emma's ass twice, and she would have to complain about it. I would have to sexually harass someone."[5] Apparently, a single grab is acceptable.

In the same video, we showed Trevor LaFauci, a Hillary campaign coordinator in Florida, telling a Veritas journalist posing as a campaign worker that he would not report the worker's ripping up of three voter registration forms "as long as you don't make a habit of it."

In the video we produced, I juxtaposed the sound-bite of Donald Trump saying "Grab them by the pussy" and Mao saying "Grab them by the ass twice." When our video was released, Mao deleted his Twitter account. Always opportunistic, Laura Loomer, then with Project Veritas as a communications associate, sent out a spot-on tweet aimed right at his boss: "Looks like @WylieMao deleted his Twitter. @HillaryClinton taught him well. #VoterFraud #VoterID #SexualAssault @PVeritas_Action @HFA."[6]

As Saul Alinsky reminded us, "Keep the pressure on." We kept digging. We kept tweeting, and the audience kept growing.

First we found another clip in the hours of footage where Mao admitted, "I used to make fakes in high school. This is my work." Then, with some help from J. Christian Adams at Election Law Center, we identified the Federal Election Commission Form 3X report of receipts and disbursements showing that Mao was paid $1,249.95 by the Democratic Executive Committee of Florida for work done around August 30. This made him a paid employee. I made a screengrab of the disbursement form and sent a tweet with a link to the screenshot: "@Wylie Mao @HillaryClinton Staffer who likes talking abt grabbing ass; #VoterFraud is paid by Democratic Executive Committee of Florida."[7]

We also tweeted, "Tomorrow our hidden cameras go inside a top donor fundraiser to see what a certain Senate candidate really thinks . . ."[8] Then it happened. I went to log in to my Twitter account only to discover that I was locked out. "We have determined that you have violated the Twitter Rules, so you will need to wait some time before using Twitter again," said the Twitter administrator. At the time I checked I was told that I could reuse Twitter in eleven hours and fifty-three minutes. Maybe. The administrator added a note, saying, "You may need to complete some additional tasks to resume using Twitter."

Additional tasks? What was Twitter expecting? I wondered. Would I need to confess my thought crimes in the public square? Do a hundred hours of community service? Name names? I suspected that some select Twitter engineers were sitting in a room somewhere making political decisions, on their own or with help, about what should be allowed on the platform. Could it be the Wylie Mao content hit too close to home? A later investigation into Twitter would seem to confirm my suspicions.

This was not my first censorship rodeo. Facebook banned my account when I crossed the Rio Grande dressed like bin Laden. At the time, I alerted David Martosko of the *Daily Mail*, and he sent a strongly worded inquiry to Facebook headquarters. They restored my account within ninety seconds. I had a similar experience with the Planned Parenthood videos years earlier. When Planned Parenthood sent a "cease and desist" letter threatening to have me and Lila Rose jailed for filming them breaking the law, I forwarded the letter to Bill O'Reilly. He read it on air. The harassment ended. Sunshine works.

This time I would have to leverage the power of Twitter against itself. Without Twitter, there would be nowhere else to go. "If they boot us off this platform," I told my chief of staff, "it's game over for us." In July 2016, Twitter permanently banned gay conservative provocateur Milo Yiannopoulos for "inciting targeted abuse of individuals," in this case, black *Ghostbusters* star, Leslie Jones.[9] Milo had three hundred thousand followers at the time. Although he had said nothing racist, some of his followers had. In an election year, that was excuse enough for Twitter.

Hoping to avoid that fate, I promptly sent out a press release to the media: "Releasing hidden camera videos on a US Senator tomorrow inside a fundraiser. Twitter is trying to block our journalism. We're too effective—and there are bombshells coming out all week."[10] I then asked my Twitter followers to contact Twitter CEO Jack Dorsey and ask him why his people had chosen to block me at such a critical moment. That they did, sending at least twenty thousand tweets to Dorsey. We also sent an email blast to tens of thousands of people with an auto-tweet option that read as follows: "@jack Censoring speech violates your mission statement. Unlock @jamesokeefeiii's account so he can SHARE HIS IDEAS #FreeJames."[11]

A strange thing started to happen throughout the Twitterverse—people were literally sending hundreds of messages to the Twitter CEO. Some samples follow:

@WeStaywithTrump Use Hashtag #FreeJames and #FreeOKeefe to spread the word of Twitter's censoring. This is getting ridiculous. Keep fighting for the USA.[12]

@Rightlyaligned And @Project_Veritas twitter account has been locked down by @jack WHY?? #FREEOKEEFE #Trump #TrumpTrain #MAGA #tcot[13]

@Jack Why do you continue to silence those you don't agree with? #freeokeefe[14]

Even Fox contributor Guy Benson chipped in: "@Seriously, why was @jamesokeefeiii's account suspended by Twitter? #FreeOkeefe."[15] The barbarians were at the social media gates, and the public outcry was enough to prompt Twitter engineers to seek a truce—but with terms. To save face, they insisted I remove the tweet about Wylie Mao and how much he made. If I pulled that information, Twitter would give me back my platform.

For posterity's sake, I turned the camcorder on and recorded myself deleting the tweet. As soon as I did, up popped the message, "Thank you for addressing the issue. Your account is now available for use. To prevent future lockouts or account suspension, please review the Twitter Rules and help us maintain a safe environment for everyone on Twitter."

I am not quite sure how tweeting public information about Mao's payouts or his comments about "grabbing ass" threatened Twitter's "safe environment." Kathy Griffin, for instance, had no fear tweeting out the image of her holding Trump's decapitated head. She had been sending outrageous tweets for years without consequence, like this 2009 tweet about Sarah Palin: "Oh, Palin, ur goin down so hard, you'd better just stay in Wasilla w ur retarded baby."[16]

I also thanked my followers for making Twitter back down. Then, of course, I tweeted the video of me deleting the Mao tweet with the simple message, in full caps, "I'M BACK."[17] In short, we did a full Alinsky on Twitter. Twitter's stated mission is "to give everyone the power to create and share ideas and information instantly, without barriers."[18] We made its executives live up to that mission statement and then used the medium they had created to advertise their hypocrisy. Although the social media giants were all in the tank for Hillary, they were being hoisted on their own empty rhetoric.

The Feingold video that Twitter hoped to block was not earth-shaking, but it revealed what we already suspected—Democrats want your guns. The savvy ones, like Feingold, know the time is not yet right to say so, at least not in public. Nearly a million people saw the Feingold video, with a disproportionate amount of those in Wisconsin. Feingold lost his bid for a Senate seat by 3 percent. Hillary lost the state by 1 percent. The video may have made a little dent. For sure, we made a bigger dent in Wisconsin a few days later when we introduced key Wisconsin political operative Scott Foval to the voters of the Badger State. And this story is still not over.

Closing Up Shop

As the 2016 election approached, we had a plan, an unusual one. We were going to burn every single one of our undercover reporters at the same time, 1:00 p.m. EDT, October 14.

This is not the norm in intelligence work. We were not using cutouts the way intelligence agents who put their lives on the line do. In the language of that community, "a cutout is a mutually trusted intermediary, method or channel of communication that facilitates the exchange of information between agents. Cutouts usually know only the source and destination of the information to be transmitted, not the identities of any other persons involved in the espionage process."[1]

In our case, however, all of our journalists could be connected through one giant introductory chain: Steve Packard, our consultant, to Charles Roth, our philanthropist, to Michael Carlson, our British overseas investor, to Angela Brandt, the philanthropist's niece. If one person gets burned, they all go up in flames—or so we thought. As things turned out, our operation turned out to be complex enough that Robert Creamer failed to make the connections.

We contacted the Sinclair Broadcast Group, a large, Republican-friendly news organization. Sinclair was historically open to the stories we had been running in various states over the last several years, most recently the Feingold fund-raising story in Wisconsin. I met with one of their executives. They listened to our plan, reviewed our footage, and signed on to broadcast our work. Unlike the major media brass, they were not in bed with the Clintons. Satisfied with our work, the execs turned the job over to Circa Media, their investigative journalism arm.

At the appointed hour on D-Day, October 14, Circa reporter Raffi Williams and his crew planned to confront Creamer on a Washington street and ask him to comment on the record about what he had told us. To remind him, Williams had plenty of video footage to show. Incorporating Circa's encounter with Creamer and video highlights from our material, Sinclair was to release a video package on all of its news stations across America at noon on Monday, October 17. The stations would promo the package on the Sunday night news. Although the opposition dominated the national media, this plan would allow us to subvert that control through the use of local news nationwide.

We knew exactly where Creamer would be on October 17: the Tosca Ristorante on F Street in Washington. We knew because he would be meeting with our foreign investor, Michael Carlson, the British orthopedic surgeon with the posh accent that Roth recommended. That meeting would end at 1:00 p.m. Once confronted, we expected Creamer to make his staff aware of the bust. We wanted all of our operatives out of harm's way when he did.

On October 14, a Clinton victory seemed imminent. A Reuters headline that day read, "Clinton Leads by 7 Points as Trump Faces Grope Claims."[2] Given that likelihood, Carlson's plan to explore purchasing access in the incoming Clinton administration seemed credible. More immediately, Carlson wanted to get Creamer to take credit for the violence at Trump rallies. In the best of all worlds, Creamer would implicate Hillary in the planning of violence as well.

Creamer had already told us it was "the future president of the United States, Hillary Clinton, that wanted ducks on the ground." We were hoping it was she who ordered thugs on the ground as well. We had even flirted with the idea of keeping the investigation going given how well our operatives had penetrated Democracy Partners, but time was getting precious.

After some innocuous chitchat, Creamer mentioned that he had run into Charles Roth. "I arranged for him to have a tour of something at noon," said Creamer.

"What's he doing, tour of what?" asked Carlson disingenuously.

"Oh, he wanted to see Media Matters," said Creamer, "which is an organization here. Apparently his significant other is particularly fond of, and I think was a spousal political requirement, that he . . . so he can go back and say, 'I went by there and saw it was great.'"

At that very moment, thanks to Creamer's intervention, Roth was indeed across town at Media Matters. There, on the sixth floor of that faceless glass and steel building, he was meeting with then president Bradley Beychok, a diminutive young redhead who favored orange-framed glasses. As Beychok and Roth toured the offices, Beychok discussed some hit pieces Media Matters was putting together on Donald Trump. Roth wanted to learn if Media Matters would be interested in a compromising photo of Trump from *The Apprentice* set that he hoped to see published.

At Media Matters, anything was possible. A month before this meeting, the founder of Media Matters and operator of Correct the Record super PAC, David Brock, had posted on Correct the Record's website a request for damaging video or audio of Trump. As Brock noted, he was willing to "provide some compensation" for anyone who could provide useful footage.[3] This move troubled even NBC. "Posting a bounty for dirt on a political opponent is highly unusual in modern politics and seems to cross a new line in the rules of war," observed reporter Alex Seitz-Wald.[4]

In his conversation with Roth, Beychok showed he had the stuff to follow in the founder's footstep, bragging about how he was able "to take [Trump's] MVPs and put them on the sidelines." The first notch on his belt was veteran Republican consultant Roger Stone. According to Beychok, Media Matters tracked every book appearance that Stone made. "We took everything that was crazy in his book," he boasted, "and made sure that people knew it was sourced even in the crazy material." To Beychok and his media allies, "crazy" was anything they disagreed with.

The Media Matters staffers parsed out Stone's tweets by interest group and privately reached out to the networks to make sure their producers knew what groups Stone might possibly offend. "Hey," Beychok claimed he told the networks, "are you aware you have had this guy on twelve times in the last four months and he said these three things?" Beychok succeeded in getting Stone banned even from Fox News.

While Roth moved in on Beychok, Carlson continued his discussion with Creamer back at Tosca. Creamer had a couple of inside guys who, presumably for a price, could help Carlson's imaginary clients work out some of their problems. The first one Creamer suggested was "probably one of the best immigration lawyers in the country, for your Syrian guy." Roth's "Syrian guy" wanted to get out of Syria and into the United States. If anyone could make that happen, Creamer's guy could: "And he is eager to talk to whoever, okay?"

Roth's second overseas client had some trade issues that needed to be resolved. Creamer could take care of that as well. He had high-level lobbying friends who had worked with Speaker of the House Dick Gephardt and who were "wired up to a network of people." Said Creamer, "They are all eager to talk to whoever you bring. So just have them be in touch." When the conversation got around to Barack Obama, Creamer boasted, "I've known the president since he was a community organizer in Chicago." He told Carlson he did a lot of work with the White House on issues such as immigration reform, the healthcare bill, and "trying to make America more like Britain when it comes to gun violence issues."

Perhaps aware of the time crunch, Carlson did not press. As the hour wound down, he and Creamer mostly just gossiped about the Clinton campaign. At the appointed hour, he parted company with Creamer. Creamer headed down the sidewalk on F Street, looking dapper in his navy blazer, slightly buzzed from the red wine. Meanwhile, across town, after checking his watch, a disappointed Roth realized he did not have the time or opportunity to probe Beychok about the Trump photo.

At the moment Creamer headed down the street, Roth donned his shades and slipped out of Media Matters. At that same time, at the Democracy Partners office, Angela Brandt informed the secretary she was leaving and briskly walked out without explanation. There were no cutouts to protect their identities. Everyone had to get out of Dodge. No one was sure exactly what would happen next.

Curiously, our best source on what did happen was a lawsuit filed by Creamer in June 2017 against Project Veritas among others. According to the suit, as soon as Creamer and Carlson left the Tosca, a video crew from Circa Media accosted Creamer. Raffi Williams, the lead reporter, volunteered to show Creamer two video clips that we recorded of him, likely in conversation with Angela. Circa's Raffi Williams knew to find Creamer at Tosca, the suit claims, because I had told Williams that Creamer would be there.

Later that day, Williams called Creamer and asked him to sit for an on-camera interview so he could respond to the videos. Williams apparently told Creamer that Project Veritas had provided his network with hundreds of hours of raw tape. He also told him that Sinclair agreed to syndicate four nightly news pieces on these videos beginning the following week. This was all fairly accurate.

Back at Project Veritas headquarters, we sat in the production room patiently waiting to see the outcome of how this plan played out. What we got instead was a call from Creamer's assistant, a woman named Lauren Windsor, wanting to speak to Charles Roth. The call came into the cell phone of our executive producer, Joe Halderman. On a few occasions, Joe had played the role of Roth over the phone. This is why Windsor had his number. He picked up. Windsor told him there was an emergency involving his niece.

"I'm her uncle," said Joe, genuinely concerned. "What is the emergency? Has she been hurt?"

Windsor hedged, "We believe she is involved in some sort of infiltration in our office."

"Okay," said Joe, "Like, I don't understand."

"I know," said Windsor. "We don't understand either, but she has left the building and has a security keycard to our office. We believe she was surreptitiously recording events that were taking place in the office."

When Joe asked why she might have done this, Windsor refused to say and pressed him on whether he had seen Angela. She wanted the Democracy Partners property returned and an "explanation for these activities." Windsor's tone hardened. She was obviously not worried about Angela's well-being. She was worried about the well-being of Democracy Partners.

"This an emergency for our office," she told Joe, "and I assure you that if we find sufficient evidence that she was involved in recording any of the partners or any activity in our office illegally there will be action."

The call astonished us. We did not think Windsor was trying to bait us. The investigation was sufficiently complex and well played that Creamer seemed to be unaware there was no "Charles Roth III." He must have thought Roth's niece betrayed her poor Uncle Charles.

Spiking the News

The same evening we shut down our operation, Creamer agreed to meet Circa Media's Raffi Williams at the DC law offices of KaiserDillon. At this meeting, Creamer and his attorney viewed roughly three hours of videos that showed recordings of Creamer, other Democracy Partners staff, and Aaron Black, as well as clients of Democracy Partners and Creamer's Strategic Consulting Group. The Sinclair people had the video. It was their call.

Sinclair was to release a trailer Sunday night, followed at noon on Monday with a video package on campaign violence. Tuesday at noon Sinclair would release the voter-fraud package. We would follow these releases, of course, with an all-out blitz on social media. All weekend we had waited to see Sinclair's packages and promo pieces. Nothing aired. We were less worried than we should have been. On Monday October 17, at 10:00 a.m., two hours before we were scheduled to go live with the first bombshell tape, I received a call from an executive at Sinclair.[1] I took the call in the production room. I was sitting with Joe, our producer, and Fredy, our editor. We were assembling the storyboard for the first video.

"So, here's the state of play on Sinclair's side, and it is what it is," the executive said. From his tone I knew the news was not going to be good.

"We weren't able to get the approval we need to go with these stories," he continued, "certainly not today or tomorrow from what I've seen." He conceded that our journalistic work was solid, but the decision was made above his head. "It's funny," he added. "We have Creamer in our offices right now. We're interviewing him."

Maybe it was the state of shock I was in, but I didn't think "funny" was exactly the right word choice. According to the lawsuit, Creamer and his attorney were indeed meeting that Monday morning with Sinclair's management at Sinclair headquarters in Arlington, Virginia. In the meeting, those present reviewed additional footage—no big deal—and "Creamer's attorney discussed legal and factual issues relating to the videos"—big deal.

I had been running around all morning getting everything ready. The takeout breakfast I had grabbed on the way in sat cold on my desk, but it was not nearly as cold as the words from our executive friend. With two hours to go before launch, Sinclair had undone our entire strategy. The video package we expected to lead with was no more. A CBS veteran, Joe had been down this road before. His news instincts kicked in. While I was on the phone with the Sinclair executive, he put his hand on my shoulder. I put the phone on mute, frustrated that Joe was interrupting my call with the executive.

"What is it?"

Joe answered softly but intensely, "So fuck 'em. Let's just get on with producing the story."

"I'm on the phone," I said. "I'm finishing the conversation with Sinclair. Just give me a second."

Joe pointed to the other journalists in the room and to the clock and to Fredy who sat in front of a large monitor furiously assembling the story in the video timeline.

"Can you give *us* a second?" Joe said pointedly.

Yes, I could. I gave them the go-ahead. As I walked out of the room, the entire production team at Veritas frantically scrambled to put the finishing touches on this game-changing story much the way network crews do in movies like *Broadcast News* or in TV series like *Newsroom*. I genuinely believe our team is the best in the business.

We had already assembled the relevant undercover video selections. To that we had to add my introduction and explanatory narrative. We would put the package together ourselves and meet the noon deadline we had promised our followers. In that moment, my respect for my team increased tenfold.

After a quick pep talk, I headed back into my office to hear out Sinclair's meandering rationalization for why its execs would not run our story. At the time, they really could not tell me or would not. I have a lot of respect for the Sinclair people, still do. They ventured further than any other media company would, but they blinked and spiked our story. I needed to find out why.

Breaking Through

B y 2016, social media had matured, and we had much more control over the information flow. "Flow" here is the apt word. There were multiple streams in 2016—Twitter, Reddit, 4chan, Facebook—and together they had dramatically more power than social media had just four years earlier. On October 16, the day before our breakthrough videos were to be released, I tweeted, "T minus 24 hours. The way to defeat and overcome a corrupt and complacent media . . . is to become the media."[1]

Our two most powerful videos in the "Rigging the Election" series were to drop on Monday and Tuesday of that week, October 17 and 18. The first of the two focused on the orchestration of violence at Trump rallies. The second focused on voter fraud. Each made ample use of our conversations with Scott Foval, Robert Creamer, and others.

Our principal conduit remained Twitter. The temporary Twitter ban five days earlier had, as Twitter execs should have figured, the opposite effect of what they intended. Sometimes things that you think are bad turn out to be a blessing. Once the ban was lifted, I was adding 10,000 followers a day. By October 17, I had 120,000 followers. I know. Kim Kardashian has more than 50 million followers, but no one checks @JamesOKeefeIII to see what I am wearing that evening. People follow me because they want real information they are not going to get elsewhere.

If the streams had strengthened since 2012, so had the dam holding them back. It bears repeating that for the first time in the broadcast era, the major media threw its collective weight shamelessly and unapologetically behind one candidate and against another. Not a single major newspaper in America endorsed Donald Trump. The news pages at Google, Yahoo!, and AOL—and these were seen by scores of millions of people every day—unmistakably slanted their news against Trump. So did every major magazine and every broadcast network, except Fox News, and Fox was chockablock with NeverTrumpers.

As I learned that very morning, even our would-be allies in the broadcast media were afraid of coming to our aid. It had been three and a half years since I had appeared on the editorial side of Fox News and more than six years since I appeared with Eric Shawn to explain my arrest in New Orleans. I had not appeared on the news side since.

Millions of Americans sensed the reluctance of the conservative media to break news. These people were looking for a dam-buster. Andrew Breitbart had that potential, but he died unexpectedly four years prior. His news organization prospered, but it had no public face. In 2016, in fact, there was only one person in America with the charisma, the face time, and the will to hammer away at that dam. I am convinced it was that will to power, more than any other factor, that made Donald Trump the Republican nominee. Who knew what he believed in?

One thing that had not changed in the last four years was the primal Veritas rule, the rule that had guided our destiny from the beginning: "Content is king." On October 17, we had that content, the most damning content we had ever gathered, and the most potentially consequential. Near noon—the final editing was still in process—we were going to pour that content into the existing streams and see what happened. In the meantime, I wanted to make sure our allies were still on board.

I called Joel Pollak, the senior editor-at-large for Breitbart. He was out of the office for the next few days. Out of the office? Three weeks before the election? What? Someone reminded me that Pollak was an Orthodox Jew. October 17 and 18 were Sukkot, the Feast of the Tabernacles. I tried to contact Drudge. He was offline, probably asleep. As I did with Reddit's AMA, I held up a whiteboard with my face and the time to assure him it was me. Drudge keeps odd hours. For all of his clout, he is the most elusive dude on the planet. He responds to no one

I know. His responses often come in the form of updates to his website text thirty seconds after he receives a message from you. That is how he communicates.

I called Alexander Marlow, the Breitbart editor in chief, a Berkeley grad, younger than I am. I wanted to reassure myself that no one had threatened Breitbart. No one had. Marlow was still all in, just waiting for our video. Noon was approaching. Our guys were still uploading the video.

Breitbart would help, but we had to be our own destination. My guys assured me the website could handle the anticipated traffic. I paced around. "What would really suck bad," I said to our fully engaged communications team, "is if the electricity went out, or if there was another ISIS attack."

Noon came. We were still not up. Our followers were chomping at the proverbial bit. One guy who posted a tweet at 12:01 was demanding we let the corruption out of the bag. Just a minute behind schedule, and our guys were bitching. "Damn!" I said. "It's much more fun to be the underdog."

At 12:05 we launched. At about 12:10 the website crashed. "What's going on?" I asked the tech guys who were huddling around a computer monitor. "We're jammed," one said. "We'll give you an update in thirty seconds." I couldn't wait that long. "I need it now," I said. Our business model depended on having a viable site. Yes, the video was running on YouTube. In fact, it was running crazy on YouTube, about a hundred thousand views in the first five minutes, but that ad revenue went to YouTube, not to us. Plus, YouTube was not about to solicit donations on our behalf. I was going to send a link along with a personal email to Drudge, to Rush Limbaugh, to Hannity, and Gavin McInnes. I did not want to send them a YouTube link. Fortunately, our guys quickly got it fixed. Using NotePad, they wrote the code for that page by hand, inserted the YouTube embed script, and uploaded it to the website, greatly reducing the server load.

I called our contact at Salem Radio for reassurance. Lee Habeeb, Salem's VP of content, is one of those many guys on the right who shreds the stereotypes. An Arab American, he graduated from the University of Virginia Law School, lives in Oxford, Mississippi, and has a daughter named Reagan. Go figure. Salem, Lee told me, was solid. Its news service provides content for some twenty-two hundred affiliates across the country, all of them Christian and/or conservative.

The Federal Communications Commission, Lee explained, was always eager to shut Salem down, but the company had learned to negotiate around it. The media companies most vulnerable, I was learning, were those that were publicly owned and traded, especially those that lacked a genuine mission. With these companies, the threat of a major lawsuit, an FCC action, or even a bluff from the Department of Justice could roil the markets and cost shareholders millions. Breitbart was not publicly traded. Nor was it subject to the FCC. Plus, like its founder, Breitbart had chutzpah. It was now our go-to site. I called Marlow back.

"We're going to send you a link. You'll get a shitload of traffic. You still good to go? You sure?" I paced around as I spoke, the nervous energy pushing me through the day.

Marlow was sure. He would build a story around the video and, if it was as solid as promised, give the story top billing. "The internet is our friend," I told him, "the best friend we have." This was uncharted territory.

I heard back from Gavin McInnes. McInnes was born in England to Scottish parents and grew up in Canada. Somewhat of a libertarian bad boy and provocateur, he had cofounded VICE with Shane Smith and embraced the nickname "the godfather of hipsterdom." The Gavin I know is a reckless, comic, creative genius with conservative tendencies and an incapacity to sugarcoat.

When I first met Gavin a few years prior, he told me in the way of either a compliment or encouragement, "We need journalists with balls." It was probably both. "You're on a quest for truth in the age of media obfuscation," he would tell me when I needed to hear it and make me laugh at things I knew I shouldn't laugh at—like his own wicked self-description as "Wilford Brimley with AIDS."

Gavin had me on as a guest of his radio show just before noon. Now he had seen the video, and he was tweeting about it: "Biggest scoop of the election so far."[2] It was fitting such a moment occurred with him.

Laura came up with the idea of taking some of the more damning quotes out of the first "Rigging" video and embedding them in their own individual tweets. There were some good ones. I favored Scott Foval's anthemic, "It doesn't matter what the friggin' legal and ethics people say, we need to win this motherfucker." The tweet quickly received six thousand retweets in the first few minutes. I had never seen such traffic. Yeah, we were chopping the video up, but I remembered what Andrew Breitbart told me: "I don't care if they cannibalize content. It needs to get out there."

The actual video was about sixteen minutes long, or about fourteen minutes longer than most Americans were willing to watch anything online. A good thirty-second sound-bite could reach millions that the long-form video would not. The strategy worked better than we had planned. The retweets were burning up the internet.

Since the first tweet worked so well, we embedded another quote from Foval: "The media will cover it no matter where it happens. The key is initiating the conflict by having leading conversations with people who are naturally psychotic. Honestly, it is not hard to get some of these assholes to pop off."

This one netted seven thousand retweets, five thousand likes. The story was getting out! You could feel the energy on the tweet deck. All of this was happening days after Twitter executives decided to ban me, then reinstate me. We felt suddenly unstoppable. "Now we're in business," I told Laura. "Keep going. Awesome."

I heard back from a top executive at Sinclair. His tone was icy cold.

"We're not running it," he said of the video package. "You should go forward with your plans for publishing it. We're just not prepared to move forward at this point."

"You're not prepared what?" I was trying to make sense out of what we were being told.

"To move forward at this point."

"Is there a reason why?" I asked. I pushed the mute button while the executive struggled to come up with a plausible answer.

"It sounds like a gun is pointed at his head," said one of our guys during the pause. Metaphorically speaking, a gun *was* pointed at Sinclair's head. Robert Creamer's attorney was holding it.

I needed some good news. I checked Drudge. We weren't up yet. Drudge was probably still sleeping. I turned on Rush. He wasn't talking about us either.

About 1:18, a little crack appeared in the dam. Donald Trump Jr. retweeted the video. So did popular conservative commentator Michelle Malkin. We were getting fifty tweets a second now. I posted our stream on one side of the computer screen and Kim Kardashian's on the other. We were outpacing her. This was historic. At about 1:30, Sean Hannity's people called. They wanted us on his radio show. Only Rush Limbaugh has more listeners.

Laura and I went over our talking points before the show began. One question we entertained was whether I should ask Sean on air why Fox News seemed to be blocking me. By the time I got on, we had not yet come to a conclusion. I took the call in my office. Sean had seen the video. He was impressed. He said on air that this was our "best work to date" and described me as someone who is "doing what the old media used to do." Before the segment was over, I encouraged him—nicely—to get us on the air. He mentioned the lawyers and made no promises.

I was beginning to feel like Al Pacino's character Lowell Bergman in *The Insider*. I pulled the relevant clip up on my monitor and watched it while being recorded. I explained to the Project Veritas staff the similarities between our mission and Bergman's. "Staff, it's what you do right now that will matter for the future of journalism."

I played the clip to remind us of the risks we ran: "And Jeffrey Wigand, who's out on a limb, does he go on television and tell the truth?" says Pacino as Bergman to the suits at CBS. "Yes. Is it newsworthy? Yes. Are we gonna air it? Of course not. Why? Because he's not telling the truth? No. Because he *is* telling the truth. That's why we're not going to air it. And the more truth he tells, the worse it gets!"

We tweeted the clip out with my commentary. The pace was picking up. I called Marlow back at Breitbart. "This is the best thing you've given us in years," he told me. "It's an absolute monster." We were breaking Breitbart's traffic record even without a link to Drudge.

This was truly remarkable. Years earlier, when we released the story about obtaining Attorney General Eric Holder's ballot, Breitbart's

Steve Bannon told me nothing much happened without a Drudge link. "The strategy is basically to get it on Drudge," he confided. As political writer Mark Halperin observed with some accuracy, "Matt Drudge rules our world."[3]

Drudge was still silent. So was Rush Limbaugh. His three hours passed without a mention. "If not today, he will talk about it tomorrow," I assured Laura. But it was now 3 p.m. The dam still held. I tried to remind myself that the story had only been alive for three hours, but in this era, three hours passed like three years.

Just ten days earlier, when the *Washington Post* released the Trump/Billy Bush tape, the tape became the number-one story *in the world* within one hour. I believe the content of the "Rigging" videos was more relevant, possibly even more incriminating, but our media streams led to a dam. The *Post* stream led to an open sea.

The *Post,* which helped create the dam, was indirectly involved in its most spectacular breach. The opening of this breach can be traced back to 1994 when reporter Michael Isikoff left the *Post* after a flare-up with his editors. The *Washington Times* reported Isikoff's departure in a story headlined "Post Sex Story about Clinton Gets the Spike."[4] The sex story in question involved allegations made by Paula Jones in Arkansas that Bill Clinton, when governor, had exposed himself to her. Although Isikoff insists he left the *Post* for more complex reasons than the *Times* headline might suggest, the Jones story was at the heart of it.

After leaving the *Post,* Isikoff went to work for *Newsweek* magazine, which was owned by the *Post.* In January 1998, history repeated itself and then some. Isikoff was about to break the story on Clinton's seamy Oval Office affair with intern Monica Lewinsky when his editors, depending on whom you believe, either delayed it or spiked it.[5] Unfortunately for *Newsweek,* the media landscape had shifted dramatically between 1994 and 1998. In 1994, only one in nine American households had internet access. By 1998 that number had tripled, and all major media had an online presence.[6]

Then, too, in 1994 Matt Drudge was an unknown twenty-seven-year-old working as a manager at a CBS Studios gift shop in Los Angeles. Concerned about Matt's lack of direction, his liberal father bought him a computer. A born aggregator of other people's news, Drudge began sending out emails regarding gossip he had gleaned at CBS. He soon turned to politics, and in January 1998, the Drudge Report hit paydirt when someone gave Drudge Isikoff's suppressed *Newsweek* story on Lewinsky. It was too hot, too powerful, too sexy for the dam to contain. The story made Matt Drudge, and he never slowed down. During the 2016 campaign, Drudge was getting as many as *1.5 billion* page views a month.

Not surprisingly, the same publications that suppressed stories about Clinton's accusers, allegedly for lack of corroboration, had no qualms about giving Trump's accusers front-page coverage. The first of these women went public on October 13, just four days before our launch. She claimed that Trump groped her thirty-seven years earlier on an airliner. There were no witnesses, no video, no evidence. Who cared? Within hours, she received more major media attention than I had in my entire career. For all the power of the social media, we were still very much the David facing the major media Goliath.

What made resistance even fiercer is that we were implicating Goliath in the story we were trying to break. Foval and the others incited violence at the Trump rallies for one reason only: the media would report the story the way the provocateurs wanted it reported. "When they're outside the rally, the media will cover it no matter where it happens," Scott Foval relayed conspiratorially to our undercover reporter in the first clip. No major media reporter would bother probing the roots of the violence, and no editor anywhere would want it known that Foval counted on this. America's newsrooms were content with the story the way it had been told and sold. Our reporting would only subvert that narrative.

Knowing all this only made me jumpy. I contacted everyone I could contact, worked on the next day's voter-fraud videos, and monitored the social media. As the afternoon wore on, the dam showed little sign of cracking. My staff and I debated the wisdom of directing our social media followers to pound Fox News and demand they have me on. "Don't burn this bridge yet," one of my guys implored me.

We decided to burn it anyhow. With nowhere else to turn, and much too dependent on social media accounts that could be suspended at any moment, we asked our followers to contact the Fox hosts and encourage them. It was time for them to shed their fears of Hillary and do the right thing.

I had our cameraman film me at my desk. Looking straight into the lens, I implored our citizen audience to "tweet at the anchors at places like Fox News, @BretBaier, @MegynKelly, @OReillyFactor, @SeanHannity. Tweet this video at them with the hashtag '#Veritas.'" While our folks got busy on this, I did a quick radio interview with Simon Conway, a British radio host working out of Iowa's monster WHO Radio. "The people of the country are pissed, and they have nowhere to go," I told him, pacing while I talked. "You are seeing the collision of two monumental forces." By this time, I could hear the anxiety in my own voice.

More bad news. I had been scheduled to appear on Stuart Varney's show on Fox Business. His people called and canceled. No reason given. We had been assured earlier that Fox Business played by different rules than Fox News—apparently not. Then some good news. James Golden called. A stocky black fellow who sports a variety of dashing chapeaus, Golden could show up at a CPAC convention and not merit a second look. Even if he introduced himself, few would take heed. If, however, Golden used his *nom de radio* during that introduction, everyone would want a piece of "Bo Snerdley." The head producer for *The Rush Limbaugh Show*, Golden may be the most influential gatekeeper in the media.

"James," I sighed, "Fox News just booked me and canceled me."

"Un-fucking-real," said Golden.

"The video is everywhere," I told him. "It's got to break somewhere, I don't know where."

Golden had some ideas, good ones. We proceeded to talk media strategy for nearly half an hour. He shared all his contact information, major and minor. That info was priceless. And yes, he promised, Rush would indeed talk about the videos tomorrow. Okay. We were making progress.

As frustrating as the day was, I would be lying if I said I didn't love the action. In ten years, I had never had a day quite like this. After a while, we all got kind of silly, including, apparently, Fox News. Several of our monitors had the channel on in the background.

"Look at this," one of our people said.

Here we were, three weeks before the most critical election in anyone's memory, and Fox was showing a segment called "Corgi vs. the Stairs." This clip was lifted from the Instagram account "Cobee theCorgi." The video showed a puppy trying and failing to get up the first step in a flight of stairs. This was immediately followed by a segment called "Feline Fun" in which two cats were playing patty-cake in slow motion. They were pretty good at it actually.

The irony was palpable. These segments had less to do with journalism and more to do with business, efficiency, and economics, or as Noam Chomsky and Edward S. Herman put it, "a matter of cost." Wrote the authors, "Taking information from sources that may be presumed credible reduces investigative expense, whereas material from sources that are not prima facie credible, or that will elicit criticism and threats, requires careful checking and costly research."[7] In short, CobeetheCorgi was a more economically useful source than Project Veritas.

"Film the television, Get me in front of those cats playing patty-cake," I told our guys. They did, and we embedded it in a tweet that read, "Greg Gutfeld, why are you showing cats playing patty-cake instead of airing our bombshell report"?[8]

"Shame them all!" said Laura for the ages.

Our followers sent thousands of tweets targeting these hosts, anchors, and producers. We needed all the help we could get. On the same day, on the same afternoon, as our "Rigging" videos were becoming the most trafficked video on YouTube, these corporate mainstream media outlets were refusing to air the story. Other than Fox News, they were not even considering running them.

CNN's Jake Tapper tweeted at 2:53, "Trump Slams election 'rigged,' offers no evidence."[9]

"Here's Part 1 of the evidence," I tweeted back to Tapper with a link to our "violence" video.[10]

"Shame on them," repeated Laura, my one-woman Greek chorus.

Our tweets and posts kept contradicting a blithely complicit media. We were winning a war of words, but victory was bittersweet, sweet because it was just, bitter because the media had yet to acknowledge our attack, let alone their defeat.

Our strategy of tweeting at the Fox anchors was getting under their skin. Brit Hume tweeted at 6:42, "James O'Keefe is beefing his latest video not being played on News Outlets. That's because it needs to be checked out before being aired."[11] One of our followers fired back, "That's never stopped you before Brit."

"The hell it hasn't," responded an irritated Hume. "Buddy you have no idea. Stuff pours in over the transom here all the time. It has to be checked out."[12]

"For the record," I tweeted back at Hume, "I reached out to Fox News reporters a week ago willing to have them take a look at everything. I'm waiting for a call back."[13]

I tweeted Bret Baier, "Bret, what happened? The videos were going to air on multiple programs and @FoxNews canceled last minute. Why?"[14]

"We are still investigating all elements of it and will update tomorrow," Baier responded. "Thanks."[15]

"I'm having so much fun," I enthused, and it was getting better. I knew in my heart the second-day video with Foval saying "We've been busing people in to deal with you fuckin' assholes for fifty years" was so damning it might force reporters to cover it just so they could look in the mirror the next morning.

Things were picking up. Mark Levin's people called. They wanted me on his national radio show. Now. I was ready to go. Levin introduced me as a "brave young man." I think "crazy" is perhaps more accurate than "brave," but I'll take a compliment where I can get one.

"I've got a smoking-gun video of how they incite violence at Trump rallies," I told Levin. "The grassroots are on fire, and I am trying to get this out on the major media." He was all ears and fully supportive. There were no major cracks in the dam yet, but the pressure was building.

Day had already turned to night, but our sky was brightening. Twitter could no longer ignore the traffic we were generating and finally listed us as "trending." Up to that point, "Power Rangers" was trending with eight thousand tweets, but we had ten times that number and were not trending yet. Better still, Drudge had woken up, and there we were. In bright red. I hugged Stephen Gordon. "We're doing it," I said. "We're doing it."

Before leaving for the night, I cut an up-to-date intro for part two of our series. This part on voter fraud was as powerful as the one on inciting violence. We were punching through. I could feel it, and I felt the overwhelming need to share that feeling. "You guys are watching history being made," I told the production crew. They knew that without being told.

That evening, Sean Hannity stepped up to the plate in a major way. He had his staff call Americans United for Change. He learned that Foval had been fired. For us, this was huge. Foval's termination was inarguably *news*. At 8:05 p.m., I followed up with Hume. "Brit," I tweeted, "now that they've fired the operative for inducing violence, you're safe to report the fact he's fired. It's real."[16]

To their credit, Fox News anchors were talking about whether they were going to air the story. CNN was still mute, even on social media. Charlie Kirk, executive director of Turning Point USA, pointed out on Twitter that night, "Zero tweets from @CNN on the bombshell @JamesOKeefeIII story. Censorship. They want Clinton to win."[17]

The guy who gave Foval the axe was his boss at Americans United for Change, Brad Woodhouse. Unbeknownst to Woodhouse, he would soon be featured in one of our videos accepting a $20,000 donation from overseas. Woodhouse's statement on Foval read in part, "[We] have always operated according to the highest ethical and legal standards." To us this sounded like a punch line to a joke, knowing as we did Foval's memorable declaration, "It doesn't matter what the friggin' legal and ethics people say, we need to win this motherfucker."

Then came a breakthrough. Overriding the lawyers at Fox News, as he would later tell me, Sean Hannity was showing our video on his TV show. Radio was great, but video was our game. To see is to experience on a much more visceral level than to hear. To keep the suits happy, Hannity threw in qualifiers such as "if true" and the like, but he punched the most significant hole in the dam to date.

Sleep did not come easily that night, but I wasn't needing much. Four hours would prove plenty. Adrenaline served as a useful substitute. I got to my office next morning and did a radio interview with the fearless Laura Ingraham. She was not afraid to say what we were up against. It wasn't just about winning, she explained: "They are in this to humiliate and crush Republican opposition." It was the first opportunity I had to thank Hannity on the air. "Credit Sean Hannity," I told her. "He's a good man for doing what he did. They fired Scott Foval." We owed Hannity a major debt. The man put his reputation on the line for a story no one else wanted to touch.

After Ingraham, I did radio interviews with Rusty Humphries and Salem's Mike Gallagher—both good and reliable guys. "I need your audience to tweet this video at the media and say, 'cover this,'" I told Rusty about part two of the "Rigging" series, which we were just about to drop. "What tape [the media] choose to air is going to determine who wins the election." On certain stories in the past I would have begged to get on the radio shows whose producers, today, were calling us. Most of them I had to turn down. I hated to do it, but there was much to be done.

I spent a good deal of time that morning chewing over a decision that I never expected to face. Trump's people had called. They wanted us in Las Vegas for the third and final debate. That debate was *tomorrow*. Vegas was at least five hours away. I called in my senior staff. These guys had seen more of the world than I did, and I needed their advice. I had two major questions to answer: should I go and, if I did go, how the hell would I get there?

My one concern was of seeming too partisan. Yes, of course, just about all of us were pulling for Trump to win. All politics aside, the way we figured it, our enemy's enemy was our friend. Then too, Trump had been a donor—not a big one, but all our donors were our friends.

The guys who had been to debates before described just how much media exposure I would get as a guest in the Spin Room at a presidential debate, especially given the fact that the first "Rigging" video had been the most-watched video in the world during these last twenty-four hours. They convinced me I could not turn the opportunity down.

While this debate was going on, CNN called. It was reporter Drew Griffin. From the tone of his voice, he sounded like he would rather be covering school board meetings in Prince George's County than talking to me. He objected immediately to being on speakerphone. He wanted to see raw tape. He was sure those involved would say that their words were taken out of context. Yes, yeah, yeah! I had little patience for his demands. Still, as annoying as the call was, I could hear in Griffin's snark the fissures in the dam cracking open. It took twenty-three hours to get the attention of the non-Fox media, but now they were calling.

Part two in the "Rigging" series dropped at noon. And good things really started happening. Drudge kicked in with seven separate links, all of them above the mast, several in red. Drawing my attention away from Drudge was the memorable opening theme music from *The Rush Limbaugh Show*. I headed out to the common area where the show was being streamed on a large overhead monitor. As soon as I heard my name mentioned, I shouted out, "Turn it up."

Now just about the entire staff gathered in front of the monitor. Rush began by replaying his own broadcast from last March during which he speculated that the violence at the Chicago Trump Rally had been staged. "Make no mistake. This is all on the Democrats," he had said back then. "This mob had been bought and paid for."[18] He was feeling vindicated.

"Let's go now to the Project Veritas video," said Rush, and our people spontaneously cheered. Over the last year, eight of these journalists had put everything into this effort. This was a risky business. Unlike other journalists, for them there was no guarantee of a byline. In fact, when they started, there was no guarantee there would be a story worth telling. But they had pulled it off. I could see in their faces the joy, the pride, the relief. The work they had done for the last year, the career they had chosen, just got a whole lot easier to explain to friends and family.

The day kept getting more and more interesting. Although Foval was history, Robert Creamer clung to his job. Earlier we speculated that the Dems would not dare ditch Creamer given his congress-woman wife and his White House connections. An email I received that afternoon would prove us wrong.

The email came from Madelin Fuerste, a local TV producer in Chicago. She wanted me to respond to a statement by Creamer. The statement read, "I am unwilling to become a distraction to the important task of electing Hillary Clinton, and defeating Donald Trump in the upcoming election. As a result, I have indicated to the Democratic National Committee that I am stepping back from my responsibilities working with the campaign." DNC head Donna Brazile later offhand-edly told me she fired Creamer, but that afternoon I was totally okay with "stepping back." A scalp is a scalp.

"Creamer fired!" I shouted throughout our newsroom. Before I even responded to Fuerste, I took a screenshot of the Creamer statement and tweeted it out. The Veritas twitter feed lit up like a slot machine in jackpot mode, buzzing, popping, and clicking so frequently I could scarcely keep track. Two top Democratic officials had been fired for getting nabbed trying to rig the election, and, to this point at least, no one in the mainstream news media had reported on the story.

That was about to change. The sacking of Creamer forced the media to cover a story most were hoping to avoid. I looked up at the six monitors inside the Project Veritas newsroom. Each was turned to a different station. And every broadcast—Fox News, CNN, MSNBC, even local media—were playing video clips and discussing our "Rigging the Election" series.

Even CNN's Anderson Cooper got dragged into it. Broadcasting from Las Vegas that evening, Cooper said without a trace of enthu-siasm, "Video emerging of a group of pro-Clinton political operatives talking about stirring up trouble and provoking violence at Trump rallies." That got our attention. He added the mandatory mainstream caveat that I had a "less than stellar reputation for accuracy." That established, Cooper conceded, "Some of the things you'll hear on the tape are certainly hard to ignore, enough we're learning for one person to be fired, so far another to resign."[19]

Every one of the staff members inside Veritas at 8:00 p.m. was frozen in place. As hopeful as we were, it shocked us to witness such a turn of events. "Angela Brandt" stared up at Cooper shaking her head in awe. "All the nights transcribing video," she said quietly, "all the days writing after-action reports leads to this. Even Van Jones is defending us. Van Jones!" True, Jones did refer to me as "Pinocchio," but he called out Foval's activities as "horrific."

Cooper and his crew were broadcasting outside in a public space. As sweet as Cooper's words were, one single image that evening was sweeter still. To this day, I choke up when I think about it. Clearly visible behind Cooper was a citizen whose name I will likely never know. He was surely one of the 14 million who watched the videos on YouTube, and I suspect he tweeted out at least a few of the "Rigging" series' 100 million tweets. Proudly and defiantly, the man walked back and forth behind Cooper in full view of the millions of CNN viewers. He was holding a sign above his head. The sign said simply, "#ProjectVeritas."

Weaponized Autism

In the lead-up to the 2016 presidential election, our geek allies had a ton of nervous energy they hoped to put to good use. During elections past, all they could have done was to consume news or at best redistribute it. By 2016, they could help create it. Perhaps the most usefully creative of all sites was Reddit.

Although most Americans over thirty have not even heard of it, Reddit has quietly become the eighth most popular online destination in the United States. Its methodology is a mystery, and its internet-amped collection of memes and verbal mischief is incomprehensible to all but its legion of "redditors." Despite those seeming limitations, Reddit is changing the culture.

What registered redditors do is post text and/or a direct link to an article and see if they can generate a community of users around their post. Other users vote the item up or down. Those posts that gather the most "up" votes ascend the page. Users can add their comments to the post, often playing off one another. Most conversations do not get much beyond commentary, some of it less enlightened than others, but our redditors wanted to do more than talk. Many found their voice on what is called a "subreddit," an interest community on which people communicate with one another.

Specifically, it was on the subreddit "The_Donald" where the self-described "online mob of rabid self-organized supporters" became a genuine countercultural force. On a daily—no, hourly—basis, they gleefully subverted the cultural institutions the left holds dear. When, for instance, WikiLeaks dumped the John Podesta emails late in the campaign, the redditors scrambled through them like rats at the city dump looking for a choice morsel or two. If it took one rat a thousand hours to find everything worth finding, it would take a thousand rats just one hour. In today's media, time is everything.

Among other self-descriptions, the redditors call themselves "weaponized autists" and "centipedes." The social media geek who came up with the phrase "weaponized autism" meant no offense to the autistic. If anything, he was celebrating the hidden virtue of having a singular focus in a world of distractions.

One of the most accomplished autists, Charles Johnson of GotNews, admits to being "neuroatypical," which is somewhere on the autism spectrum.[1] Another borderline case was my mentor, Andrew Breitbart. He would tell me the internet "cured" his ADD because it put his wandering mind to good use navigating tabs and Twitter text boxes. His shortcoming was now a virtue.

The idea of the "centipede" suggests a hundred individual agents working together as one, feeding off each other, boosting each other's spirits, occasionally correcting the redditor who takes a wrong turn. At their best, redditors can outperform any newsroom in America. They pore obsessively over publicly available data and connect dots. The internet, of course, makes all this possible. The fact that virtually every other newsroom is looking in another direction or not looking at all makes their job that much more satisfying.

In the lead-up to the launch of our "Rigging" series, we came up with the idea of teasing the release on Reddit's "Ask Me Anything" (AMA) forum. Redditors describe this no-man's-land as a place "where the mundane becomes fascinating and the outrageous suddenly seems normal."[2] I think of the place as a hive for angry, motivated bees, all hot to pollinate. With less than a month to go before the election, the hive was buzzing. The Twitter ban on my account had stirred them up. The redditors, in fact, were instrumental in getting Twitter to undo the ban.

These were my cyber-Contras ready to subvert the collectivist establishment wherever they could find an opening. I needed to live up to their expectations. I announced we were planning on doing an AMA on Friday evening. Typically, people do not do AMAs unless, as one sage told me, "they have something to say." What I was promising was huge, and I could not afford to disappoint. If I did disappoint, the redditors would never let me forget it.

I wrote that our videos directly involved Hillary. I was referring here to Creamer's admission that Hillary was the one who insisted on putting "ducks on the ground." I wrote, "I know people want me to clarify that the footage directly involves HRC. Again, the answer is yes. And it's more than that. We've exposed the whole network. The dirty tricks, how they commit the voter fraud, illegal coordination— is delegated from the top down. And we have all that on tape. And we're releasing different tapes every day." If Hillary was not pulling the strings herself, it was people very close to her.

The redditors' appetite could not be satisfied so quickly, especially after the teases they had seen in the weeks prior. On September 28, for instance, I put in a plug for the power of visuals: "Congressional hearings, IG investigations and other Govt spectacles are a waste of time. Catching the bastards on tape is all that matters!" Their hopes raised, they wanted action. One user wrote, "This is the only important question. If it's not directly involving Hillary (i.e., her own words) then it's literally nothing."[3]

Another followed in the same spirit, "Look, 'this guy from Hillary's camp is doing corrupt things' trash won't stick. Stop hyping this trash up, it won't even dent Hillary's campaign. If it's not Hillary's own words, it's not shit."[4]

I knew we had the goods. It may not have been exactly what the redditors wanted, but I was confident that they would not be disappointed. Days earlier, October 10, right before we dropped the New York elections commissioner video, I tweeted, "Our first tape drops tomorrow."[5]

"Don't fuck with me James, better be good," Cybork91 snapped.[6]

I responded, "This week we drop smaller bombs across the country. Next week we drop atomic bombs."[7] The plan was to lower expectations on the current releases and build anticipation for the next one. This was happening under the very noses of a major media that scarcely knew the subreddit thread "The_Donald" existed, but our people were paying attention.

Many redditors despaired nonetheless. Melissa Gott from North Carolina tweeted back that in Hillary Clinton's case, "even a video or paper trail does not matter."[8] I reassured her that in a country as free as ours, however unlevel the playing field, the game was far from over. In a rare direct reply I wrote, "Wrong. We have tape of them demeaning and disparaging black people in the worst ways. That will matter. Coming in October."[9]

The tweet went viral. Twelve hundred retweets at the time was a near record for me. After the first two "Rigging" videos were released, however, I came to expect that many retweets every five minutes. In retrospect, I should have been more precise. I did not mean to imply that Hillary had been caught disparaging black people. That honor went to a major Democratic donor at an event for US Senate candidate Deborah Ross in North Carolina. In a conversation about Ben Carson with one of our undercover journalists, the donor said, "You know the issue of the Holocaust? Do you know the SonderKommandos? Jewish guards who, in effect, helped murder Jews in the camps so they could live a little longer? So blacks who are helping the other side are seriously fucked in the head."[10] The donor pointed to his head to get the message across.

Ben Carson, of course, was the pediatric neurosurgeon who ran for president as a Republican and is, as of this writing, secretary of housing and urban development. The donor in question, Benjamin Barber, was no ordinary yahoo. He was a Harvard grad and political theorist, best known for his 1995 bestseller *Jihad vs. McWorld*. True to form, he had a glass of chardonnay in his hand when he slandered Carson and the million-plus African Americans who voted for Donald Trump.

Even without Hillary Clinton, the footage was powerful. At Veritas we use a "content spectrum"—the weaker the target, the more powerful the content has to be. This was a relatively weak target, but the content was insanely powerful. If a Republican had said what Barber did, it would have been a career ender.

In that we had not yet released the *Sonderkommando* video, the redditors were free to imagine what was on it. Quickly, it became the "Hillary N-word" tape on Reddit, Free Republic, TigerDroppings. com, Twitter, and 4chan. There is a deep hunger for content that runs contrary to mainstream media narratives. Even the *notion* that such content existed created a news buzz in the pro-Trump counterculture.

The *New York Times*'s Thomas Friedman likes to describe the internet as an "open sewer of untreated, unfiltered information."[11] His take on the internet was pretty much the norm in America's newsrooms, especially after the election. What these critics fail to understand, however, is that the interactive forums on the right almost inevitably self-correct. "O'Keefe said he has a clip of someone in the Clinton campaign disparaging black voters that's what he said. He never said Hillary, never said nigger."[12] Yes, thank you! In any event, I did not want to let these guys down for the Ask Me Anything forum. After the release of the "Rigging" videos, I was confident they would not let me down, and I was right.

To begin, I held up a whiteboard with the time of day and my picture to verify that I was, in fact, James O'Keefe. User PrinceCamelton quickly confirmed, "This is verified to be James O'Keefe." We logged in and wrote a headline, "TONIGHT: James O'Keefe, award winning journalist and writer, will be joining us for AMA at 7:30 PM EDT!!"[13]

At 7:30 p.m., I promptly logged in, first to thank the redditors for spreading the word about my Twitter situation. The pressure they helped bring ended my lockout after twelve hours. From the very beginning of this AMA, I felt at home with this community. The "weaponized autists" greeted me with a steady stream of strong, encouraging messages. I had been knocking around the internet in a major way these last seven years, but I had never before seen a right-of-center community show a will and energy comparable to that of the political left. Some sample greetings:

"Doing God's work good sir. We are going to win . . . *The whole world is against us.*"

"THIS IS INFORMATION WARFARE!"

"Based Acorn destroyer!!! Dude, just drop all of them. Let us autists take care of the rest."

"WERE BREAKING THE CONDITIONING."[14]

What the redditors called "conditioning" others might call the "Overton Window," the range of facts and policies that are viewed as politically acceptable to discuss. We were breaking that window indeed. The_Donald redditors were a force to be reckoned with, and whether Trump won or lost, the redditors in many ways had already won. Despite the pounding propaganda from the major media and the peer pressure from their fellow millennials, they found their way through the haze and formed a community of like-minded souls. Together, they had the power to accomplish incredible things.

During the week of October 17, 2016, they did just that. The technique they employ is often called "crowdsourcing," that is, encouraging a bunch of unrelated people to solve a problem. On the day we dropped the first "Rigging" video, the redditors crowdsourced the heck out of it. They developed news stories, added to existing stories, and verified each other's posts.

Take the case, for instance, of Zulema Rodriguez, a seemingly minor figure in our "Rigging the Election" video released on October 17. On one occasion, as I've mentioned, we captured her saying, "So [Aaron Black] and I did the Chicago Trump event where we shut down like all the, yeah. . . ." On another occasion Rodriguez says, "We also did the Arizona one where we shut the highway down."[15]

When we put this video together, we did not know for sure whether Rodriguez had done as she claimed or was simply boasting about doing it. Our redditor friends decided to answer this question for us. No sooner did we post the first video than the leads came pouring in. The first really good one came from user NotWTFAdvisor. He found news footage of Rodriguez apparently faking an illness during the Arizona highway protest on March 19. In the video you can clearly see guys from the local fire department putting her on a stretcher and taking her away in an ambulance. You can also see her car being towed off the highway.

"Let's find the public records," NotWTFAdvisor encouraged his colleagues, and they responded.[16]

Trumpfan75 went into Zulema's Facebook page and found a photo posted that same day. He compared the jewelry. "It's definitely her, folks!" he said. User Rex-Super-Universum found proof she was actually called Zulema Rodriguez and worked with the Center for Community Change, "the site in charge of writing the Trump Duck article." Rex was referring to an article in the *Huffington Post* that featured a photo of a duck and gave the photo credit to "Zulema Rodriguez."[17]

WeTheMediaNow identified Zulema's California license plate. It was a rental car. He called the towing company but hit a wall trying to trace the rental back to the Clinton campaign. That information could not be released. FrootAVator found earlier video footage of Rodriguez sitting in her car pretending to be blocked. "I'll move my car . . . if you move [arrest] them!" she told the police as though she were not part of the "them."[18]

The redditors kept digging. They learned that Rodriguez collaborated with "Trump Ducks" in Miami, that she was reimbursed for $1,108.97 by MoveOn.org on May 24, that she was given an airline ticket worth $830.95 by Stand Up for Ohio PAC on May 19, that she was paid $17,500 by that same PAC on June 10, a PAC that received $63,750 from MoveOn.org in June.[19]

Another redditor, 2moreEyez, plowed into the WikiLeaks documents and found an email from Democracy Partners honcho Robert Creamer to DNC communications director Luis Miranda reminding him of a "Trump Rapid Response/Bracketing Call—Today-Tues-May17–1PM Eastern."[20] This was two days before the Arizona protest. 2moreEyez reminded his colleagues that in part one of "Rigging the Election" at 10:59–11:04 Rodriguez says, "I just had a call with the campaign and the DNC. Every day at one o'clock."[21] She was not just bragging. She knew whereof she spoke.

"Dang, our people are like Colombo," said DescendingLion. "Jesus you guys are amazing researchers," added Deplorabetty. "I think the FBI is obsolete at this point," said Americascicero. "Crowdsourced investigation is getting scary good."[22]

The major media underestimate the ability of social media users to correct bad information from their own side. In the Rodriguez case, for instance, one redditor thought he spotted her at the Chicago Trump protest. NotWTFAdvisor corrected him. "False alarm," he said. "This is someone else—check the teeth."[23] The teeth! If the right side of the internet has profited more from this phenomenon than the left, it is for the simple reason that folks on the right have no more than one news-room doing the work for them.

Meanwhile HaroldStassenGhost came up with another WikiLeaks confirmation. This was a May 10 email from Eric Walker to Miranda regarding "action in front of RNC on Thursday morning for Trump/ Ryan meeting." He had "discussed with Creamer et al. today" and was sharing their plans. These included a demonstration, "a sepa-rate action in front of the NRSC," and the distribution of signs to the rent-a-mob, his favorite being, "Donald Trump: Dangerous, Divisive, Disgraceful."[24]

Then came the bombshell. PepeTheRacistFrog—his name an ironic taunt aimed at the thought police—found proof that the Hillary Clinton campaign had Rodriguez on the payroll. This was huge! He posted the relevant spreadsheet from the Federal Election Commis-sion website and said, "Going rate for a rioter: $1,610.24 and a free phone. To the top!"[25]

"The date she was paid & had a phone was 2/29. 11 days later Trump's rally was cancelled in Chicago," added a fellow redditor. "She clearly admitted she was part of the trump rally violence / shutdown in Chicago. Hillary directly paid her on 2/29, to protest & cause a dis-turbance on 3/11. Pedes, get this to the top. Weaponized autism at its finest. LOCK HER UP!"[26]

The Rodriguez angle alone should have made for a major news story. Here was a woman provably on the Hillary Clinton campaign payroll caught on camera helping stage a highway shutdown and then later caught bragging about it. Tucker Carlson's *Daily Caller* was one of the very few publications to run with it. The article was headlined, "Activist Who Took Credit for Violent Chicago Protests Was on Hil-lary's Payroll."[27] Said user Colorado-living to Pepe, "They copied your work almost verbatim and took credit for it. At least it's out there."[28]

On October 18, WaterBuffalo—where do they come up with these names?—posted the White House visitor log. We had seen this and talked about it, but as one redditor observed, "People need to SEE it too. They need the visual confirmation, the illustration of how this extends all the way to the top." Another chimed in, "The first entry on the whitehouse list just posted shows Cramer [*sic*] going to see POTUS at the Residence. Tell me that's a low-level anybody. (It's not.)" He definitely was not. Said ImWithHEarse, "I'm loving this. Presidential campaign turns into community hacktivism turns into getting regular folks into becoming lethal computer forensicators."[29]

I was loving this too. My staff and I were checking these updates in real time. They were not just advancing our story. They were keeping us entertained and reminding us we represented one very creative community of forensicators and hacktivists. These were the nameless, faceless counterrevolutionaries who were helping Project Veritas crack the dam and flood the countryside with real information. Genuinely moved, I sent out as many tweets as I could. As expected, the traffic on every tweet was two or three times what it had been just days prior. More than once, I found myself posting, "Look what the good people at @reddit just found!" And I meant every word of it. "Credit 1, Sean Hannity. Credit 2, Subreddit, The_Donald."[30]

Going Viral in Vegas

About 6:00 a.m. on Wednesday, October 19, I was riding in an Uber on the way to Newark Airport when I heard New York radio host Frank Morano talking about our videos. In the last few days we had received scores of requests for me to speak on the air, and it pained me to turn so many down. These stations were hungry for content. Wanting to oblige, I texted Frank and—bingo—I was on the air. The Uber driver turned the radio off and listened in. He had heard stranger things I am sure.

I was hoping to sleep on the flight to Vegas. I had very little of it in the previous few days, but I was still too wired. CNN anchor Erin Burnett was sitting behind me. I did not speak to her, but I did speak to the Norwegian reporter sitting next to me. He knew who I was and asked if he could interview me. Later he emailed me, "Hi James, good meeting you on the plane today. The story is being read very well on our website now—thanks for the interview!"

While I was winging westward, the *New York Times* published an article on our efforts. They even took a screengrab of the YouTube video during the moment Scott Foval said, "If you're there and you're protesting and you do these actions, you will be attacked at Trump rallies. That's what we want." This was certainly a success, getting covered by the *New York Times* in a relatively fair article. That said, the headline—"Right-Wing Video Suggests D.N.C. Contractors Schemed to Incite Chaos at Donald Trump Rallies"[1]—was more of the pigeonholing we had gotten used to. They could call us "right wing" if they liked, but unless exposing political corruption was now a "right-wing" phenomenon, there was nothing ideological about the video in question. The *Times* used that descriptive to alert its readers not to take us seriously. The article was laced with qualifiers. Our videos were "creatively edited." They only "appeared to show" Creamer and Foval plotting violence. O'Keefe "considers" his investigators "to be journalists" and, the sine qua non, "He has also had legal problems of his own."

Most of the article was dedicated to denials of wrongdoing. DNC chairwoman Donna Brazile described Scott Foval as a "temporary regional subcontractor," one who does not "represent the values that the committee holds dear." What is more, she added, "We do not believe, or have any evidence to suggest, that the activities articulated in the video actually occurred." Creamer agreed. He assured *Times* readers that "none of the schemes described in the conversations ever took place" and dismissed Foval's comments as "unprofessional and careless hypothetical conversations." Never took place? Trump had to cancel the Chicago rally, Zulema and pals tied up the Arizona highways for miles, and Shirley Teter made headlines for appearing to get punched out by a Trump supporter in North Carolina. As for himself, Creamer "was stepping away from the campaign to avoid being a distraction."

Following the denials, the *Times* turned back to me, reminding its readers that I pleaded guilty to misdemeanor charges in New Orleans six years earlier and had paid $100,000 to settle an ACORN lawsuit in California. What the *Times* did not do is what the redditors did—see if the actions boasted about actually occurred. Forced to cover the story by the termination of Foval and Creamer, the *Times* used the occasion to discredit Project Veritas and our efforts. Nevertheless, half a page in the *New York Times* wasn't bad.

That same morning, October 19, Anderson Cooper was in Las Vegas, leading a panel discussion on the videos.[2] Cooper led off by reminding the audience of my "less than stellar reputation for accuracy." He did not provide examples. He then introduced CNN reporter Drew Griffin, the same guy who grudgingly called me in my office the day before. Griffin referred to me as a "discredited conservative activist" so casually you'd think it was my job title.

After claiming I had "zero credibility," CNN political contributor Maria Cardona showed her own credibility to be less than zero. "He is the one who did the doctored videos of Planned Parenthood, which were completely false. He is a criminal, right?" No, Maria, not exactly. Although I had done a Planned Parenthood video years earlier, she was referring to a recent series done by activist David Daleiden. The videos were not "doctored," and if they were "completely false," how do you explain that tray of baby parts the Planned Parenthood clinician sorts through so casually in video five?[3] Cardona had no need to explain. Nor did Griffin or Cooper. CNN had never showed the videos.

On that same October 19, Adam Raymond of *New York* magazine wrote an article headlined, "James O'Keefe's Latest Videos Cost Two Dem Operatives Their Jobs." Again, these two high-level players were not forced out because of our selective editing. They were forced out because of what they had said and done. Raymond must have known this. The headline indicates the same.

In virtually every sting we have done, of course, the culpable party claims that what he said was taken out of context or somehow distorted. Cesar Vargas, one of the stars of our "Rigging" series, did just that. "Given O'Keefe's history of selective editing," wrote Raymond uncritically, "Vargas's claim should probably be taken seriously."[4] No matter how many heads roll because of our journalism, no matter how many funding sources dry up, no matter how many laws are changed, no matter how many arrests are made, the media never weary of this accusation.

Meanwhile, back at the White House, a Fox reporter asked Obama spokesman Josh Earnest a useful question. He wanted to know how it was that a convicted felon who had just been sacked by the DNC for campaign mischief had managed to visit Obama's White House 340 times, 45 of which were with Obama himself.

Earnest knew these were legitimate numbers. They had come from the White House logs. Rather than answer the question, Earnest chose the well-trodden media path of attacking Project Veritas. "I've been asked about the videos that have come from this outlet in the past," Earnest snickered, "and each time I've tried to urge people to take those reports not at face value and not just with a grain of salt, but with a whole package of salt."[5] As was normative during the Obama years, no other reporter followed up on a tough question from Fox.

After arriving in Vegas, I tried to sleep at the hotel but could not manage it there either. By the time we arrived at the University of Nevada at Las Vegas campus for the third and final presidential debate, I felt as if I were spacing out. Sitting there before the debate started and looking around at the various anchors in the booths above us, I had this weird sensation that they were talking about Project Veritas. I thought maybe it was just sleep deprivation, but the closer I looked, the clearer it became that they actually were talking about us. I could see the "Rigging" videos playing on their monitors. I decided to scan the shows on my iPhone.

I was able to pick up the conversation between Clinton campaign manager Robby Mook and CNN's Jake Tapper. To his credit, Tapper was asking some tough questions. To his discredit, Mook was giving nonsense answers. Yes, of course, Mook told Tapper, the actions described in the video were "unacceptable," and he was prepared to speak out against them. What he also wanted to speak out against was my implication "that people's votes won't really be counted and that the system is fraudulent." Where did Mook get that? On our videos, the only ones who implied the system was fraudulent were Scott Foval and his pals.

Mook concluded, "Republican secretaries of state are the ones coming out condemning the things Donald Trump and James O'Keefe are saying." I tweeted from my seat, "#RobbyMook excuses #VoterFraud & attacks me. He's literally a professional excuse maker." I added, "You're witnessing history in the making. The power of citizen journalism and social media is greater than the firewalls at the MSM #debate."[6]

While I waited for the debate to begin, I read an article by Dave Weigel that had just gone up on the *Washington Post* website. Weigel did little more in the article than parse, Bill Clinton–style, Scott Foval's use of the word "it." Weigel conceded that Foval did seem "to be mentioning the idea of fraudulent voters,"[7] but since some of the edited clips were not "100 percent clear" on what "it" meant, the videos could be safely ignored. In a subsequent tweet about "the B.S. Project Veritas video," he made his contempt clear.

"Did the higher ups at @washingtonpost tell you to bury/spin this, @daveweigel?"[8] I tweeted back.

"Now, if you end up proving that Obama had dozens of meetings on how to steal elections, I will shine your Pulitzer,"[9] Weigel replied.

If any single quote summed up the state of the current media, that was it. The *Washington Post* has a $500 million annual budget.[10] That is at least one hundred times greater than ours. In his article, Weigel claimed that "years of investigations" have shown in-person voter fraud to be insignificant, but I am hard pressed to recall a single serious investigation by the *Post* or any major media outlet. Back in the day, *Chicago Tribune* reporters had no trouble finding tons of it. The fraudsters were still at it. The journalists weren't.

"Shouldn't this be YOUR job at the @washingtonpost to expose?" I responded. "I'd never accept a bs Pulitzer from such a corrupt media."[11] To make the job easier for Weigel, we posted the log of Foval's White House visits. I did not expect him to follow up. Voter fraud is not a story Weigel and his fellow travelers want to explore.

I'll admit it. I watched the debate itself with a different expectation than the rest of the audience. They cared about how their candidate would perform. I cared about whether Donald Trump would mention our videos. He did not disappoint. After a few false starts, Trump seized an unlikely question about his sexual behavior to weigh in on dirty Clinton campaign tricks in general.

"I believe it was her campaign that [recruited his female accusers]," said Trump of Hillary, "just like if you look at what came out today on the clips where I was wondering what happened with my rally in Chicago and other rallies where we had such violence. She's the one and Obama that caused the violence. They hired people. They paid them $1,500, and they're on tape saying be violent, cause fights, do bad things."[12] Trump segued back to the female accusers and then returned to the "criminal act" captured in our videos. Said Trump, "They're telling people to go out and start fistfights and start violence—and I'll tell you what. In particular, in Chicago, people were hurt and people could have been killed in that riot. And that's now all on tape started by her."

I was sure that at that very moment the Project Veritas staff and all those who helped spread our message cheered loudly. "One small step for Veritas," I tweeted, "one giant leap for citizen journalism."[13]

When the debate was finished, Gentry Beach, the Trump staffer who invited me, escorted me to the red-carpet area where the media were gathered. This whole experience overwhelmed me. I felt sort of like *The Hunger Games'* Katniss Everdeen must have in her first visit to the crazed, decadent Capitol.

I saw Sean Hannity interviewing Donald Trump Jr. Hoping to get in the shot, I wandered back and forth, phone in hand as though I were on a call. I wasn't. When they began talking about the videos, I moseyed over to get in on the conversation, which I barely managed to do. If the shot looked half as awkward as it felt, it will probably make someone's blooper reel.

Then the *really* awkward part began. I and the others strolled around the red carpet taking questions from the literally hundreds of media gathered there. To be more specific, the others took questions. I just strolled around looking stupid. There were only a few of us, including the Trump family, walking on that red carpet. There were hundreds of flashing cameras and scores of reporters with their arms extended. This scene looked like something out of an old Hollywood movie like *King Kong*.

Laura, our social media specialist, was watching from afar. "Why aren't you talking to people?" she texted me. The real question, I asked, was why were they not talking to me? I suspect they were unwilling to give our cause any more airtime than they absolutely had to. From their perspective, no question they might ask would result in a politically useful answer, so better not to ask any questions at all.

Here I was with the hottest video in America, one that the president addressed during the debate, one that all the anchors talked about that evening, and the reporters treated me as though I had head lice. As I passed, some of them looked down, some looked away. Remember the friendly Norwegian guy who interviewed me on the plane and wrote a story about it? Even he acted as if he did not know me.

Although no one spoke to me, I noticed this one slight little guy checking me out. At first I thought he was some blogger. He looked young enough and nervous enough as he repeatedly zoomed in his camera on me. Then it dawned on me who he was: Bradley Beychok, president of Media Matters. Upon reflection, I suspect he was terrified of what he might have said on tape to "Charles Roth," our undercover rich guy who had recorded video of him in his office. Once Creamer learned he had been busted, he must have told Beychok. The last few days had to have been a nightmare for him as he waited for the videos to drop. Boss David Brock would not be happy. As squirrely as they are, I have a certain odd respect for Beychok and Brock. Unlike their media colleagues, they were at least open about their role as propagandists.

The award for best post-debate question went to Megyn Kelly, then still with Fox News. She was interviewing DNC head Donna Brazile.[14] For most of the ten minutes, Brazile ducked and dodged as best she could, but Kelly kept nailing her. The best exchange was this one:

BRAZILE

When you have a convicted criminal sneaking around your office . . .

KELLY

Are you referring to Bob Creamer, head of Democracy Partners?

Later in the interview, Brazile tried to claim the tapes were falsified. After all, she insisted, "Mr. O'Keefe enjoys falsifying records." She actually said that. If the tapes were fake, Kelly asked, why was it that the Democrats "fired" two staffers?

"Stepped aside," said Brazile. "Stepped aside." Brazile later admitted, in her book, *Hacks*, about the exchange: "I was not fast on my feet that day. I didn't have my usual wry smile and quick capacity to turn the subject around."

Days after the election, I ran into Brazile in the elevator of a Florida hotel. We gave each other that "Are you who I think you are?" look. She saw me reaching to turn on my iTalk recording device and said, "Before you reach for your recording device, let me just say that I am so pissed off with all that happened and especially Debbie Wasserman Schultz and all of it."

Wow! This opening gambit threw my game off altogether. Upon leaving the elevator, we talked. She asked if I was "filming" her, a reasonable question. I honestly told her I was not. She did not ask if I was recording her on audio. That I was. Brazile was surprisingly charming and pleasant in person compared to her media persona. This made me question the artifice that surrounds many of these personalities on television. For a moment, I almost let my guard down. It would not have mattered. I had nothing unethical to confess.

Brazile's interest in speaking to me was to find out whether we bugged the DNC offices. "That's illegal," I told her. I reassured her we never do anything illegal. I may have even convinced her. As to the fate of Foval and Creamer, she told me, "I did what I had to do."

"Which is firing?" I asked.

"Of course," she said. "I made sure that happened." So much for the "stepped aside" bit. The public side of these people can be so much different from their private side.

The circus left Las Vegas that Wednesday night, but not without a final walk on the high wire. At an impromptu press conference on Hillary's campaign plane before its departure, a female Fox News reporter sneaked in a question about the violence at Trump rallies. Hillary interrupted her in mid-question. "I know nothing about this. I can't deal with every one of [Trump's] conspiracy theories," she said dismissively, "but I hope you all have something to eat and something to drink on the way back to New York."[15] With that Hillary turned her back on the reporters and walked away. No one would ask her about the campaign violence again.

The following morning the *New York Times* had another story up. To be fair, the news-gatherers at the *Times* feel more responsibility to history than do those at CNN. *Times* men and women, after all, consider the *Times* to be the paper of record. On October 20, reporters Steve Eder and Jonathan Martin noted that 8 million people had already seen the two "Rigging" videos.[16] Although they did not say as much, the "paper of record" no longer had the option to slight a story millions had seen and Donald Trump had discussed before millions more.

After rehashing the various Democratic denials and disclaimers, the reporters conceded: "The videos were an embarrassment for Mrs. Clinton at a moment when she is trying to frame Mr. Trump's claims of a rigged election as nothing more than the fevered dreams of a conspiracy theorist." The DNC offered a new evasion, claiming it had contracted with Creamer only to provide "bracketing," the term of art for staging an alternative event to distract from the opposition's planned event. The reporters, however, weren't quite buying. "The tactics described went far beyond mere distraction," they acknowledged.

In the way of follow-up, the reporters contacted Shirley Teter, the sixty-nine-year-old woman tethered to an oxygen tank who was knocked down during a Trump rally. Foval claimed he trained her. Of course, Teter denied it. As mentioned earlier, this case was later thrown out of court. "The last thing in the world I want to see is Trump getting elected to be our president," she told the *Times*. "It is the first time in years that my heart actually ached, and I felt I had to do it." And that's how the article ended. Still, we had broken through, proving once again that even in the land of the blind, content is king.

In the major media bubble, none of this was significant enough to be held against Robert Creamer. Within a few months after the election, all was forgotten. Creamer was able to sit in the front row of President Obama's farewell speech without media comment. So he had to leave the campaign in disgrace. So he had already served a prison sentence for bank fraud. Creamer did his dirty work and kept his mouth shut. That was apparently enough for the media to forgive and mostly forget. They never questioned the propriety of his sitting there so prominently.

Operatives like Creamer are hard to shame, even harder to subdue. They always seem to reemerge in some new incarnation, if not unscathed, then close to it. Their resilience troubles the sane half of America. When I do speaking engagements, my audiences ask how to deal with a force that refuses to die or to stay dead. I respond by saying, "More of what we've already done."

Marcus Luttrell gets it. The *Lone Survivor* author understands what it takes. I had the good fortune of seeing Luttrell speak at the Republican National Convention in 2016. His voice shaking, Luttrell ignored the words on the teleprompter and said from his heart, "To the next generation, this is for you. Your war is here." He reaffirmed what I had been sensing around the country, "Your people are afraid."

Luttrell did not stop there. He delivered a powerful and moving call to action: "Who among you will love something more than you love yourself? Who among you will step up and take the fight to the enemy because it is here?"[17] When I tell you the enemy is on our own soil and not in a desert overseas, don't take my word; take the word of Navy Cross–decorated Marcus Luttrell.

Anticipating Hillary

Fearful as they are of lawsuits, media companies have even more reason to fear the federal government. Radio and TV stations all require government licenses to operate. The government must also approve all mergers and acquisitions. If anything, large and growing media corporations are more vulnerable to government harassment than small stable ones. This is the inverse of the way federal regulation usually works. Typically, the big guys can afford the cost of it, and the little guys suffer. But in the media world, the FCC more or less owns the airwaves. The more waves a company acquires, the more beholden it is to the owner.

Media executives expected Hillary Clinton to be elected president in 2016. Just about everyone did. Once sworn in, she would control the appointment to the Federal Communications Commission. A media executive did not have to be paranoid to believe that an extremely damaging story on Hillary would lead to the imposition of regulatory obstacles at the federal level. Sinclair had benefited from the FCC during the Bush and Obama years as the agency remained largely apolitical. Under a Hillary Clinton administration, Sinclair management did not expect to fare quite so well.

Sinclair was on an ambitious growth curve. In the fall of 2016, it is likely that management already had its eye on Tribune Media, for which it would make a $3.9 billion bid in May 2017.[1] The fact that some Republicans held prominent positions in Sinclair's hierarchy was trouble enough. Had Sinclair broken a story from Project Veritas, a group that most Democrats considered reckless and borderline criminal, company brass knew they could face reprisals.

Executives had to choose between running a story that required what Herman and Chomsky would describe as "careful checking and costly research," or spiking the story. The prudent decision was to put the bottom line first, avoid making enemies, and spike it. In retrospect, I am surprised we had come as close as we did to having it released.

Although American libel law favors the journalist, the judicial process favors those with the money to see the process through. In the 1990s, the process got more complicated as news agencies sacrificed their independence to merge with corporations larger than themselves.

The most celebrated of these internal conflicts unfolded in 1995. At the time, CBS's storied *60 Minutes* was prepared to air a candid interview with Jeffrey Wigand, a former vice president at Brown & Williamson Tobacco Corp.[2] Wigand was a reluctant witness. He had been prodded to come forward by veteran CBS producer Lowell Bergman. The story Wigand had to tell was explosive. He accused Brown & Williamson CEO Thomas E. Sandefur Jr. of lying to Congress when Sandefur claimed to have been unaware of nicotine's addictive power.

Before the Wigand interview could air, however, CBS "corporate" got to *60 Minutes* executive producer Don Hewitt. The lawyers warned him that Brown & Williamson could sue CBS for billions if *60 Minutes* followed through with the Wigand interview. CBS execs did not expect to lose the suit, but they were looking at a potential sale of the network to Westinghouse. They reportedly did not want to hang a billion-dollar albatross around their necks while the network was on the market.

Al Pacino played Bergman in the 1999 film *The Insider.* What follows is the section of dialogue in which Bergman comes to grips with the deep-sixing of his story.[3] Eric Kluster was the president of CBS News at the time. Laurence Tisch was the CEO of the CBS network. Mike Wallace, of course, was the legendary CBS newsman. If you get a chance, watch the movie. With few exceptions, visuals, even dramatizations, have more emotional power than the printed word.

BERGMAN

If Tisch can unload CBS for $81 a share to Westinghouse and
then is suddenly threatened with a multibillion-dollar lawsuit

from Brown & Williamson, that could screw up the sale, could it not?

KLUSTER

And what are you implying?

BERGMAN

I'm not implying. I'm quoting. More vested interests . . .

(reading from SEC filing)

"Persons Who Will Profit From This Merger . . . Ms. Helen Caperelli, General Counsel of CBS News, 3.9 million. Mr. Eric Kluster, President of CBS News, 1.4 million . . ."

HEWITT

Are you suggesting that she and Eric are influenced by money?

BERGMAN

Oh, no, of course they're not influenced by money. They work for free. And you are a Volunteer Executive Producer.

HEWITT

CBS does not do that. And, you're questioning our journalistic integrity?!

BERGMAN

No, I'm questioning your hearing! You hear "reasonable" and "tortious interference." I hear, "potential Brown & Williamson lawsuit jeopardizing the sale of CBS to Westinghouse." I hear, "Shut the segment down. Cut Wigand loose. Obey orders. And fuck off!" That's what I hear.

HEWITT

You're exaggerating!

BERGMAN

I am? You pay me to go get guys like Wigand, to draw him out. To get him to trust us, to get him to go on television. I do. I deliver him. He sits. He talks. He violates his own fucking confidentiality agreement. And he's only the key witness in the

> biggest public health reform issue, maybe the biggest, most-
> expensive corporate-malfeasance case in U.S. history. And
> Jeffrey Wigand, who's out on a limb, does he go on television
> and tell the truth? Yes. Is it newsworthy? Yes. Are we gonna air
> it? Of course not. Why? Because he's not telling the truth? No.
> Because he is telling the truth. That's why we're not going to air
> it. And the more truth he tells, the worse it gets!

I cannot tell you how many times I have watched that scene. For me, it speaks like no other to the paralyzing force of corporate media inertia. That is the reality that Bergman faced in 1995 the year he coaxed Wigand forward. There were only 16 million internet users worldwide, less than half of 1 percent of the world's population. If CBS did not air Wigand's interview, no one would. The government did not need to control America's corporations. Those corporations more or less controlled each other.

The problem Bergman faced many others had faced before him. In his 2012 memoir *They're Going to Murder You: My Life at the News Front*, legendary local reporter Clarence Jones described his attempt to report the truth about railroad influence in Jacksonville, Florida. The problem was that both the local newspapers, the *Times-Union* and the *Journal*, were lobbying tools for the railroads. So tight was the railroads' control of the media that the running joke was, "In North Florida, trains don't hit cars. Cars hit trains."

As a twenty-five-year-old reporter, Jones got it into his head that if he put together an air-tight exposé of a government official, his paper, the *Journal*, would be forced to run it. So he and a friendly editor set up a dummy corporation. Soliciting bids through the corporation, they learned what a certain microfilming process cost. It was one-fourth what a former city commissioner was charging Jacksonville. They submitted the story about the commissioner's scam to the executive editor who sat on it for weeks. Finally, he called Jones and his partner in. The newspaper's politically wired attorney had convinced the executive editor to spike the story.[4]

"Those who make the final money decision in media conglomerates have no grasp of journalistic ethics or the original concepts that gave the press Constitutional protection," wrote Clarence Jones. "They have abandoned the old persistent, righteous indignation that throws bad guys and business moguls out of office and into jail."[5]

That opinion seems widespread in the industry. "They only give a shit about their bottom line," one of the top journalists at Fox News told me. "These higher-ups, well, I don't know what the fuck they are. I don't know what the fuck they want."[6]

This is the reality that journalists face. As the major media corporations consolidate, those who work within those companies, even the best of them like Sinclair and Fox, can expect to see their toughest stories spiked, not because they lack truth but because they have too much of it. Those of us who work outside the major media must stay vigilant lest we become the very people we warn our staffs about, the inverse of what Clarence Jones called "bosses with balls."

Fleeing Philly

o! Go! Go!" I told Gio, my "transporter," as I hustled into our Chevy rental. "The lady's coming after us." A veteran street racer, Gio did not need much prompting. He gunned the engine and roared down the street, treating stop signs like yield signs and red lights like yellows.

The lady in question was a formidable and very angry election worker named Sarah. As far as I could tell, she ran the show at the polling station from which we were speeding away. Minutes earlier, armed with a button camera and dressed as a bum, I had wandered into her station and asked for help in deciding on a candidate. She readily obliged.

"Can I get this man some literature so he knows who he's voting for?" she asked her colleagues. Not waiting around for an answer, Sarah headed outside and got me some "literature." I looked at it and smiled. It read "Official Democratic Ballot." Looking for voter fraud in North Philadelphia was like shooting fish in a barrel—no, not fish, dolphins. Only problem was, in Philly, you never knew when the dolphins were going to shoot back.

I went back outside and recorded what journalists call a "stand-up." Speaking into a mike, I showed the "ballot" and explained to the camera why the transaction I had just recorded was illegal. The law is clear: no election officer, when giving instructions, should "seek to persuade any such voter to vote any particular ticket or any particular candidate." Sarah had boldly ignored the law. Matt, one of our undercover journalists, had gone in with me and gotten even more explicit instructions from another poll worker. "Yeah, yeah, vote for Hillary," she told Matt. "Vote for Hillary?" Matt asked. "We're not supposed to tell you who to vote for," she said with a wink. "Vote for Hillary?" Matt asked again. "Yes," she affirmed.[1]

To get more footage I went back inside and there ran into an enraged Sarah. She sensed she had been stung and was coming after me. This was not a place I wanted to hang around. North Philly has a history. On Election Day 2008, two members of the New Black Panther Party stood guard outside a polling station and threatened voters. One of the two men carried a nightstick. Both wore paramilitary gear and shouted racial slurs. "You are about to be ruled by the black man, cracker!" one of them yelled at a would-be white voter.[2] There was nothing subtle about this. The bullying was captured on video and witnessed by veteran civil rights workers. They had never seen intimidation quite so flagrant.

This was serious business. The Justice Department had more than enough evidence to file a lawsuit. Just weeks before Barack Obama was to be inaugurated as president, its attorneys charged the New Black Panther Party and three of its members with violating the 1965 Voting Rights Act. When the accused failed to respond, the DOJ fully expected to win the suit by default and mete out punishment accordingly. That did not happen. In May 2009, the newly appointed brass in the Department of Justice overruled the six career attorneys who managed the investigation and let the suit drop. The New Black Panthers walked away unpunished, and the media chose not to ask Obama why.

Emboldened by the media silence, Obama took to questioning the very existence of voter fraud. At a White House press conference three weeks before the 2016 election, he insisted that "instances of significant voter fraud are not to be found."[3] Significant? Sounds like something of a hedge, no? Days later at a Miami rally for Hillary Clinton, he upped the absurdity level. "You are much likelier to be struck by lightning," he told a cheering crowd, "than have somebody next to you commit voter fraud."[4] The media happily joined in the mockery.

From our experience on the ground, we at Project Veritas knew better. In many localities we had been finding fraud—or the possibility of it—everywhere we looked, and no city offered a more target-rich environment than Philadelphia. The 2012 election offered ample evidence to anyone who cared to know. According to the *Philadelphia Inquirer*, not exactly an alt-right publication, fifty-nine voting divisions failed to register a single vote for Republican presidential candidate Mitt Romney, not one. The total count from these divisions was an astonishing 19,605 votes for Obama to 0 for Romney.[5]

Think about this for a second. By best estimates, Romney received 6 percent of the black vote nationwide. For argument's sake, let's assume he got only half that number in Philadelphia. Even with that handicap, if only twenty-three people had voted in those divisions, the odds would have favored Romney getting at least one vote. With nearly twenty thousand people going to the polls, Romney would have had a better chance of getting struck by lightning while being eaten by a shark than striking out with every single voter.

Having teased with the numbers, the *Inquirer* skipped the probability theories and moved directly into the defensive crouch that had become reflexive during the Obama years. "These are the kind of numbers that send Republicans into paroxysms of voter-fraud angst," jibed the trio of *Inquirer* reporters who covered the story. Assuring the reader that there was "little hard evidence" of fraud, they implied that the real problem was Republican paranoia.

By 2016, the major media and their well-funded allies in the blogosphere had gone all in for Hillary Clinton. They weren't even faking objectivity anymore. Although they professed confidence in the outcome of the election, I sensed a desperate edge to their reporting and a crude sharpness to their attacks, and all of this was coming to a head on Election Day.

The evening before the election, I was talking with Stephen Gordon, Laura Loomer, and some people close to Veritas we had flown in from around the country to help with media. When going out to cover the potential for voter fraud, it's a safe bet to know you will come back with video content, but it is very difficult to predict exactly what you will get. They wanted a theme for the next day that would stick no matter what our journalists came back with.

We toyed with a couple of ideas and then went back to one we started during the primaries: #VeritasIsEverywhere. Around 6:30 p.m.

I tweeted: "WARNING: If you don't want to become a viral YouTube sensation tomorrow, don't commit any #VoterFraud!!! VeritasIsEverywhere."[6] A supporter tweeted back, "Everyone has cell phones with cameras. #VeritasIsEverywhere should be a movement! You see something, report it."[7] While the hashtag had been used sparingly before, a new minor movement was born then and there.

Gio slowed down after putting a few blocks between us and the polling station. Ahead of us we chanced upon an old van whose back window was marked with the kind of crude, paste-on letters you might buy at your local Dollar General. The words were in Spanish. Happily, Gio was fluent. Although born in the United States, he spent a good part of his childhood in Guatemala. I had hired him during the summer to help me paint my sailboat. Just eighteen at the time, he proved to be such a good worker I asked him to join us at Project Veritas. With his studded earring and wiry good looks—in the movie version, a young James Franco—Gio fit no one's stereotype of a right-wing activist. In fact, almost no one at Project Veritas fits that stereotype. Our median age is about twenty-five, and our politics are all over the place.

The key word on the van in front of us was "Iglesia," meaning "church." I could have probably figured that out, but it was good to have verification. What struck Gio as odd was that there was no designation of which church. It was simply "Iglesia." Suspicious, we followed the van for a while and discovered that the driver was taking people to the polls. It looked like a classic knock-and-drag.

I shot a video of the van and posted the footage along with my commentary on Twitter. "So we're behind this bus, which is like a pastor bus busing people around to polls in Philadelphia, and we're going to be releasing video today showing some people doing some improper things—busing people around, maybe they shouldn't be doing it? Stay tuned . . . [We're] all over the country undercover on Election Day, and we're going to be busting the whole thing open."[8]

From past research we knew, too, that these vans did not always stop at one polling place. In one of the more notorious recent incidents, a New York State grand jury uncovered a voting conspiracy in Brooklyn that had persisted for at least fourteen years. One witness told the grand jury how he bused a crew of eight people from one polling station to another, each member of the crew voting at least twenty times in a given day. On the Election Day in question, this was one of twenty such crews in Brooklyn alone.[9]

No sooner had I posted my tweet about the pastor bus than the attack dogs in the alternative progressive media came back snarling. What follows are some sample headlines:

Slate: "James O'Keefe Stalks Van of Voters, Alleges Fraud, Is Himself Possibly Breaking Law."[10]

Salon: "James O'Keefe is spending Election Day following vans around Philadelphia. Not a single 'pastor bus' in the city of Philadelphia is safe from the snoops over at Project Veritas."[11]

TPM: "James O'Keefe Spends Election Day Stalking Vans of Voters around Philly."[12]

RawStory: "James O'Keefe Films Himself Committing Voter Intimidation by Stalking a Church Van Bringing People to Polls."[13]

Protected by a major media that nurtures them, these left-leaning outlets do not get half the critical attention of their less privileged right-leaning equivalents. That said, they have resources and connections I can only envy. For instance, Microsoft helped launch *Slate* twenty years ago, and eight years later the Washington Post Company bought *Slate* and remains involved to this day.

According to Jeremy Stahl, who posted his *Slate* article at 1:28 p.m. on election day—two hours after my tweet—I had a lengthy history of unfounded voter fraud accusations, a history I took to a "creepier level, stalking potential voters and bragging about it." In this brief time window, Stahl had tracked down a law professor from California who assured *Slate*'s readers that the "shady James O'Keefe" was the real problem. "It is legal to give people free transportation to vote," said the professor. "It is illegal to hassle people for voting. Once again, O'Keefe's efforts to find election crimes may be creating them." Stahl concluded his piece with a patronizing touch of millennial snark, "Nice work, James."[14]

None of these publications asked the most basic of questions: although it is obviously legal to give free transportation to would-be voters, is it legal for a pastor to give free transportation? According to the IRS code then in play, 501(c)3 organizations—and that includes churches—cannot "participate in, or intervene in, any political campaign on behalf of/in opposition to any candidate for public office." In short, pastors and church staff should not be using church resources to engage in political campaigns.

The dominant media profess to believe this. Consider this unremarkable opening sentence from an approving 2012 CNN article: "Americans United for the Separation of Church and State has sent a letter to the Internal Revenue Service accusing Pastor Robert Jeffress of violating the law when he posted his endorsement of presidential hopeful Rick Perry on the First Baptist Church of Dallas website."[15] A 2014 *Washington Post* article carried this alarming headline, again about conservative preachers, "Political Pastors Openly Defying IRS Rules on Candidate Endorsements."[16] More recently, the Americans United for Separation of Church and State urged its friends in Washington, "As 2016 Presidential Campaign Gets Under Way, IRS Should Act to Enforce Non-Profit 'No-Politicking' Rule."[17]

It is not at all unfair to say that the thrust to separate church and state has come almost exclusively from the left. Lyndon Johnson was responsible for the IRS provision in question. Donald Trump has since annulled it. Given this fact, one would think progressive politicos and their media allies would appreciate our efforts to warn America about potential violations of the IRS codes by the Iglesia van. They apparently did not.

As we knew and the media should have, there is nothing nonpartisan about these pastor buses. On that same day, November 8, we posted a video assembled from undercover footage that Project Veritas journalists had recorded in Gary, Indiana. Posing as political consultants, they met with a Reverend Marlon Mack, pastor of Gary's nicely named Sweet Home Baptist Church. Mack proved forthcoming and more than a little boastful. That first meeting led to a second meeting with the Reverend Mack and a crony, the Reverend Marion Johnson, to discuss plans for Election Day. It took very little prompting to get them to open up.

"The thing is," bragged Johnson, "if we get our people to the polls, they know who to vote for. It's not going to be, 'Oh who do I vote for?' Because we're going to tell them who to vote for."[18]

"I say I'm voting for Hillary Clinton. And that's automatically telling our congregation to vote for Hillary Clinton," Johnson continued. "And you see all these vans rolling to the polls with the name of the church and the pastor's name on the side. And they know that the pastor's providing that. They know who they're voting for." Added Mack, "I mean literally, we can have twenty vans roll up." There was no nuance to their boasts. They said what they said, and after the video was posted, they did not try to deny it.

Inner-city pastors of all shades have been intimidating voters in Democratic-controlled cities for years. Personally, I had trouble with the IRS code that prevented church involvement in politics, but the left has supported that measure. At least they did in theory. In reality, the left-leaning media have chosen not to notice when pastors drive busloads of voters to the polls to elect Democrats. In reality, they openly embrace the wholesale vote harvesting, legal and otherwise, that undermines democracy in America's cities. In reality, they delight in smearing organizations like Project Veritas whose reporting protects the integrity of the electoral process.

People talk about an "echo chamber," but in the era of Obama, "power chamber" made more sense. Obama called voter fraud a myth and hinted that those who exposed it had racist motives. The major media amplified the message throughout the progressive imperium. Their colonial outposts in local and alternative media, here and abroad, sharpened the edge of the message and struck out at the opposition. Finally, the faceless minions in social media channeled the power of the White House and America's newsroom and savaged those who challenge that power, especially on Twitter. I was called a "piece of shit," a "little bitch," and was asked to crawl back under my rock any number of times.

I get this a lot. The thinking is that since I did not go to a journalism school and did not work in a major newsroom, I have no business venturing into the public arena. The Twitter trolls would rather I rejoin my fellow vermin, including the soon to be humiliated Donald

Trump, under whichever rock we emerged from. In the early afternoon of November 8, they were feeling the power, certain they had at
least four more years to abuse it. They were so sure that they called in
outside muscle to serve up the vengeance that was their due. "Thanks
for everyone who tweeted us this," the ACLU said about my "Iglesia"
post. "Please contact @LawyersComm if you see voter intimidation."[19]

As they became more and more excited, the trolls were tweeting
furiously enough to get my name trending on Twitter. It was less of
an honor than it used to be. Not too long ago "trending" meant you
were among the top ten news stories of the hour. That gauge, however,
was too objective, especially in an election year. A reliable cog in the
progressive power machine, Twitter now admits that the number of
tweets "is just one of the factors the algorithm looks at when ranking
and determining trends."[20] Whatever the algorithm was on November
8, Twitter allowed me to trend. The trolls were quick to remind me
that my critics were driving that trend.

I had no time to fret about these petty snipes or the future of the
nation. I had to get the "Sarah" video edited and posted that afternoon
while it still had legs, and I had to get back to New York for what I
believed was a private election watch party. New York and Philadelphia are only a hundred miles apart, but on the New Jersey Turnpike,
on a late weekday afternoon, only God knows how long that could take.

I was driving now. Gio was sitting in the front seat producing the
video on a laptop. He had gotten better journalism training in the last
four months than a student at the vaunted Columbia Journalism School
would get in four years. Hell, he had gotten a better education in this
single day. Even before he fell in with us, Gio had no interest in college. From what I have seen of the tyranny of political correctness on
college campuses, I could hardly blame Gio for keeping his distance.

Making History

Happily, we made it through the Lincoln Tunnel without losing too much time. I drove uptown to an Equinox gym, turned the car back over to Gio, and headed down to the showers to clean up and change into something presentable. Gio came back to pick me up and drove me crosstown to the Hilton. I got there about 6:30 and took the escalator up to the ballroom.

Damn! This wasn't some private watch party. The room was huge, no *yuuuuge*. Young people in red "Make America Great Again" caps wandered about excitedly. Older people in business attire milled around nervously. A large screen in the center of the stage was tuned to Fox News. Rows of American and state flags graced the stage to the left. The stage to the right had a single microphone. This was the real show. Win or lose, history would be made here in just a few hours.

I stood wide-eyed at the entrance. I did not know quite what to do. I did not have a pass. Hell, I did not even know about the event until a few hours earlier. Then a Trump surrogate, Josh Whitehouse, spotted me.

I met Josh in Vermont about a year earlier when no one thought Trump had a prayer. After a Trump stump speech, his only one in Vermont, Josh escorted me backstage. This is where Trump called me "wild man." At the ballroom entrance, I told Josh my predicament. I didn't have a VIP pass. I didn't have any pass for that matter. I wasn't sure whether I needed a security clearance. I wasn't even sure if I should be standing where I was. He looked at me as if I had three eyes.

He reached down, grabbed a VIP pass, and scratched out the name that was on it.

"You're James O'Keefe," he said. I nodded. He wrote my name on the pass and handed it to me.

"James," he said, "You won the election for us. You can stand wherever the fuck you want."

Crazily optimistic, I thought, and something of an overstatement about my role perhaps, but I'll take it. I wandered in. The room was colorful but smaller than I would have imagined, the right size, I supposed, for a "moral" victory, much smaller to be sure than the hall at the Javits Center where excited crowds waited eagerly to see glass ceilings shattered. I made my way through the anxious mass of rabble-rousers, red cap–wearing late-stage adolescents, and outsiders of a thousand different stripes. They all looked surprised to be there and happy despite their trepidations. The exuberance was tangible.

"Mr. O'Keefe," said a young guy approaching me, "I went to Rutgers too. Mind if I get a picture?"

"No problem," I answered. "My alma mater would never have me back." The ice broken, other young guys approached. I was busily signing T-shirts, programs, and, of course, "Make America Great Again" hats. I'd be lying if I said I did not enjoy the attention. I am much more introverted than I ought to be for doing what I do, but the Hilton that night was my world.

Not everyone shared in the slowly growing anticipation that the night might break Trump's way. Here and there I spotted establishment types—consultants, pollsters, pundits. Some had come to experience the punch line of the Trump joke, the anticipated moment when all their warnings were realized and their establishment wisdom vindicated. For them, a Clinton victory meant four years of talk show bookings where they could sound off, look smart, and patronize their less savvy compatriots. They had made their peace with the deep state. If the swamp prevailed, so be it.

The idea of a Trump win unsettled them. Throughout the evening I overheard their random insider comments—"I was with Frank Luntz earlier"; "Chris Christie was telling me"; "Clinton wins Virginia"—and sensed their unease. For the last few weeks, few months really, even on

Election Day itself, the media had been predicting not just a Hillary Clinton victory but a Hillary landslide.[1] Now, these skeptics were not so sure. The world was shifting under their feet, and more so by the minute. For skeptics and true believers alike, there was this dawning sense that Trump might actually win. For the believers, this would be their first real taste of heaven.

"Where are we?" some enthusiastic young guy asked behind me.

"We're 254, and we need to get to 270," came the answer.

In the VIP section, a giant image of Brit Hume loomed above us. His voice echoed loudly as the state returns came in. In between announcements he killed time. No Trump fan, Hume worried out loud about the effect on the markets if Trump should win.

"Oh, please!" said a Wall Streeter standing next to me. "What's going to happen tomorrow? Nothing! The ups and downs are all fake. It's Brexit, basically. Markets responded when FBI info came out, but they bounced back in a day. Stocks are going to bounce back obviously."

And then the word came down. The AP was reporting that Trump had won Pennsylvania. Hillary's path to victory had narrowed to the vanishing point. Trump was going to be our next president. The confetti flew. The tears flowed. The young men screamed into their smart phones and waved their red caps.

Although I try to keep my distance from partisan politics, what I realized during the campaign was that Trump's people were our people.

"I tweeted every single video of yours during the election," one guy said.

"Dude," another laughed ecstatically, "you're the reason we won."

I meant every "thank-you." Every handshake I was offered, I shook back harder—with appreciation. When someone hugged me, usually awkwardly, I hugged them back. My hugs were as sincere as theirs, maybe more. They tweeted my stories out. They made it happen. It can be hard to express gratitude to people you've never met, but not that night. That night it all came easy.

Laura grabbed a screenshot of me and tweeted it out with the message: "Watching a historic power shift, not just in government but in media. You can bypass them now."

The media were a mess. Laura and I looked up on the elevated podium where hundreds of journalists gathered, their lights beaming down like those of the aliens in *Close Encounters of the Third Kind*. And aliens these media people now were, strangers in a strange land, their estrangement from the crowd below palpable. They hunched over their phones in shock or pulled at their hair or sobbed unashamedly. This election was about them—they knew it—and they lost. A few actually accepted responsibility and expressed something like contrition. In the Showtime series *The Circus*, John Heilemann offers a belated mea culpa. "I was wrong," says the ace political reporter. "They are going to be talking about this for years, the greatest political upset of our lifetime."[2]

Down below, above the din, I found myself in a few sobering conversations. One was with Sidney Powell, a DOJ whistle-blower, truth-telling author, and former federal prosecutor. She seemed to sense what I was thinking and walked over to me to talk about it.

"First thing everyone always asks me," she said, "is, 'Aren't you afraid of the DOJ? Don't you have someone starting your car for you?' I have a feeling you get the same questions."

I just stared at her and murmured, "All the time."

Powell had written about prosecutorial misconduct, specifically how prosecutors often conceal the evidence that might free a defendant, and they do so with impunity. I knew something about this phenomenon. In New Orleans in 2010, the arresting officers confiscated my computer and cell phone without permission. The exculpatory information contained therein was not shared with the court, but someone did leak my private communications to the media in order to poison public opinion. Several prosecutors on our case were later forced to resign when it became clear they routinely used aliases to post comments critical of their investigative targets on the website of the *Times-Picayune*.

"I just tell them I'm not going to live in fear," said Powell of those who questioned her sanity. "I'd rather be mad. But fear is why some people quit."

Man, did that hit home. I thought about quitting so many times— the arrest in New Orleans, the three years spent on federal probation, the accusations of sexual assault by a woman I never touched—which I describe in detail in *Breakthrough*—the occasional half-baked sting that went nowhere. Worse, every failure, every setback, was cheered by gloating, vindictive journalists. But then, just when I was convinced I was spinning my wheels, that no one really noticed or cared, some worldly advisor would whisper in my ear, "They attack you because they fear you, because they respect you. Press on!"

I spoke with a few military veterans that evening. In each case, theirs was a measured celebration. Yes, we had secured a beachhead on enemy territory, but there was a long slog ahead.

"This is a phenomenal night, a big victory," one Special Forces guy told me, "but now the hard part really begins. The establishment will dig in their heels and try to fuck us every which way they can."

The bond we shared in victory gave me the nerve to ask a question that I had been chewing over since Marcus Luttrell first raised it at the Republican National Convention.

"I've never understood," I asked, genuinely perplexed, "why soldiers in our country are willing to make the ultimate sacrifice. They go to hellholes like Iraq and Afghanistan knowing they just might die for their country. But here, almost no one is willing to sacrifice anything for his country."

The soldier got it. "For all the soldiers we have with the moral courage to get it on overseas," he said, his voice rising, "not one fucking careerist FBI agent had the stones to stand up and say, 'Here's what's going on with DOJ.'"

He was referring to those many FBI agents who leaked their displeasure about Director James Comey's bewildering refusal to bring charges against Hillary Clinton in the email scandal. Yet for all the backstage grumbling, not a single agent chose to risk his career by bucking the DOJ and going public with his discontent.

"Why is that?" I asked. "I don't understand." This was the heart of the matter for me. The question that would answer so many other questions about how we got where we were as a country.

"Cowardice," said the soldier. "It takes two of kinds of courage to fight a war. You need individual soldiers willing to attack a position and leaders willing to commit to an attack, even when the outcome is uncertain."

"So, is it harder," I asked, "to confront some bureaucrat who might fire you than to confront an enemy who might kill you?"

His answer cut through all the jubilation around us and fixed itself in my heart.

"A firefight lasts for minutes," he said. "The decisions you make, you make in seconds. And you know someone's always got your back. But in government it takes years to build a reputation and a ton of moral courage to put that reputation on the line. Plus, you've got lots of time to stew about the decision, too much time."

"And no one's got your back," I said.

"Probably not."

"You've got to be pretty naïve to take this fight on, I suppose."

"It helps," he said with a wry smile, then nodded and walked away, my suspicions confirmed. I got to see this duality up close. Not too long afterward, I was talking to a would-be Project Veritas recruit who hoped one day to be a Marine. He was less afraid, however, of getting injured in Afghanistan than he was of being burned by the *Huffington Post*. The fear of exposure troubled this young guy. As you might expect, we didn't sign him.

In *The Righteous Mind,* Jonathan Haidt argues that "the most important principle for designing an ethical society is to make sure everyone's reputation is on the line all the time."[3] In a firefight that certainly holds true, but in public life it is just too easy to compromise your principles and slink away from a fight. If you're a Republican, the media will even praise you for "growing" in office.

When Trump finally came out in the early morning hours at the Hilton, it just didn't seem real. I felt like I was watching some kind of pageant that Trump himself had staged, a "Mr. President USA" contest.

"Sorry I'm late," he said with a smile, "had very important business." Watching him speak over the sea of red hats in front of me and knowing that millions of others were watching on TV left me feeling like a witness to history.

After his speech, I headed for the exit. A line of NYPD officers met me as I stumbled out of the building. This wasn't New Orleans. These guys wanted to shake my hand, and they weren't shy about it. "You're the guy who did those videos," said one. Yes, I was. I suspect they saw in Trump what I did. On the campaign trail at least, he didn't always make sense, didn't always say the right thing, but he never backed down. In the immortal words of Steve Bannon, "Honey Badger don't give a shit." What these cops respected about him was that he stood against the grain and defied the same elites they and I had been defying for years.

Targeting the Media

A
s the election proved to all who cared to see, the press was in a state of crisis. Its reputation, its business model, its power over the people were all at risk. It was the victim of a now undeniable reality: much of the public had given up on the credentialed journalists of the establishment media and were turning to citizen journalists and alternative media sites, not just for opinions but for news.

If the press was stuck in time—the anachronistic word "press" suggests as much—the social media were altering the course of global events, rewriting history, rewiring human society. Diversified and decentralized, these media have wrested control of public imagery away from the powers that be. No force can stop the truth from emerging, and no cabal can shape the national consciousness the way it once did.

A late April 2017 poll showed only 29 percent of those surveyed trusted the political media, a figure less than those who trusted President Trump.[1] The social media were largely responsible for those numbers. By 2016, spending on social media advertising surpassed that of television or print, and all major brands were running videos on various platforms. From 2014 to 2017, money invested in social media advertising increased nearly 150 percent to an estimated $41 billion per year, with Facebook and Twitter getting the greater part of that revenue.[2]

The once formidable barriers to entry were no more. Although some in Congress may try to dictate just who is a journalist, no degree is needed to launch a podcast or start a blog. No license needs to be filed. No one's permission needs to be sought. Good content usually finds an audience, and content is king.

The swamp class has watched all this with dismay. Thomas Friedman spoke for his class the week before Trump's inauguration in 2017 when he lamented, "A critical mass of our interactions had moved to a realm *where we're all connected but no one's in charge.*" The italics are his. Friedman saw this state of affairs as "downright scary."[3] At Project Veritas we find the concept of "We the People" downright liberating.

Despite the trend toward social media, we are teetering back and forth on what Malcolm Gladwell calls a "tipping point." The paradigm has not completely shifted yet as evidenced by the media's continued shaming power over the Republican Party. As Friedman recognized—he too used the phrase "tipping point"—the shift is well under way.

No one has figured this out quite like Donald Trump. The democratization of the media allowed him to go right to the people. He became his *own* assignment editor. He was also the media's assignment editor. The fact that he and his supporters could communicate "without editors, fact-checkers, libel lawyers or other filters" disturbed Friedman and others of his class to no end.

In some ways, Trump turned the access paradigm on its head and twisted it into something unprecedented. With his direct Twitter connection, he gave the press pool an unfettered feel for what he was thinking. This directness, combined with a Bannon-inspired strategy of always being on the offensive, made it difficult for the media to focus on anything but Donald Trump.

This was true from the moment Trump declared for the presidency. During the primary campaign, he accumulated more earned media than all the other Republican candidates combined. Trump was good for ratings, but, even better from the media's perspective, he seemed to be wrecking the Republican Party. This was a big win-win—until it wasn't.

"Trump has caught the press in something of a double bind. To ignore what the President does or what he says he intends to do would be journalistic malpractice," wrote Politico's Jack Shafer during inauguration week. "For now, Trump has his glittering saddle on the press, is fannywacking the beast's butt with his crop, and is driving the day."[4]

As became evident in November 2016, the truth was drifting away from what the political class preferred to report and far away from what it predicted. Allan J. Lichtman, the one major political historian who accurately called the presidential race, put it thusly: "Punditry has no scientific basis but simply reacts to the latest polls, which miss the fundamentals of an election and what really drives our politics."[5]

As to what does drive our politics, there is a brutal reality that those immured in our capital cities refused to face right up until election night. The day after the election, the *New York Times*'s Jonathan Martin finally conceded, "Voters have had it with the artifice, emptiness and elements of corruption that pervade the country's politics."[6] Was that not obvious?

The major media were profoundly wrong throughout 2016. They missed the drive and pulse of this country in the run-up to an election of extraordinary consequence. The condescension toward Trump and his supporters started at the top and flowed downstream to the entertainment media, most notably to the once-funny *Saturday Night Live*. On October 23, two weeks before the election, America's beloved actor Tom Hanks showed how far he had strayed from his "everyman" roots when he played a Trump supporter as a marble-mouthed conspiracy theorist so dimwitted he believed the election to be rigged.[7] The audience laughed and cheered. What *SNL* was attacking here was not only Trump and his followers but also their communication streams. If Hanks's character got his information from the internet or wherever, the real Hanks got his information from the major media. That is why he was in a laughing mood. At least he was before the election.

In an unusually honest commentary two days after the election, CBS's Will Rahn admitted that he and his colleagues "spent months mocking the people who had a better sense of what was going on." This, said Rahn, was "symptomatic of modern journalism's great moral and intellectual failing: its unbearable smugness," a smugness he traced to a "profound failure of empathy in the service of endless posturing."[8]

Unfortunately, few in the mainstream media proved to be as honest as Rahn. The election of Donald Trump was a repudiation of their credibility and thus their relevance. They took it hard. They had reason to. Said Kelly McBride, a media ethicist and vice president of the Poynter Institute, "Everything the media does is based on the notion it has relevance. The whole business model falls apart if you're irrelevant."[9]

In the aftermath of the election, a CNN senior producer in Atlanta confirmed to one of our undercover reporters his network's growing fear of irrelevance. "Like, if you look at our ratings and our numbers, we don't have enough of an audience," he told our journalist. "Like, even if you combine Fox, MSNBC, and CNN all together, you're talking about 2 million people in a country of 300 million people. Like, our ratings, alone are not enough to swing an election."[10]

The producer sensed that the tipping point had already been reached. He acknowledged that the "social media," more specifically "the conservative media," prevailed on Election Day. "It's like Town Hall, Breitbart, those people really helped Donald Trump get elected. I mean, we have 250,000 people watching us on our best night." Those numbers, he conceded, were "not enough to change the behavior of a nation."

"The business model for mainstream journalism is in crisis," wrote Nicholas Kristof of the *New York Times* in a spiteful postelection column headlined, "Lies in the Guise of News in the Trump Era." Other than his observation about the business model, Kristof got just about everything else wrong. His takeaway message was that "fake news is gaining ground, empowering nuts and undermining our democracy."[11] This kind of sentiment is precisely what Rahn had in mind when he called out the "unbearable smugness" of the mainstream media.

In reality, the business model is "in crisis" because for years the media have been passing off their analysis and opinions as journalism. When this "journalism" is shown to be as spectacularly misguided as it was on Election Day, citizens have reason to wonder whether they should believe anything the media might say about the Trump administration going forward.

Trump advisor Steve Bannon was echoing the sentiments of millions of distrustful Americans when he dared to say, "The media should be embarrassed and humiliated and keep its mouth shut and just listen for a while." Bannon defiantly said this on the record, adding, "The media here is the opposition party. They don't understand this country.

They still do not understand why Donald Trump is the president of the United States."[12] Almost universally, the media reacted as the *New York Times* did, putting the "keep its mouth shut" part in the headline and feigning outrage over an imagined threat to the First Amendment. Columnist Derek Hunter got it right when he wrote in response, "Outrage is cheap and self-reflection is hard."[13]

I thought Hunter's quote and McBride's above about "relevance" were so spot on I tweeted them out. One of my Twitter followers tweeted back, "The moment they begin to publish truth is the moment they become relevant."[14] Truth appears to be something the media are not yet prepared to handle. After a few semi-honest days of post-election soul searching, the media doubled down on the spin. Why? As Dinesh D'Souza tweeted during the height of the Russian hysteria, "The media instinctively knows that either they or @realDonaldTrump will survive this—it's a political fight to the finish."[15]

Instead of dispassionately reporting the facts, the major media, with the *Times* and the *Post* leading the way, slipped into a self-righteous frenzy, feeding their own wounded pride and their audience's bewildered angst with whatever made everyone feel better, truth be damned. More annoyingly, they took to posturing as defenders of the First Amendment, chest-thumping all the way. The *Washington Post* adopted a new motto and proudly displayed it on the paper's front page, "Democracy dies in darkness." The *New York Times* launched a major ad campaign called simply, "The Truth." For the first time ever, the paper ran an ad during the Oscars. The ad took several explicit shots at Trump and concluded, "The truth is hard/the truth is hard to know/ the truth is more important than ever," followed by the logo of the *New York Times*.[16] "Now more than ever, our mission is clear," reads CNN's new promotional mission statement. According to the Daily Wire, "The self-promotional ad frames Donald Trump's presidency as ushering in new heights of mendacity in national politics, with CNN's operatives committed to delivering truths to its audience."[17] The smugness kept getting more and more unbearable, but behind it was the media's sad search for relevance and even survival.

The major media have entered an unprecedented new phase. Their corporate survival model now demands that they feed a beast increasingly hungry not for truth but for revenge. To preserve the self-image of all involved, the resulting vendetta has had to masquerade as a defense of the First Amendment. Any one of us, whether citizen journalist or the president himself, who tugged on the mask of the producers of this bizarre dumb show risked reprisal.

Since the creation of Project Veritas, the major media have impeded us at almost every step and continue to do so. I have to agree with President Trump that the "fake news media" are not his enemy but "the enemy of the American People."[18] As an enemy, they remain formidable. Their reign will end, I suspect, not with a bang and not with a whimper but with a tantrum. We have been experiencing that phase every day since the election.

Manufacturing Consent

In my previous book, *Breakthrough*, I argued that modern journalists fail to properly inform the American population for several reasons—lack of access to their sources, fear of seeming different, and shared political ideology with their subjects high among them. In the years since, I have had to add a few more reasons for journalistic failure—corporate and market pressures, managers without integrity, and, perhaps most critically, fear of being sued.

It is so much easier today to aggregate information and take shortcuts than it is to dig deep, take risks, and spend the time and money needed to do serious long-term investigative journalism. In their 1988 book *Manufacturing Consent: The Political Economy of the Mass Media,* Edward Herman and Noam Chomsky argued that the media relied overly "on information provided by the government, business, and 'experts' funded and approved by these primary sources and agents of power."[1] In the thirty years since, the major media have become even more dependent on those sources. At the same time, media executives have become increasingly wary of sources "that are not prima facie credible, or that will elicit criticism and threats."[2] These sources tend to add time and expense to the fact-checking process and anxiety among upper management.

What Herman and Chomsky did not anticipate was that the internet would shift the balance of informational power. Today, I have more raw information within easy reach than the entire *New York Times* newsroom did twenty years ago. The corollary evolution in video technology has given people like me the ability to create and distribute video that three networks controlled as recently as thirty years ago. As a result of these power shifts, conflict was inevitable, especially since the media establishment was much more willing to abandon traditional American values than was the citizenry. The task of preserving those values was left almost inevitably to people operating outside the existing power structure, *Samizdat* journalists like Project Veritas.

On June 1, 2017, Robert Creamer made good on his earlier threats and served us with a lawsuit. He and Democracy Partners and the Strategic Consulting Group were suing me, Project Veritas, Project Veritas Action, the real Angela Brandt, and the real Charles Roth. The allegations were that we had violated federal wiretap laws, intercepted oral communications, trespassed, fraudulently misrepresented ourselves, engaged in a civil conspiracy, and forced dogs and cats to live together. Only the last charge was made up—the others just seemed that way. Creamer's attorney, Yael Bromberg, represents the Institute for Public Representation at Georgetown Law. That his institute would throw in with the powers that be against a small operation like ours shows just how much the truth has threatened what economist F. A. Hayek called "the whole apparatus."

On July 28, 2017, we filed a motion to dismiss. We began with an affirmation of the First Amendment: "Undercover journalism plays an important role in creating positive social and legal changes. Without it, many frauds perpetrated upon society would go undetected and rampant abuse would remain hidden. From revealing the sad state of affairs at slaughterhouses to exposing medical fraud, America is a better place because of undercover journalism."[3] As of this writing the Creamer suit is still pending. We are waiting for the judge to set a hearing date, but there is no deadline for the judge to act.

Yes, we did engage in a civil conspiracy, a pretty clever one, to show the world the truth. And the truth hurt. Nowhere in the lawsuit did Creamer deny saying anything we caught him saying. Of course, we were not the first truth-tellers to get sued. Nor will we be the last. One of the cautionary tales journalists tell about undercover work concerns the supermarket chain Food Lion. In 1992, two ABC producers took jobs at a particular Food Lion store. Their source had told them that Food Lion was selling spoiled meat. That information proved to be accurate. Using cameras hidden in their hats and bras, the producers recorded workers repacking expired meat as though it were fresh. They aired the fruits of their work on ABC's *Primetime Live.*

If the exposé were in print, a large corporation could calm an ocean of unease just by denying everything—one man's word against another. But video is the rock to print's scissors. Rock beats scissors every time. Paper covers rock, but only if that paper comes from a process server.

The larger the corporation, the more dangerous the rock and the more expensive the paper. After ABC aired its program, Food Lion's stock plummeted a whopping 15 percent. To compensate, the grocery store chain launched a campaign alleging ABC had distorted the truth. Company president Tom E. Smith said something we hear after every successful sting: "It was pretty obvious that a lot of that was faked."[4]

In the next sentence, Smith claimed the employees with the hidden cameras "had an axe to grind against Food Lion." This claim was not true, but Food Lion hoped to position ABC not as a truth-teller but as a corporate giant with a grudge. Having been embarrassed as badly as the doctors at Nellie Bly's Bellevue, Food Lion executives promptly sued ABC for $4.7 billion. They did not argue that ABC had falsified the report in the way NBC News famously did when it staged a fuel tank explosion on a General Motors vehicle. Rather, the execs claimed the producers had falsified their job applications.

At trial, the jurors were prevented from watching the video. Lest they be swayed emotionally by the imagery, the jurors were instructed only to comment on the technique, and yes, the producers had falsified the information on their job applications. It seemed the journalism was almost beside the point.

The case against ABC slogged on for five expensive years. Finally, the Fourth US Circuit Court of Appeals in Richmond, Virginia, overturned a huge jury award granted by a lower court. In its decision, the court ruled that Food Lion failed to demonstrate lasting damage from the *Primetime Live* report, but that same court scolded ABC for the trickery involved in its investigative technique.[5] If Food Lion did not exactly win, ABC News and other news agencies clearly lost. Food Lion showed just how much pain a large organization could inflict on a news-gathering agency for a story of minimal scope. As a result, ABC eventually stopped doing hidden-camera journalism.

In 1994, CBS News had to go to the Supreme Court to get permission to air videotape secretly shot at a South Dakota slaughterhouse. Judge Harry Blackmun approved the use of the footage just hours before it was scheduled to be shown as part of a *48 Hours* episode called "Bum Steer."

The road to the Supreme Court exacted a heavy toll. Unlike the Food Lion story with its plants from ABC, for the *48 Hours* episode an employee of the South Dakota packing plant had shot the footage of contaminated meat for CBS. He had to falsify nothing. That did not stop federal beef processors from suing. A South Dakota circuit court issued a court order blocking CBS from showing the footage on the mind-boggling grounds that it would hurt the company's business and the South Dakota economy. The South Dakota Supreme Court upheld the injunction.

Blackmun had little patience for the lower courts' arguments. "For many years," he wrote, "it has been clearly established that any prior restraint on expression comes to this court with a heavy presumption against its constitutionality." He noted, for instance, that in the 1971 case *New York Times v. United States,* the Supreme Court refused to suppress publication even of those documents stolen from the Pentagon.[6]

Emboldened perhaps by Blackmun's decision, ABC returned to South Dakota and in 2012 ran a series of broadcasts exposing Beef Products Inc. (BPI), specifically its lean finely textured beef. ABC used the term "pink slime" more than 350 times on its various platforms to describe the product. The broadcasts almost destroyed the company. This time, with ample evidence of ABC's recklessness and bias, BPI sued ABC, and in July 2017 ABC settled the suit for a huge but undisclosed sum. ABC, CBS, and NBC responded by circling the wagons. None of the networks covered the settlement of the suit either on a broadcast or on a website.[7]

I cite these suits to put in perspective one of the "Bingo" charges constantly dredged up to discredit our work. As late as June 2017, the *Washington Post* was reminding its readers that in 2013 "O'Keefe agreed to pay $100,000 to a former ACORN employee who said he was illegally recorded."[8] In the world of media litigation, this was lunch money, but journalists were still feasting on it years later.

In the case in question, ACORN fired a San Diego staffer named Juan Carlos Vera after our undercover video captured him advising us on how to get underage sex slaves across the border. Vera claimed he called the police after our visit, but ACORN fired him despite that claim. We believed—and still do—that an organization dependent on public money had no expectation of privacy. As we were learning, however, the legal environment in California is as hostile to reform as it is in New Orleans, and so we settled.

As we were coming to see, the Creamer suit may represent something of a strategy. In August 2017, the League of Conservation Voters initiated a legal action against us in California, specifically asking for my criminal prosecution. The suit contends that three people who *might* be associated with Project Veritas *may* have used a hidden camera to record them. In October 2017, the Michigan chapter of the American Teachers Federation initiated a legal action against us because they think that a person who *might* be connected to Project Veritas *may* have recorded them with a hidden camera and *may have* taken confidential documents. Both of these organizations are affiliated with Democracy Partners.

Creamer learned in October 2016 what United Airlines would learn in April 2017 when video captured one of its passengers being dragged off the plane screaming. United, however, had no one to sue. Besides, the image had too much visceral power to leave in the hands of a jury, no matter where the trial was held. Creamer did have someone to sue, and he was confident he would have the media establishment behind his suit. Project Veritas was pure irritant to the deep state—seemingly right wing, fake, criminal, discredited. If Creamer succeeded in securing a jury trial in a city that gave Donald Trump 4 percent of its vote, he might even win. I suspect, though, that his real goal was to discourage operations like ours from reporting the truth and to punish those who dared. He was loyal enough of a Democrat to play the long game.

We are scrappy enough to play the long game as well. As a nonprofit, Project Veritas does not have to worry about its shareholders the way ABC and CBS did. Unlike those networks, we have literally millions of Americans behind us who believe in our mission. We do not see these people as customers. We see them as compatriots, and we are no more likely to roll over than they are.

On occasion, to be able to do our job, we have to make a preemptive legal strike. On March 4, 2016, we did just that in Massachusetts federal court. Eight months after we filed suit to challenge Massachusetts' restrictive recording laws, just four days before the presidential election, we got our day in court. Our suit went by the name *PVA v. Conley*. The "PVA" is Project Veritas Action. The "Conley" is Suffolk County, Massachusetts, district attorney Daniel Conley.[9]

Many states have two-party consent law. This usually means we cannot record a conversation without consent of everyone involved. The exception is if we are in a place where there is no reasonable expectation of privacy, such as, say, the middle of a crowded restaurant. Legislators inevitably claim they pass these laws to protect the privacy of their constituents. Some legislators may actually believe that, but the more cunning among them know that these laws do more to protect the legislators than the taxpayers.

No state protects its own the way Massachusetts does. Massachusetts prohibits citizens from secretly recording oral communications in any situation, whether there's a reasonable expectation of privacy or not. The law is so broad you could be penalized for secretly recording someone giving a speech in a park. No joke. The commonwealth's Supreme Court has, in fact, described the recording of such a speech as "unequivocally banned."

This law essentially prevents PVA from doing any work at all within Massachusetts. If we were caught violating the law—which would not be hard to do since we publish the proof online—we could face up to $10,000 in fines and imprisonment of up to five years. That is just the half of it. The "victims" of our crime could bring civil lawsuits against us. With the mainstream media at their back, I am confident they would.

The federal First Circuit Court of Appeals has issued several opinions that call the Massachusetts law into question. In a 2011 case, *Glik v. Cuniffe*, the First Circuit ruled that "[t]he filming of government officials engaged in their duties in a public place, including police officers performing their responsibilities, fits comfortably within [First Amendment] principles."[10]

From the media's perspective, however, police are fair game just about anywhere. Election officials, we have learned, are not fair game. The reason is simple enough. The established media have repeatedly declared there is little or no voter fraud. "How does a lie come to be widely taken as the truth?" the *New York Times* opined in September 2016. "The answer is disturbingly simple: Repeat it over and over again. When faced with facts that contradict the lie, repeat it louder. This, in a nutshell, is the story of claims of voting fraud in America—and particularly of voter impersonation fraud, the only kind that voter ID laws can possibly prevent."[11]

There you have it. So, in our many stings in which we have shown just how pathetically porous the safeguards are that protect the vote, the media have almost inevitably attacked *us*. Our crime was undermining their narrative and embarrassing them. If the media sympathize with a given cause, they will put a not-so-subtle pressure on judges to favor that cause. We had little reason to believe the First Circuit would protect us if we violated existing commonwealth law. We figured it was more prudent to challenge the law preemptively.

When we filed in March 2016, five years had passed since the *Glik* ruling, and during that time Massachusetts made no progress toward amending its unequivocal ban on citizen interception. Keep in mind that many of our biggest scoops have occurred while recording individuals in public spaces. These are all felonies in Massachusetts, and we would not put it past the state to bring charges. As our attorney Stephen Klein observed, "It is no comfort for PVA to litigate under the Civil Rights Act after its journalists are charged under an unconstitutional law."

Our suit was bold and straightforward. In it, we asked for more than the right to record government officials engaged in public duties. We argued for the right to record secretly *anyone* who did not have a reasonable expectation of privacy when speaking. We had no interest in subverting legitimate privacy protection. Our goal was to ensure the free flow of information and hold institutions accountable for their actions.[12]

After much back-and-forth, our case was assigned to Chief Judge Patti Saris. The setting was the federal courthouse in Boston. The building is impressive in a monstrous kind of way. It has a huge glass front that faces out over the Boston waterfront with spectacular views from the hallways outside of courtrooms. It looked awfully damn expensive to build.

Klein, a First Amendment advocate based in Virginia, was exactly the lawyer we needed to complement our attorney, Benjamin Barr. Klein's free-speech work spanned the nation in cases big and small, from successfully challenging a yard sign ordinance in Wyoming to helping overturn the unconstitutional money-laundering conviction of former majority leader Tom DeLay in Texas. Klein viewed his work with us as cutting edge and took our case seriously.

Judge Saris, under her big mop of dark hair, looked like the kind of woman who would feel at home in seventeenth-century Boston. A Boston native and a federal judge for nearly twenty-five years, she would have to rule between our dueling motions. The AG's office wanted to dismiss our case. We wanted an injunction against the Massachusetts law.

From the outset, Saris gave the state's attorney, Ryan Ferch, a hard time. She questioned what PVA would have to do to get standing in the court. Perhaps, she said with a bit of a bite, PVA might draw up an affidavit saying, "I plan to use this news story and I plan to use this technique, and I am afraid?"

Ferch protested, "Journalism doesn't give you a right to do journalism in any way and in any manner that they so choose." Ferch's interpretation of the law was as bizarre as his grammar.

"Have you seen these people?" Saris countered. "I mean, they do this. I mean, this is not just some—they're pretty prominent in doing this." In reading this again, my heart swells. That was the nicest thing a judge had ever said about our work. Saris got it. She recognized that we did our work carefully and methodically and had the successes to show for it. We were "prominent" in our field. Hell, we just about invented it.

History showed that there would be no shortage of worthwhile investigatory targets in the commonwealth. Massachusetts was effectively dominated by a single political party and had a justice system so politically tinged that it let at least one elected official abandon a young woman to drown and walk away unscathed.

If that was not enough, Billy Bulger presided over the Massachusetts senate during many of the same years his hit man brother Whitey presided over the commonwealth's most lethal crime family. These were not the kind of public officials who welcomed a free flow of information. Left to their own devices, they would never roll out a red carpet for Veritas or any kind of undercover news-gatherer. "The irony is that the most corrupt states have these two-party consent laws," I told a legal publication at the time. On reflection, I am not sure "irony" was the right word.

After putting Ferch in his place, Saris turned to Klein. He explained how our suit was intended not just for our benefit but for the benefit of "anyone within the commonwealth who seeks to record secretly." Klein also addressed the impracticality of us submitting an affidavit to get approval for a sting in advance. News-gathering depends on serendipity, he told Saris. He shared with her how our Democracy Partners project—"10 million hits on YouTube between two videos"—got off the ground.

"That all began with a happenstance meeting in a bar in Wisconsin with a guy rambling to his heart's content to the point where everybody around could hear him, and the PVA reporter was wearing a hidden recording device," said Klein. "So this idea that PVA can lay out this game plan strikes me as just asking far too much."

In Massachusetts, Klein continued, we would be prevented from doing this. If, to comply with the law, we told our subjects, "By the way, I'm recording this," they would never open up to our journalists. Then Klein neatly summed up the rationale for our modus operandi.

"I think that those claims," he told Saris of the boasts by Foval and others, "had they been written down, had they been recorded in any other form, would simply have been plausibly deniable and in fact incredible. There is a power to video, and audio in particular. There is a power to having truth; hence, the name Project Veritas." Yes, exactly! This guy understood us.

When asked to sum up his position, Klein asserted once more, "Here we have an unequivocal ban on PVA's activities." That ban, he argued, should not be allowed to stand. In fact, he used the word "Kafkaesque"—one of my favorites—to describe how the current statute has been used to suppress free speech in Massachusetts. Kafkaesque or not, Judge Saris eventually decided the state law would stand and denied our injunction.

Project Veritas's history shows the importance of undercover recording in exposing public corruption. Saris's ruling assured that public corruption was safe from such exposure in Massachusetts.

The appeal in our case will not likely be heard in the immediate future. If need be, we will take the case to the Supreme Court. Happily, with some small help from Project Veritas, that court is more friendly to the Constitution than it might have been otherwise.

Freezing the "Anti-Fascist" Fascists

The first stirrings of the umbrella coalition known as "DisruptJ20" are a bit sketchy, but it is said to have come together in July 2016. The purpose of the organization was implicit in its name: disrupt the events of January 20, most notably the inauguration of the new president. Not surprisingly, the group lurked well off stage until after Donald Trump was elected, at which point it emerged from the wings to become downright fashionable.

DisruptJ20 went public with its intentions on November 11, Veteran's Day, three days after the election. "The idea," said self-described "glam anarchist" Legba Carrefour, was "to undermine Trump's presidency from the get-go. There has been a lot of talk of peaceful transition of power as being a core element in a democracy and we want to reject that entirely and really undermine the peaceful transition."[1] Had a group made a similar declaration upon the election of Barack Obama every newsroom in America would have shuddered with outrage. DisruptJ20 stirred no such emotion.

The various police agencies—the FBI, Secret Service, DC municipal police—paid more attention than the media, but their ability to infiltrate groups such as this one was limited by the age, the visibility, and the general squareness of their respective agents. At one meeting, a so-called "Action Camp" staged at American University in Washington, a Veritas undercover spotted a couple of guys standing in the rear corner who might as well have been wearing "Blue Lives Matter" T-shirts. For one, they were the wrong age, late thirties. The protesters tended to be in their twenties or in their sixties, a generation meld that spoke to forty years of complacency between Nixon and Trump. Then, too, these guys dressed wrong—jeans, Merrell boots, flannel shirts with light pullovers. If they needed one more giveaway, it was their hastily grown beards.

One of the Disrupt organizers, Colin Dunn, a sober, thirtyish fellow with sandy hair and a respectable haircut, scoped these guys out within minutes. As soon as he made them, he walked right over to where they were standing, spoke to them for no more than fifteen seconds, and escorted them out of the room. They did not come back.

Our people fit the protester profile much better. When we started getting tips about the various actions DisruptJ20 was planning, we mobilized. I was particularly concerned about their rumored plans to shut down the wonderfully named DeploraBall. It was to be held at the National Press Club on the eve of the inauguration, and I expected to be there.

Infiltrating a group like DisruptJ20 is both harder and easier than it might seem. It is easier because our undercovers are typically young and well versed in the protest subculture. Plus, they usually don't have much of a paper trail, more literally a cyber trail. It is harder for the same reason—they don't have much of a cyber trail, which throws up red flags on background checks. They all, of course, establish a social media presence under their assumed names—"Tyler Marshall," say, or "Adam Stevens." The presence includes Twitter, Facebook, and email at the least, but those who cared to check would see just how superficial the presence was. The question the DisruptJ20 leaders had to ask themselves was, how could a person be active in the protest community without a history? On top of that, our u/c's left no Google crumbs leading anywhere. In the spy world, the wealth of social media outlets makes the absence of accounts all the more glaring.

It is not hard to create a web presence for a fake organization—we have created a few ourselves—but to create a credible online "legend" for an undercover with a new alias is a challenge. As a result, going undercover requires elaborate subterfuge. It also requires that the u/c appear confident enough to temper the suspicions of fellow protesters. In any case, he or she has to tread very carefully.

There is a quote often attributed to legendary Louisiana governor Huey Long that goes, "When Fascism comes to America, it will be called anti-Fascism!" Long could have predicted the names of the groups that rallied under the DisruptJ20 banner—Refuse Fascism, Smash Racism, DC Anti-Fascist Coalition, etc. For the record, "anti-fascism" as a movement has a long and distinctive pedigree. In the mid-to late 1930s, the Soviet propaganda arm, the Comintern, sought to coalesce various left-wing groups and parties worldwide. Since many of them were reluctant to be labeled "communist," Soviet propagandists used the term "anti-fascist" to unite them in a broader "Popular Front." The apparent goal in the 1930s was to stop Hitler. The apparent goal in 2017 was to stop Trump. The larger goal in both cases was to advance the progressive imperium. On a more personal level, activists then and now gained an identity and a sense of belonging.

In 1939, the Soviets and Nazis made life emotionally difficult for anti-fascists when they threw in together to divvy up Poland. If, however, the liberals with conscience were taken aback, the serious leftists kept pushing forward. The hardcore understood the Popular Front to be a propaganda fraud from the beginning. The hardcore radicals our reporters met were using Trump the way the Soviets used Hitler, namely to rally support for their progressive/anarchist agenda. As their conversations revealed, they resembled Hitler's Brown Shirts much more closely than did the Trump supporters they tiresomely called "Nazis."

After our people had attended some preliminary meetings around the country, we decided that a good place to make new friends would be at the anti-Trump protest at the early December 2016 Army-Navy game held in Baltimore. President-elect Trump was scheduled to attend. Four of our young male journalists attended, including "Adam" and "Tyler." They met up with their fellow hundred or so protesters at McKeldin Square in Baltimore's Inner Harbor on an overcast morning. There, they mingled. This was a good, open environment at which no one could screen them. From McKeldin Square they and their new pals marched down a busy Pratt Street to the M&T Bank Stadium, chanting along the way such welcoming slogans as, "No hate. No fear. Immigrants are welcome here" and "We reject the president-elect."

Once at the stadium, they marched around several times, still chanting, still mingling.

As a newly formed coalition, DisruptJ20 signed up many participants new to the organizers and new to each other. To pull off their
planned actions on January 20, organizers needed bodies, the more
the merrier. This need left the door open to our u/c's, a number of
whom were able to find their way into one or more of the coalition
groups. In less than two months, they attended scores of meetings
from coast to coast, shot tons of video, and recorded several key phone
conversations. Time was obviously a factor here. We had to learn what
kind of disruptions the Disrupt people planned and, ideally, to prevent
any disruptions we could.

Through the contacts made at the Army-Navy march, the guys
wangled an invite to a mass meeting the following day called a "spokescouncil"—anarchist talk for a council of representatives from the various radical subgroups. The meeting was held at St. Stephen and the
Incarnation Episcopal Church, a "welcoming, progressive, multicul-
tural faith community." According to its literature, St. Stephen's provides space for "events that benefit our community." DisruptJ20 was
using that space to subvert the inauguration of the new president, violently if need be. How that would "benefit the community" was not
clear, but looking at the church's website, I had trouble imagining any
progressive cause this "center of liturgical experimentation" would not
embrace.

Three of our journalists attended the spokescouncil meeting. All
that was asked of them was their email. They estimated at least a hundred or more people in attendance, virtually all of them white and
millennial with a few old peaceniks thrown in to season the mix. Anarchy was in the air, not just in the speech-making but in the running of
the show. Like so many of these events, organizers jostled with each
other to assert power and establish agendas. Speakers talked about the
need to shut down DC during the inauguration, but at this stage it was
mostly just talk.

"Tyler," a twenty-four-year-old southerner, arranged a meeting
with a rough-edged organizer named Samantha Miller. They met one-
on-one in a DC bar a few days after the spokescouncil meeting. At this

meeting Tyler floated the idea that he had a rich relative who might want to invest in DisruptJ20's activities. This struck Miller as sufficiently unusual that Tyler chose not to pursue the angle, but it likely left Miller a little suspicious.

A week after the spokescouncil meeting, Tyler was invited to a small meeting with three members of the DC Anti-Fascist Coalition at, of all places, the legendary Ping Pong Comet Pizza, the alleged—with all emphasis on "alleged"—mothership of the District's left-wing pedophile ring. Two weeks earlier, a young nutjob from North Carolina came to the restaurant armed with an AR-15. He told friends he was "going to raid a pedo ring, possibly sacrificing the lives of a few for the lives of many."[2] He fired off a few rounds, but fortunately he did not shoot anyone. The activists held the meeting there with Tyler in solidarity with the owners.

Tyler was the first to arrive. "Scott Green" soon followed. They spoke mostly about music while they waited for the others. Green's real name, we learned later, was Scott Charney, a "foreign policy expert," or so his LinkedIn page would have one believe. Lean and bespectacled, Charney had let his hair grow in the not-too-distant past, presumably to look less like a wonk and more like an anarchist.

Charney could not match Luke Kuhn, the next to arrive, for authentic derangement. Wild-eyed and wild-haired, Kuhn reminded me of the Scorpio Killer that Clint Eastwood hunts down in *Dirty Harry*. Colin Dunn joined as well. The three of them crowded into a small booth with Tyler.

With a football game blaring behind them, the activists were able to speak in normal tones. Casual diners had no reason to suspect anything amiss unless, of course, they happened to overhear Kuhn's gems such as, "We do not recognize the city government. If you try to close us down, we will look for your house, and we will burn it," or "We will physically fight the police if they try to steal one of our places. We will go to war, and you will lose."[3]

One subject of conversation was how best to disrupt the Deplora-Ball, which was to be held at the eleven-story National Press Club building in the center of Washington. The plan that seemed most feasible involved butyric acid, a highly disruptive kind of stink bomb.

Said Kuhn, "All you got to do is pull the pin, press the plunger, and the whole thing discharges."

"If you get it into the HVAC system, it will get into the whole building," said Dunn.

"The best possible location to get to it is the air intake grille of the entire HVAC," added Kuhn, who sounded like he had done this before.

"You want to case the place?" asked Charney.

"I can do that," Dunn volunteered.

"Yeah, if you had a pint of butyric acid, I don't care how big the building is, it's closing," said Kuhn.

"And this stuff is very efficient. It's very, very smelly, lasts a long time, and a little goes a long way," enthused Charney.

Rarely, I suspect, has a federal crime with a potential five-year prison sentence attached to it been discussed so blithely. These budding anti-fascists would later say they were just leading our reporters on. I don't believe them, and neither did law enforcement. They just felt so snug in the broad embrace of the Popular Front circa 2017 that they carried on with seeming impunity. The conversation then turned to the sprinkler system.

"I'm trying to think through how to get all the sprinklers to go off at once. There's usually a piece of like fusible metal or a piece of glass with liquid in it that will blow," said Dunn. "I need to research and make sure that we can actually get them all triggered if we trigger one." He then conjured up an "added benefit." Said he, "Everybody is going to walk outside in the freezing cold."

Disrupting the Disruption

Tyler soaked all the plans in and recorded the conversation on his button camera. A few days later, he left DC for a scheduled Christmas vacation with his family. He had, however, made an impression. People would remember him. At a subsequent meeting held at a private home in the Columbia Heights neighborhood near St. Stephen's, Adam listened in awe as activists talked about Tyler. They were anticipating Tyler's return from vacation. They had already integrated him into their plans.

The private home in question was the nesting place for the so-called "Love + Solidarity Collective." According to its literature, the collective hosts an "open space discussion group" where issues—presumably like shutting down the inauguration—are discussed "in a welcoming and respectful way." One of the organizers our journalists met at the collective was a black homeless advocate named Eric Sheptock. Sheptock recommended rounding up his charges, "the poor and homeless," and enlisting them in the planned actions. This did not surprise me. As mentioned earlier, the Democracy Partners people had used the homeless to provoke violence in the Trump protests. The homeless have served the left as props or pawns since they were first exploited in the Reagan '80s.

After the first of the year, the spokescouncil meetings picked up. There were as many as three a week, and the planning was getting more specific. The actions the organizers conceived were many and bold. The unifying word for these actions seemed to be "clusterfuck." Said Carrefour at one meeting, for instance, "We are also doing a series of clusterfuck blockades, where we are going to try to blockade all the major ingress points in the city."[1] International Workers of the World frontman, Dylan Petrohilos, was even more definitive. "Our goal is to continue to help shut down the city at like, mid-inauguration, a giant clusterfuck that day," he told his troops, adding later, "So be prepared to help make the inauguration a giant clusterfuck."

Professional activist "Patrick," last name unknown, preferred "fucking shitshow." He elaborated, "Throw them all under the bus. Just fuck it up. I like the idea of the goal being they have to pull the inauguration inside." Patrick and "comrade" Aaron Cantu had been roaming the country for the six months following the Republican National Convention, almost assuredly on someone else's dime. They spent three of those months at the Standing Rock pipeline protest in North Dakota.

These organizers were not just speaking in general. They had been making some very specific plans. On an undercover audio recording at one of the January spokescouncil sessions, we picked up Carrefour explaining how he intended to use a literal chain to secure cars on the DC Metro and basically "shut down the line."

"So, we figured out this, the trains pull up," said Carrefour. "One person is going to lock one end of a chain to an edge, and on the other end of the chain the end of the car, so on and so forth."[2] If all went as planned, within fifteen minutes he and his cohorts could tie up "every single line in the city." Better still, their work could only be undone with a bolt cutter. His plan included shutting down major bridges and highway access points as well as shutting down the DC Metro. So confident was he in the popularity of his cause he did not think these actions "arrestable."

If these guys weren't so potentially dangerous, their branding of the opposition as "Nazis" would be amusing. "Generally speaking, Nazis will only actually attack people if they have, if they strongly outnumber them, because Nazis are essentially cowards," said Smash Racism DC cofounder Mike Isaacson at an Action Camp held at American University. For Isaacson, "Nazi" was a synonym for "Trump supporter." Apparently, he had seen enough of these Nazis in action to feel comfortable stereotyping them, "generally speaking" that is. When asked how best to respond to a Nazi provocation, Isaacson said solemnly, "I would say that's where you do the throat punching."[3]

Speaking in an open classroom, Isaacson showed no apparent unease advising his charges on how best to injure their political opponents. His comfort level may have derived from the fact that he had mastered the radical look—lean with a trim beard, glasses, and fashionably disheveled hair. Several of the organizers, in fact, had mastered that same neo-Lenin look.

Isaacson was apparently in on the plan to shut down the Metro. "That is going to require some teamwork, probably a rehearsal maybe," he told a Veritas u/c in a recorded phone conversation. The organizers needed "bodies" to pull the plan off. "If you are willing to be those people," he told our reporter, "we are definitely down to have you."

Given the organizers' inclination toward things illegal, they were more alert to infiltration than many with whom we have met over the years. In fact, one of our best u/c's, Allison Maass, got stung. As we've already seen, this was not her first time. In our line of work, getting burned is an occupational hazard—not a question of if, but when. Allison had been mining an entirely different protest vein than Tyler or Adam, but her success in stinging Democracy Partners left her vulnerable.

The moment of confrontation was pretty harrowing.[4] She had set up a meeting at a Washington, DC, restaurant with Ryan Clayton, the president of America Takes Action, an organization whose "top priority is resisting the Trump regime, every day and every step of the way."

Clayton was more than merely suspicious. Knowing who Allison was, he tried to lure her into saying that her apocryphal wealthy friend—she tried that gambit, too—was willing to fund specific illegal activities. Allison danced around the question. "Like I said," she told Clayton, "we're not the idea people. So, I don't think I'm . . . we're not going to suggest anything." Unaware that she had been made, Allison tried to get Clayton to state his intentions. "So is there a line for you?" she asked. "Or are you willing to go all in?"

Unable to get Allison to incriminate herself, Clayton got tough. "Please keep your hands where we can see them," he told her abruptly.

At this point, Allison did what she had been trained to do. "I'm going to be leaving," she said, but as she tried to exit the restaurant she was confronted by a young woman named Lauren Windsor. This was the same woman who called looking for Charles Roth when his niece, Allison/Angela Brandt, skipped out of the Democracy Partners office.

"You work for James O'Keefe, right?" said Windsor. "Have you been to the rape barn too? Are you hooking up with him? Is he your boyfriend? Is James your boyfriend?"

Those who read my book *Breakthrough* know about the half-assed sting that led to the nonsensical "rape barn" story and my unlikely emergence as a sexual predator. Although the accusation was dismissed in every which way, including judicially, the left never lets go. For Clayton, badgering the opposition with unfounded sexual allegations is part of his MO. In 2011, for instance, he hounded the late Andrew Breitbart at a public meeting with a fully fabricated charge, "Have you ever slept with a prostitute, a male one, have you?"[5]

For twenty minutes, Clayton, Windsor, and their comrades pursued Allison down the Washington streets, cameras at the ready, taunting her every step of the way. "Is it like good when you go home for the holidays?" said Clayton. "You're like, 'Hey mom and dad, I work for an alleged sex molester?' Is that like fun?"

When Allison hailed a cab, Clayton tried to climb in behind her. "Do not get in this taxi," she told him. Even then he kept up his snarky banter. "Do you think it's a Christian thing to do? To lie about who you are?" Allison kept her cool, admitted nothing, and fled the scene.

About the same time as the Allison bust, a Veritas u/c working under the name "Max Hunt" learned at a Love + Solidarity meeting that the organizers were suspicious of at least two people. The challenge for Max was to figure out whether the people under suspicion were actually other Veritas u/c's or maybe even him and the u/c working with him, Marissa.

"We don't know if they are cops or right-wing traitors," said the one J20 planner of the two under suspicion.

"What?" said Max, "are they like protesters?"

"They are people that have been coming to meetings and stuff," said the planner. "To learn shit."[6]

"Oh," said Marissa, taken aback. She did not like what she was hearing.

"They've been on the spokescouncil," said the planner.

"They both kind of had this story about a rich relative that wants to donate a lot of money. But they won't tell us how much." To our people, this sounded very much like Tyler and Tara. Marissa let out a little gasp as if this were the strangest thing she had ever heard.

"Yeah, it's *really* weird," said the organizer.

"That is fishy," added Max.

"Super fishy," said the organizer, adding with a laugh, "Oh, I really wish that I had a rich relative. I wish that part."

Our people here had to walk a fine line. They could act surprised, but they could not elaborate, not embellish, not excuse, not throw suspicion elsewhere. Mostly, they just had to observe and absorb and, as soon as possible, let HQ know that Tyler and Tara were in trouble.

Upon learning he was under suspicion, Tyler had to proceed cautiously. There was a real calculus involved. His best bet was to beef up his and Tara's bona fides to allay suspicions, but if he couldn't, he had to extricate Tara and himself. If he did so too abruptly, the organizers might suspect they had been tipped off. And if the organizers came to that conclusion, they might suspect Max and Marissa as the ones who did the tipping.

As should be obvious by now, these kind of spy games get complicated very quickly. They require intuition, foresight, and a fair amount of nerve. To help our reporters, we established an encrypted chat system that allowed them to communicate with HQ in something close to real time. Understandably, they felt the need to temper their instincts with counsel from more experienced voices. If a seasoned operator was telling them something did not feel right, they would be more confident in their suspicion that the plan had gone astray.

Back at headquarters, we were figuring out how to proceed with those u/c's who, if not entirely "burned," had certainly provoked suspicion. We asked ourselves whether we could keep them in play and, if so, how. For sure, they would need a well-rehearsed emergency cover story they could deploy if pressured, such as "Soros hired us to see how easily the protest movement could be infiltrated" or "We're just making a documentary." What they could not say was that they were working with James O'Keefe.

After consulting with me, Tyler scheduled a meeting with Colin Dunn. He chose an ice-cream shop for its many windows. Before going in, however, he had Adam drive him by the shop slowly to see what was what. They got an eyeful. Dunn was sitting at one booth. Charney was sitting in a booth behind him. And off to the side was this large older fellow with a Santa Claus beard. Tyler had seen him before. He was some sort of enforcer. It looked for all the world like a setup. Adam, a former high school defensive end, was just as big as Santa, but this was a confrontation Tyler saw no use provoking. They just drove on by. Tyler called Dunn later to say his car had broken down on the way to the meeting, but he knew his u/c days were over, at least on this project.

As the inauguration approached, we had gathered a ton of material disturbing enough to warrant sharing it with the authorities. Aware as we were of the planned and potentially dangerous disruptions, especially on the Metro, we could not stay silent. Our attorney Ben Barr set up a meeting in Washington with the FBI for January 13. Tyler, Adam, and Max went with him. In the past, our engagement with law enforcement has not always been congenial, but these guys were an exception. There were four of them, three FBI and one DC Metro, all casually dressed. They had done a fair share of undercover work as well, but we had the goods, the video, and they greeted us like brothers-in-arms.

Three days later on January 16, we went public with our first finished video. This one focused on Tyler's meeting at the Comet Ping Pong. Immediately after its debut, DisruptJ20's Lacy MaCauley hit back with a press release. In it, she claimed DisruptJ20 had outed four of our journalists, including Tyler. She insisted that the activists chose Comet Ping Pong as a meeting site for "humorous" reasons. Knowing Tyler was not who he said he was, they planned the meeting to give him "false information about what they felt was the most humorous red herring available: a false plot to use stink bombs at an event called the DeploraBall."[7]

On January 17, we launched the second video, this one featuring Carrefour's plan to chain the trains. These were charges serious enough and detailed enough that even the more slanderous of the progressive blogs checked the impulse to mock us. The major media held back as well.

By the end of the day January 17, *U.S. News and World Report*, among other media, was reporting that DisruptJ20 had "dramatically scaled back plans" to disrupt the inauguration. Said Carrefour with a straight face, "By virtue of us making those claims, it whips people up into the kind of panic that accidentally ends up causing the chaos we want."[8] This strategy, he insisted, was intentional. He allegedly used Project Veritas to leak the plans to cause the commotion. I didn't buy that hogwash for a minute. Neither did law enforcement.

On January 19, the DC Metro Police arrested Scott Charney for his role in planning the disruption of the DeploraBall. As the *Washington Times* reported, "Police relied on the video turned over to investigators."[9] In a fitting bit of irony, Charney was arraigned on the charges in DC Superior Court just as Trump was being inaugurated president. In time, Paul "Luke" Kuhn and Colin Dunn were arrested as well.

In the most shocking development of all, on January 25 the *Washington Post* ran a favorable article on our efforts to infiltrate the protest and prevent potential violence. "A D.C. police spokesman has confirmed," wrote the *Post*'s Peter Hermann, "that a secret video recording made Dec. 18 by one of O'Keefe's operatives led to the arrest of one man and foiled an alleged plot to spread acid at the DeploraBall for Trump supporters at the National Press Club."[10]

"I've spent years trying to fight the mainstream media that doesn't view me as a journalist," Hermann quoted me as saying, "This is the first time that a video we shot has led to an arrest. It legitimizes what we're doing. It's a new era for us."

If not a new era, it may at least be the end of the old one. To quote one sentence from this front-page story, "The arrest validates [Project Veritas] and its controversial methods."

Backtracking in Wisconsin

Anyone who watched our "Rigging the Election" videos in October 2016 knew at least one thing: some of the most damning footage was recorded in Wisconsin and highlighted Wisconsin-specific problems with voter fraud. Organizer Scott Foval proved particularly eloquent in discussing ways to move illegal voters in and out of the state. Foval's scheming cost him his job, but it will not likely cost him his freedom. One reason why is that local district attorneys and state attorney generals, Democrat or Republican, are reluctant to investigate voter fraud, Republicans for fear of being called "racist," Democrats for fear of costing their party votes.

That said, given the millions of people who saw our videos in October, Republican attorney general Brad Schimel felt compelled to respond. The same week they were released, Schimel acknowledged he was aware of their contents. Understandably, he believed they showed "apparent violations of the law." Schimel's spokesman went on to say that the AG's office was "evaluating and reviewing available options to address the serious questions these videos raise."[1] That only made sense. On October 31, two weeks after our first video aired, we sent Schimel's office our raw tapes as well as a transcript of the relevant portions. Things went south for us from there.

The media got curious when no public action was taken. In response to an open records request by the *Wisconsin Journal Sentinel*, the AG's office released a memo on April 25 written in January by Ryan Korte, the head of Schimel's criminal investigation division. "Based on all the available facts," Korte wrote, "I do not believe there is any basis to conclude the videos demonstrate or suggest violations of Wisconsin criminal laws."[2] It was one thing not to charge Foval with a crime for what he claimed to have done, but Korte took it a step further. He questioned the reliability of the videos. He claimed the recordings were "suspect" because edited sequences began in the middle of conversations. He even questioned the location of where the conversation with Foval took place. "The recording is not clear," he wrote, "whether the conversation occurred in Wisconsin which would be necessary for any potential venue."

The recording took place inside of Garfield's 502, a Milwaukee bar. With five minutes of phone calls and Googling, Korte could have verified the location. In fact, any two-bit investigator worth his or her salt could have glanced around the room in which the video was shot and deduced the identity of this well-known Milwaukee watering hole. Trust me, there would have been no confusion if this had been a standard homicide investigation, but our case was radioactive, and Korte was unwilling to get burned.

His gamesmanship did not surprise me. I have become all too familiar with the way prosecutors work the media, whether it be the New Orleans prosecutors leaking false information about the Landrieu case or the Brooklyn district attorney claiming our ACORN videos were "selectively edited" or California attorney general Jerry Brown burying the fact that California ACORN had engaged in "highly inappropriate behavior." As described earlier, these "criticisms" are inevitably hyperbolic and usually evidence free.

For the media and the Democrats, getting the Korte report was like finding a pony under their tree on Christmas Day. They loved the new angle.[3] They could forget what their lying eyes told them about Foval and turn a Democratic scandal into a Republican one. "Today's news makes it clear that Attorney General Brad Schimel is either woefully incompetent of the laws he is supposed to enforce or he intentionally used his office for politics," said state Democratic Party spokesman Brandon Weathersby. "This is beyond partisan politics," claimed Scot Ross, executive director of the liberal group One Wisconsin Now, "this is abuse of power by Schimel." According to Ross, Schimel suppressed evidence that would have proved his original assertion of potential criminal violations to be "false."

When the Associated Press called my office, no doubt for a "comment" about how these officials were "cleared" of wrongdoing, I knew I had to push back immediately. Two days after the release of the Korte report, on the morning of April 27, we posted a video in response. It reminded viewers what Foval had said and explained how we had cooperated with the AG's office.

I called Korte's claim of being unable to verify the location of the recording "laughable." I questioned, in fact, whether Schimel's office did any investigation at all or whether Schimel had even watched the tapes we sent him. "If the state of Wisconsin is not going to do their job," I said to Schimel via video, "you should be investigated. We should investigate you and you should lose your job."[4] This video takedown led to a remarkable series of events.

On that same morning, the *Milwaukee Journal Sentinel* posted a follow-up article headlined "Conservative James O'Keefe Threatens to Investigate Attorney General Brad Schimel over Video Flap."[5] As the reader will note, I was identified as a "conservative" in the first word of the headline. This was a routine way of slighting our work, but here the designation serves an additional purpose. It tells the reader that if a conservative is attacking Schimel, the *Journal Sentinel* cannot be accused of liberal bias for piling on. In the third paragraph, readers are reminded, as they almost inevitably are, that I had once "pleaded guilty to a misdemeanor."

I followed up with an email blast to eighty thousand supporters at 2:15 p.m. on that same April day with a request to send a tweet to the Wisconsin Department of Justice. Embedded was my video and the tweet, "@WisDOJ Why did Roy Korte refuse to investigate voter fraud? Korte did not interview @PVeritas_Action or Foval/Creamer. Why? #Veritas."[6] Within a matter of minutes, hundreds of tweets aimed right at the attorney general's office echoed my tweet. Some added their own unique spin, such as this one from LaurenNann: "yes, @WisDOJ WHY?! @PVeritas_Action stay on these crooks!"[7] And even the haters pitched in with the predictable "O'Keefe as criminal" theme: "Because you've thoroughly established that Veritas' work is untrustworthy. The only successful prosecution has been yours."[8]

As this Twitter tsunami was rolling across cyberspace, Brad Schimel appeared on Wisconsin public radio, reiterating the claim that the investigation was closed. He also defended his decision in light of my pushback: "We did take it seriously and looked at this to see whether there was something we could pursue . . . and just concluded there's not anything that presented itself as a viable investigatory lead." He added unconvincingly, "If it's not specific enough that we can identify who did something, where they did it, we don't even know where to start."[9] I'm no attorney, but I have seen enough legal shows on TV to think that interviewing witnesses, maybe Scott Foval himself, might have been a good place to start.

Schimel was facing criticism from both sides of the aisle. Unfortunately, he deserved it. It probably threw NPR and the *Journal Sentinel* that their "conservative" poster boy was challenging a Republican attorney general. As the *Journal Sentinel* did acknowledge, however, this was not the first time I took on a Wisconsin Republican. In 2014, we caught Wisconsin State Senate president Michael Ellis (R–19) on hidden camera explaining how he planned to circumvent state campaign finance laws.[10] That video led him to drop out of his senate race.

In the midst of this, Steve Klein, one of our attorneys, cautioned Ben Barr, our main general counsel, about my challenging the attorney general. But at that moment, something interesting started to happen. Paul Connell, a former federal prosecutor who was appointed Schimel's top deputy in 2016, called my criminal defense attorney and told him that the AG's office was caught up in a "tempest." According to Connell, the Korte memo was one person's view, not the department's position. He added that Project Veritas was "doing the Lord's work" and was perplexed that his office had never sent anyone to interview Foval. That was about to change. Connell requested the "third" Foval video and promised a fresh start.

As that phone call was in progress, Schimel went on another radio program, this one with Mark Belling, a conservative radio host out of Milwaukee. Now, Schimel was reinforcing what Connell was telling us privately, that an assistant AG cannot close an investigation.

"I appreciate the work that groups like Project Veritas do to expose corruption and criminal conspiracies," said Schimel, "but the war of words that has sparked up in the last twenty-four hours is incited by fake news, Mark. There's no story here. There's nothing to report yet."

"Is the investigation over?" Belling asked.

"No!"[11]

I tweeted out in the midst of this fury, "WOW. Wisconsin AG appears to be backtracking as a result of our video exposing their Refusal to investigate. Good work, internet."[12]

Then came the inevitable headline from the *Journal Sentinel* a few hours later, "Wisconsin Attorney General Brad Schimel Contradicts Self, Says Voter Fraud Probe Is Open." As glad as I was that Schimel swung around, the *Journal Sentinel* was right: he did contradict himself. Life would be easier for everyone if he had not, especially Schimel himself.

By the following day, Schimel was saying the memo had been "released in error." The *Journal Sentinel* was accusing Schimel of creating "fake news," and Schimel was accusing the *Journal Sentinel* of the very same thing. The *Journal Sentinel* concluded its editorial of April 28 on this absurd note, "So we ask again: What game are you playing, Mr. Schimel? Is your job to serve justice for the citizens of Wisconsin? Or to serve the special interests of partisans who threaten you?"[13]

"Special interests of partisans?" There is a new one for an updated political lexicon. Those partisans were doing nothing more than seeking "justice for the citizens of Wisconsin." The media today are too conflicted to distinguish ordinary citizens from special interest groups and justice from partisanship.

By week's end, an Associated Press story on the controversy had found its way into both the *New York Times* and the *Washington Post*. The story had just enough negative Republican fallout to get Scott Foval and his troublemaking allies back into the news. All it took was the creation of a short video challenging a sitting AG and the balls to post it.

Editing the News

As our media betters learned on election night, there is a profound shift of power taking place in our country. All the deep state's newswomen and all its newsmen could not elect its chosen candidate again. This came as a horrible shock. For months, journalists had been smugly mocking Trump, sharing polls with their fans, predicting landslides.

By Wednesday morning, November 9, it was obvious even in America's newsrooms that the traditional media had failed in their job to keep their audiences informed. As the journalists emerged from their stupor, they were beginning to see how much ground they had yielded to the alternative media. Ordinary citizens had undermined the interests of entrenched media moguls, often through the very channels the elite introduced and now struggled to control, like Facebook, Twitter, and YouTube.

To rationalize the humiliation of the deep state–media complex, the *New York Times*'s Nicholas Kristof accused the Trump camp of "fake news," using those very words.[1] Reeling from Hillary Clinton's surprise defeat, the media imagined a surge in "fake news," much of it allegedly produced by Russia, as a way of explaining a reality that defied them. In the days since, opposing camps have been lobbing charges of fake news at each other the way armies did gas canisters in World War I. In both cases, much has gotten lost in the smoke.

Although the term has been around for at least a century, "fake news" gained currency in recent years with the emergence of Fox

News, or, as many in the media preferred to call it, the *Faux* News Network. Said *The Daily Show*'s Jon Stewart in 2003, "I do believe we need to go to a 24-hour fake news channel. Fox can't be the only fake news channel out there!"[2] In 2007, liberal journalist Eric Alterman wrote an article for the *Nation* titled "The Real 'Fake News,'" in which he too blasted Fox News for its alleged fabrications.[3] The assumption all along was that fake news, whether on Fox or elsewhere, was a phenomenon of the right. I could not begin to count the number of times our work product at Project Veritas has been called "fake" or "false" or "fraudulent" or "discredited."

Always defiant, Donald Trump turned the phrase back on the media. He focused particularly on CNN, and once he did, the use of the term by people on the right exploded. The major media proved vulnerable to the accusation if for no other reason than that they create the vast majority of new stories, especially high-profile news stories. As should be obvious, their news creators tend to advance ideas very similar to one another. Given their shared agendas, they do not do a very good job of policing their competitors.

At present, the term "fake news" is being defined in many ways, most of them irrelevant. Fully false or satirical stories die a quick death on the internet with the first salvos usually coming from the side the story is supposed to please. The most dangerous news stories are those with at least some basis in truth and generated by people or institutions with some credibility. The late commentator Christopher Hitchens offered a useful understanding of such deception in his critique of the film *Fahrenheit 9/11* by Academy Award–winner Michael Moore. Said Hitchens:

> So I know, thanks, before you tell me, that a documentary must have a "POV" or point of view and that it must also impose a narrative line. But if you leave out absolutely everything that might give your "narrative" a problem and throw in any old rubbish that might support it, and you don't even care that one bit of rubbish flatly contradicts the next bit, and you give no chance to those who might differ, than you have betrayed your craft.[4]

All journalists edit selectively. We do as well. We have to. Few people would be willing to watch hours of unstructured raw video. Many edit deceptively—Michael Moore–style. Forget the silly "Pope Backs Trump" stories floating around on Facebook. Call it fake or deceptive or selective, ideologically driven editing by the major media is the real problem with the news today.

The establishment media's contempt for the creators of fake news would be understandable if they had a deep and consistent commitment to journalistic ethics, but they do not. This was made abundantly clear in their treatment of Katie Couric's documentary *Under the Gun*.[5] In the critical scene of the documentary, aired in May 2016 to influence the election, Couric is seen earnestly interviewing several members of the Virginia Citizens Defense League, a gun-rights organization. "If there are no background checks for gun purchasers, how do you prevent felons or terrorists from walking into say a licensed gun dealer and purchasing a gun?" Couric asks. Each of the next three camera moves catches a different activist looking perplexed, if not confused, as though he or she had not heard this question before and had no good answer. After about eight or nine seconds of empty airtime, the documentary cuts to the cylinder of a revolver being dramatically locked into place.

Unfortunately for Couric, the Virginia activists had the foresight to make a recording of the interview. They also found editors willing to publish their complaint at the *Washington Free Beacon,* a largely conservative online journal "dedicated to uncovering the stories that the powers that be hope will never see the light of day."

The audio revealed Couric prefacing her question with something of a disclaimer, "I know how you all are going to answer this but I'm asking anyway." As she surely expected, an activist answered immediately. As the audio recording made clear, the activists chewed the answer around with Couric for about four minutes. Unlike Couric, they knew what they were talking about. The *Beacon* coverage forced the story into the mainstream, and the establishment media were quick to cover for Couric—remarkably quick. The *Beacon* article was posted on May 25, 2016.[6] So, impressively, was a *New York Times* article on the brewing controversy.

"A conservative news site posted . . . ," so began Katie Rogers's article in the *Times*. The word "conservative" is used here to alert readers that the charge to follow—namely that filmmakers "deliberately edited video to portray gun-rights activists as unable to answer questions about background checks"—is not to be taken too seriously.[7]

Rogers contacted Stephanie Soechtig, the director of the film, who assured her that the editing was not intended to make the activists look ignorant. "My intention was to provide a pause for the viewer to have a moment to consider this important question before presenting the facts on Americans' opinions on background checks," Soechtig dissembled. "I never intended to make anyone look bad and I apologize if anyone felt that way." Couric had Soechtig's back. "I support Stephanie's statement and am very proud of the film," she told the *Times*.

The network that broadcast *Under the Gun* lined up with all the other media worthies. "Epix stands behind Katie Couric, director Stephanie Soechtig, and their creative and editorial judgment," said Nora Ryan, the company's chief of staff. "We encourage people to watch the film and decide for themselves."

The problem for the producers was that millions of viewers did as Ryan suggested. Thanks to the internet, they were able to watch the video and listen to the audio and make up their own minds. The evidence was undeniable. Soechtig had inserted a video shot out of sequence to create a false effect. This was textbook selective and deceptive editing, Michael Moore–style. It is precisely this kind of journalistic hubris that people rejected when voting for Trump. In 2017, Yahoo! News failed to renew Couric's $10 million-a-year "Global Anchor" contract when it was purchased by Verizon. Couric made the mistake of getting caught.

Were it not for the internet and the alternative media, Couric and her cronies would have gotten away with their scam. Were it not for the internet, CBS anchor Dan Rather might well have sunk George Bush's reelection chances in 2004 with the forged documents that discredited Bush's service with the Texas National Guard. "Memos on Bush Are Fake but Accurate, Typist Says,"[8] so claimed the *New York Times* in a now famous effort to prop up a story that citizen journalists were rightfully tearing down.

This was a pivotal moment in the history of online citizen journalism. A former CBS News executive, Jonathan Klein, defined the conflict with imagery for the ages. On one side, he told Bill O'Reilly, you have a professional news bureaucracy with "multiple layers of checks and balances." On the other side, he snickered, you have "a guy sitting in his living room in his pajamas writing."[9] This taunt lit up the internet and inspired the launch of the now powerful site PJ Media. Ten years later, Hollywood tried to rehabilitate Rather with a movie improbably titled *Truth*. It seems somehow fitting that actor Robert Redford played Rather forty years after he played Watergate hero Bob Woodward. Over those years, truth has corroded as visibly in Hollywood as it has in America's newsrooms. One wonders if there is a Katie Couric movie in the works.

Journalists have been in the fake news business for quite a while. If it is okay now to blame Russia, I would trace the introduction of consciously fake news back about ninety or so years to Soviet meddling in the Sacco and Vanzetti case. Working through their Western cutouts, Soviet propagandists "framed" the two anarchist killers as innocent victims of a xenophobic America. For the next eighty years, the media routinely framed the guilty as innocent—Alger Hiss, the Rosenbergs, Leonard Peltier, Mumia Abu-Jamal. Without an alternative media, much of that fake news has become fake history. In spite of the best efforts of citizen journalists, the media have of late taken a much darker turn. Today, they are willing to frame the innocent as guilty.

In the shooting deaths of Trayvon Martin in Florida in 2012 and Michael Brown in Missouri in 2014, for instance, the media ignored all journalist canons and employed various editing tricks in a vain effort to send two innocent men to prison for the rest of their lives. The truth emerged in court in both cases, but in the court of public opinion, the men were condemned and their futures severely damaged.

Even more unmoored from reality has been the media's coverage of the Trump presidency. For a fuller rendition of the media's use of fake news to subvert the Trump ascension, I would recommend *The Smear* by former CBS reporter Sharyl Attkisson, but allow me to provide a couple of everyday examples to give the flavor.

Consider this top-of-the-fold *Washington Post* story from May 15, 2017: "Trump Revealed Highly Classified Information to Russian Foreign Minister and Ambassador." This is high-stakes fake news.[10] For sources, the *Post* turned to "current and former U.S. officials," a "U.S. official familiar with the matter," and, worse, "a former senior U.S. official who is close to current administration officials." All the sources were anonymous. It is likely that the best of them was dealing in hearsay.

More perversely still, it was not until the seventh paragraph that the reader learned that Trump did nothing wrong. "As president," wrote the *Post* reporters, "Trump has broad authority to declassify government secrets, making it unlikely that his disclosures broke the law." Said veteran columnist Daniel Greenfield of the *Post* article above, "This isn't journalism. It's a joke."[11]

The media twisting of an unremarkable cabinet meeting in June 2017 stands out for its gratuitousness. The meeting was recorded and broadcast on cable news. What made it newsworthy at all was that it was the first time, given the protracted approval process, that Trump was able to get all of his appointees to the table. To begin, the cabinet members went around the table and introduced themselves.

Andrew Ferguson analyzed the media reaction in a publication largely hostile to Trump, the *Weekly Standard*.[12] Watching *Morning Joe* on MSNBC, Ferguson was taken aback by the hosts' disgust with what appeared to be the fawning attitude of a few of Trump's appointees. "Whoa," said Joe Scarborough. "That was some sad stuff." Cohost Mika Brzezinski was even more appalled. "That was sick," she added.

Listening to NPR that same morning, Ferguson heard more of the same. A scholar, troubled by the "display," told the NPR reporter, "That's a more common occurrence in nondemocratic regimes, which are trying to portray themselves as being popular."

Ferguson turned to the *New York Times* and got more of the same: "One by one, they said their names and—as if working to outdo one another—paid homage to Mr. Trump, describing how honored they were to serve in his administration." CNN was no better, no different. "Trump planned to have *every* Cabinet member speak," wrote the CNN reporter. "And when I say 'speak' what I really mean is 'praise

Trump for his accomplishments, his foresight, his just being awesome.' You think I am exaggerating. I am not."

Often happy to pile on, Ferguson decided to watch the entire twenty-five-minute introduction rather than just selective clips. Wrote Ferguson afterward, "I discovered that every story I had read or heard or seen that morning about the cabinet meeting was, as a whole, wrong or misleading, and in many particulars, just wrong."

By Ferguson's count, eleven of the twenty-three appointees did not mention Trump at all. Almost all who spoke of him did so appropriately. Wrote Ferguson, "The 'adulation' was all in the fevered imaginations of reporters."

Ferguson summed up the fake news phenomenon. "In the eyes of the bright young things who work in the White House press corps, with their faulty educations and unearned world-weariness," wrote Ferguson, "everything Trump does must be nefarious, and if not nefarious, at least vulgar and unprecedented. It just has to be. So it is. Even when it's not."

Attacking Fox

For all their power, the major media could not prevent their citadel from being breached in November 2016. The barbarians had gotten inside the gate. At their head was Donald Trump, the vulgarian-in-chief (from the Latin *vulgus*, "the people"). To pull Trump down, strategists on the left understood they would have to subvert the media that supported him, both corporate and *Samizdat*. The corporate part was the most vulnerable.

Immediately, the media sought to undo Trump's presidency. They were not even subtle about it. From the day Trump was elected, the major media assaulted him and his allies with a ferocity and consistency no other president had ever experienced. In a useful public service, the Kennedy School's Shorenstein Center on Media, Politics, and Public Policy at Harvard catalogued the abuse. At CNN, NBC, and CBS, more than 90 percent of Trump's coverage was negative during Trump's first hundred days, his presumed media "honeymoon." At the *New York Times,* that figure was 87 percent and at the *Washington Post,* 83 percent. At the German consortium ARD, the world's largest public broadcaster, the coverage of Trump was a frightening 98 percent negative.[1] The one outlier in the Shorenstein study was Fox News. Living up to its "fair and balanced" slogan, Fox registered 48 percent positive, about 40 percent too much for the *Pravda* crowd.

For years, Fox dominated cable news for one obvious reason: it was the only television news channel that respected the views of the conservative half of America. From the beginning of his presidency, Obama made a point of singling out Fox News. It was the one network that challenged him on issues that Fox's competitors preferred to ignore: Fast and Furious, the IRS targeting of Tea Parties, Obamacare, the Iran deal, even Benghazi. In June 2009, Obama began making his discontent known. "I've got one television station that is entirely devoted to attacking my administration," Obama complained.[2] Although he did not say "Fox" out loud, everyone in Washington got it.

In a 2010 *Rolling Stone* interview, Obama got down to specifics. Yes, the problem was Fox News. Prompted by publisher Jann Wenner, he described Fox as a throwback to a time before "the golden age of an objective press," a time when media moguls like William Randolph Hearst used their outlets "very intentionally to promote their viewpoints." From Obama's perspective, Fox's viewpoint was "ultimately destructive." That said, however, he could not deny that Fox had been "wildly successful."[3]

The attack on Fox News went beyond the rhetorical. In 2010, billionaire George Soros gave Media Matters $1 million specifically to target Fox. To Soros, Fox was public enemy number one, and he was not reluctant to say so. "I am supporting Media Matters in an effort to more widely publicize the challenge Fox News poses to civil and informed discourse in our democracy."[4] (There's that word "discourse" again.)

Beginning in that same year, Obama's Department of Justice secretly monitored the personal and professional communications of James Rosen, Fox's Washington correspondent. What was troubling about the specific case, which involved the monitoring of North Korea's nuclear program, was the willingness of the DOJ to use search warrants to investigate a reporter. Worse, its attorneys threatened to prosecute Rosen under the terms of the Espionage Act "as an aider, abettor and/or co-conspirator." Said First Amendment lawyer Charles Tobin, "Search warrants like these have a severe chilling effect on the free flow of important information to the public. That's a very dangerous road to go down."[5] No one much listened. Rosen was Fox News after all.

Coming into the 2016 election season, Fox executives, like those at Sinclair, had good reason to feel spooked. As I discussed earlier, they feared the various reprisals that might follow a Hillary Clinton victory,

especially given her history of lawlessness and her taste for revenge. Without a major push from Sean Hannity, it is unlikely our "Rigging" videos would ever have aired on Fox. Had Fox blinked, the other networks could have safely ignored our videos, and Scott Foval might still have his job.

When Trump unnerved Washington by winning, Obama, while still president, assigned a major part of the blame to Fox. He found it shocking, appalling really, that Fox News aired "in every bar and restaurant in big chunks of the country."[6] He seemed unaware that conservatives are exposed to liberal media every time they open their Yahoo! or AOL or Google accounts, every time they pass a newspaper rack or a magazine stand, every time they sit in an airport waiting area anywhere in America and are exposed to just one network, CNN.

As long as Fox News remained "wildly successful," however Obama and his allies would not be able to monopolize what these citizens saw and heard. No longer able to rely on the DOJ or the FC to achieve their ends, strategists on the left turned to their frien in the media, and they set out to break Fox News by the surest w possible—subverting its success. "The public has no idea of the exte to which news is influenced by smear merchants," said former C reporter Sharyl Attkisson. "They operate from a Byzantine playbook exploit today's weak-kneed and corporate owned media."[7]

The first Fox News rainmaker to be taken out was Bill O'Rei O'Reilly was big enough that the hit had to come from an entity w equal or greater clout, and who more likely to make a clean kill t the *New York Times*. The headline of an April 1, 2017, article Emily Steel and Michael Schmidt spoke to both the reason O'R was targeted and to the precise spot of O'Reilly's greatest vulner ity, "Bill O'Reilly Thrives at Fox News, Even as Harassment Se ments Add Up."[8]

The exhaustive article provided various charts and graphs to d ment O'Reilly's importance to the company's success. "His val the company is enormous," insisted the reporters. "From 2014 thr 2016, the show generated more than $446 million in advertising enues, according to the research firm Kantar Media." The dug deeper on this story than it had on Fast and Furious or th

targeting of the Tea Party. The reporters unearthed five women who accused O'Reilly of sexual harassment or other inappropriate behavior, fewer than they had found for Donald Trump but enough to cause headaches for Fox News.

To be sure, Fox News was not eager to dispense with O'Reilly. Its executives had already sacrificed the mastermind behind Fox News, Roger Ailes, on the altar of gender sensitivity, but Ailes was near the end of his career—and his life. O'Reilly still had many productive years in front of him.

Or so he thought. On April 19, Patriot's Day, the *Times* thrilled its readers with an article simply titled, "Bill O'Reilly Is Forced Out at Fox News."[9] Schmidt and Steel were pleased to report "that more than 50 advertisers had abandoned his show, and women's rights groups had called for him to be fired." They wrote this as though the protests against O'Reilly rose up spontaneously. They did not. Whatever the merits of the case against O'Reilly, the *Times* and its allies targeted him not for his behavior—he was a choirboy compared to *Times* heroes Bill Clinton and Ted Kennedy—but for his success. Through their popularity, O'Reilly and other Fox stars forced their way into public spaces, specifically those bars and restaurants in "chunks of the country" big enough to unsettle Barack Obama and deny Hillary Clinton the presidency.

With O'Reilly's scalp on their belt, the activists next went after Sean Hannity. They were helped by an unlikely collaborator, a semi-obscure pundit named Debbie Schlussel, best known for her hardline position against Islam. On Friday, April 21, two days after O'Reilly was fired, Schlussel claimed on an Oklahoma radio show that Hannity had once invited her back to his Detroit hotel room after a book signing.[10] In listening to her gossipy ramblings after the fact, I got the impression that she bore a grudge against everything Fox. Whatever Schlussel's motives, she played right into the hands of the anti-Fox media. By the time Monday rolled around, her accusations, often amplified, were everywhere. Unlike O'Reilly, however, Hannity was not vulnerable along this line of attack. Calling Schlussel's claim "100 percent false" and threatening to sue, he counterattacked so passionately he backed the media off.[11]

It was a strategic retreat. A month later, Media Matters took the lead in attacking Hannity for the content of his show. Unlike his peers in the major media, Hannity dared to inquire whether the unsolved shooting death of young DNC staffer Seth Rich on a Washington street might be related to the WikiLeaks investigation. For the major media, the real problem with the WikiLeaks angle was that it conflicted with their equally speculative claim that somehow Trump and Russia colluded to deny Hillary the presidency. When Hannity suggested that Rich may have been involved, he stepped on their narrative. Enter Media Matters stage left. Instead of making an effort to bring Rich's killer to justice, new Media Matters president Angelo Carusone posted a list of Hannity advertisers. His goal was to pressure them into dropping Hannity's show.

"I don't think that it is censorship if a company doesn't want to associate with or give money to a personality," said the always disingenuous Carusone.[12] He can call it what he wants, but the endgame of Media Matters and its allies was to secure *Pravda*-like control over all broadcast media, which is why Hannity refused to roll over. "This is an attempt to take me out," he said of the Media Matters effort. "This is a kill shot."[13] He lost several advertisers but held on.

Despite Trump's victory, I expect the crackdown to intensify.

As of this writing, the Republicans control Congress and the White House, but their power is an illusion and not much of one. Trump received only 4 percent of the votes in the District of Columbia and 11 percent of the votes in Manhattan. He did only slightly better in Hollywood and Silicon Valley, the money from both sources having gone almost exclusively to Hillary Clinton.

The totalitarians on the left still had their hands on the levers of media power, and now they were angry to boot. They could tweak their algorithms to keep us from trending on their social media sites. They could render critical words as "hate speech" and block discussions on those subjects. They could and did dismiss us as "fake" and assure their own partisans that everything we said or did had been "discredited." Long trained to ignore alternative sources, the partisans, more often than not, chose to accept uncritically their side's version of the truth, their *Pravda*.

This is not paranoia. In May 2016, the largely apolitical tech and science site Gizmodo reported in some depth how "Facebook workers routinely suppressed news stories of interest to conservative readers from the social network's influential 'trending' news section."[14] According to Gizmodo, the "news curators" were mostly young and Ivy educated. They not only imposed their own biases on the news, but they also followed instructions from above. They told Gizmodo "they were instructed to artificially 'inject' selected stories into the trending news module" regardless of whether there was any grassroots interest in the story.

The crackdown on the alternative media continues apace with that on the corporate media. In July 2016, in pure *Samizdat* spirit, Google senior engineer James Damore circulated a memo internally describing the company as an "ideological echo chamber" with a "politically correct monoculture," one that made dissent difficult. Damore quickly found out how difficult. "We strongly support the right of Googlers to express themselves," said CEO Sundar Pichai in a company-wide memo and then promptly fired Damore.[15]

Up the coast at Twitter, cofounder and current board member Evan Williams openly regretted what many of his colleagues surely felt. He saw the internet as "broken." He had believed the free exchange of ideas would make the world "a better place." Like so many of the self-declared elite, he convinced himself that his idea of a "better place" should be everyone's. Since it was obviously not, he blamed himself for allowing people the means to "speak freely." He was especially troubled that Trump would credit Twitter with his victory. "It's a very bad thing, Twitter's role in that," he lamented. "If it's true that he wouldn't be president if it weren't for Twitter, then yeah, I'm sorry."[16] That sorrow, widely shared, will likely translate to harassment throughout the *Samizdat,* but suppression will not come quickly or easily.

American Pravda

n 2017, progressives of one stripe or another had nearly complete control of academia, public education, the advertising industry, Broadway, Hollywood, the publishing industry, large newspapers and magazines, ESPN, the comedy shows, the TV networks, the major social media sites, and, most troubling of all, the deep state. Exceptions of consequence—Fox News, the *New York Post*, the *Washington Times*—could literally be counted on one hand. The statists functioned not as a monolith the way the Soviet apparatchiks once did but more as a cartel. Their power was not absolute, but it sure as hell was intimidating.

From Berkeley to Boston, all the good people knew what to think about race, about immigration, about gender, about sexual orientation, about Islam, about social justice, about the environment, about the economy, about the climate, and certainly about the president. Although the major media outlets positioned themselves as competitors, they rarely strayed from the party line and almost never challenged each other. When President Obama singled out Fox News, they piled on. When President Trump singled out CNN, they attacked President Trump.

Trump had many enemies of consequence, but none quite as ubiquitous as CNN. "CNN Airport," for instance, operates in forty-seven major airports across North America, twenty-four hours a day. Viewers cannot change the channel. Airport managers cannot change the channel. CNN plays in virtually every public space that shows the news except deep in the heartland. Perhaps more importantly, CNN owns the world. CNN president Jeff Zucker made this clear by way of a threat the day before Trump's inauguration. "One of the things I think this administration hasn't figured out yet is that there's only one television network that is seen in Beijing, Moscow, Seoul, Tokyo, Pyongyang, Baghdad, Tehran and Damascus—and that's CNN," said Zucker defiantly. "The perception of Donald Trump in capitals around the world is shaped, in many ways, by CNN. Continuing to have an adversarial relationship with that network is a mistake."[1]

At Project Veritas, our battle from the very beginning has been against the major media. If they had been doing their job, there would have been no need for our brand of journalism. Our synergy with Trump is founded not in shared ideology but in a shared understanding of the way the media work or do not work. The major media's contempt for what we do is based not on our methods, as they often claim, but on our targets.

When I spoke briefly at the DeploraBall on the eve of the inauguration in January 2017, I made our strategy clear: "Everyone's saying, 'Who are you going after next?' I'm going to tell you right now. I'm going to make it public. I'm going after the media next."[2] The cheers rattled the room. These people did not need Donald Trump to tell them that the major media had made themselves the enemy of the American people.

As I explained briefly to the DeploraBall crowd, we had already launched an initiative that we would come to call "American Pravda." A critical modifier here is the word "American." *Samizdat* media in America such as Project Veritas have protections that Soviet dissidents could not even dream of. We understand that. Post-election, we took advantage of the freedoms we have to infiltrate the major media newsrooms, including CNN's. If caught, we would only be embarrassed, not executed.

CNN's Zucker proved as good as his threats. As the Shorenstein study documented, no major media outlet attacked Trump as relentlessly as CNN. In the first hundred days, the traditional media honeymoon, CNN slammed the president in 93 percent of its reports on the presidency.[3] These were the domestic numbers. There is no reason to believe CNN treated Trump any more fairly in its broadcasts around the world.

The hostility toward Trump was so pervasive throughout the network that its people began to lose all sense of limits, most conspicuously comedian Kathy Griffin. Griffin, who had cohosted CNN's New Year's Eve coverage with Anderson Cooper for the previous decade, had herself photographed with the severed head—happily fake—of Donald Trump in hand. So grotesque was the image that she embarrassed her own side. Once CNN brass realized no one would come to Griffin's aid, they dumped her.[4]

After a more protracted deliberation, CNN also felt compelled to sever ties with Reza Aslan, the Iranian-born host of a series called *Believer with Reza Aslan*. A few days after the Griffin termination, Aslan felt secure enough in the CNN embrace to call President Trump "a piece of shit" and "an embarrassment to mankind" on Twitter. It took a week of social media pressure from the right before CNN dumped Aslan.[5] Despite its internal dynamics, CNN positioned itself to the outside world as a middle-of-the-road alternative to MSNBC and Fox News on either extreme. Griffin and Aslan were blowing CNN's cover.

On Monday, June 26, three "prominent" CNN journalists were forced to resign after CNN execs realized they could not substantiate their story on the ties of a Trump ally to Russia. "The resignations are a black eye at a sensitive moment for the news organization, which has emerged as a regular target of Mr. Trump and his supporters," lamented the *New York Times*. For Trump, the news came as vindication. "Wow," he tweeted, "CNN had to retract big story on 'Russia,' with 3 employees forced to resign. What about all the other phony stories they do? FAKE NEWS!"[6]

At Project Veritas we knew what pressure CNN journalists were under to produce stories. A few of them had been unwittingly telling our undercover reporters about that pressure for some time. The day following the resignation of the three CNN employees, we shared what they had been telling us in the first of the videos in our "American Pravda" series.

The next two weeks turned out to be one of the more troubling stretches in CNN history. Late on June 26, I teased the series on Twitter: "Independence Day is approaching, but this year the fireworks come early. Stay tuned."[7] As soon as that tweet went out, all of us at Project Veritas realized how far the soon-to-be-released story would reach and how hard it would hit CNN. In fact, the content was so compelling that footage from the first video was leaked onto Reddit by one of our partners in the alternative media the night before the official launch.

Reddit user Mikeroolz commented on the thread, "Monday, June 26th, 2017. MARK IT DOWN! This is the winningest day since November 8th, 2016."[8] Tons of comments and tweets echoed this exact sentiment in the span of an hour. I was gratified that the raw footage was rapidly making the rounds on the internet, but at the same time I wanted our fully produced video to be seen by as many people as possible. In the official video, I primed viewers to watch for subsequent releases. Without my commentary, we lose some control over the release pattern. At Project Veritas we adhere to the Breitbart "drip . . . drip . . . drip" rule. When the media deny the content of our videos or denigrate their impact, as they often do, we come back harder the next day. I wish we could just put good footage out there when we have it, but the media force me to play their game.

I reached out to a few contacts that were linking to the raw footage on Twitter and promised a live link to the fully produced video as soon as it was ready. They took down the bootleg video, and my production team rushed to make the final touches on the official one. Laura, now freelancing, was in the office getting behind-the-scenes access of the release for an article. The media ace that she is, Laura decided to livestream the moment I clicked "Publish" on our YouTube link. Optimistically, she ended the stream by saying, "Bye-bye, CNN."

In the first video, CNN supervising producer John Bonifield confirmed what we suspected, namely that CNN's relentless narrative linking Trump and his people to Russian meddling in the 2016 election was "mostly bullshit right now."[9] Admitted Bonifield, "I think the president is probably right to say, like, 'Look you are witch-hunting me. You have no smoking gun, you have no real proof.'" Although

Bonifield's beat was health reporting, he was well aware of the larger zeitgeist at CNN. "Just to give you some context," he told our reporter. "President Trump pulled out of the climate accords and for a day and a half we covered the climate accords. And the CEO of CNN [Zucker] said in our internal meeting, he said, 'Good job everybody covering the climate accords, but we're done with that. Let's get back to Russia.'"

There is a mix of motives as to why Zucker would push the Russian narrative. The most obvious was ratings. Bonifield acknowledged as much. He told us, "All the nice cutesy little ethics that used to get talked about in journalism school you're just like, 'That's adorable. That's adorable. This is a business.'" He did not exaggerate CNN's ratings success. The stretch during which the network pushed the Russian story most forcefully—February, March, and April 2017—represented the first time in fifteen years that CNN had been a top ten network for three consecutive months.[10]

As Bonifield was well aware, however, the Russian narrative would drive the ratings only if CNN viewers were eager to hear the president being criticized or worse. "I think there are a lot of liberal viewers who want to see Trump really get scrutinized," said Bonifield, "but I think if we had behaved that way with President Obama . . . I think our viewers would have been turned off." Not all of CNN viewers were "super liberal," Bonifield added, "just a lot of them." Feeding that audience a relentless Russian narrative meant, said Bonifield, that "Trump is good for business right now."

This video went wildly viral. It was the number-one trending video in the world that day and trended on Twitter as well. As of this writing nearly 3 million people have watched it on YouTube alone. That is roughly three times the average nightly audience for CNN's Anderson Cooper. Some people of influence took notice. One was President Trump. "Fake News CNN is looking at big management changes now that they got caught falsely pushing their phony Russian stories. Ratings way down!" he tweeted on June 27.[11]

Deputy Press Secretary Sarah Huckabee Sanders chimed in as well. "I would encourage everybody in this room, and frankly, everybody across the country to take a look at it," said Sanders of the "American

Pravda" video. "I think if it is accurate, I think it's a disgrace to all of media, to all of journalism. We've been going on this Russia-Trump hoax for the better part of a year now with no evidence of anything."[12]

CNN's Brian Stelter, the network's senior media correspondent, was also paying attention. "CNN PR just issued a statement about @JamesOKeefeIII's undercover video, noting that this staffer isn't involved in Russia or Trump coverage,"[13] he tweeted in an attempt at damage control. But that's exactly what we suspected he would say.

I replied to Stelter, "That's just the reaction we were expecting and it just punctuates the video we release about CNN tomorrow."[14] Stelter followed with another tweet quoting the same statement, "CNN stands by our medical producer John Bonifield. Diversity of personal opinion is what makes CNN strong, we welcome it & embrace it."[15] What CNN did not do was deny what Bonifield had said in the video. As to the "diversity of personal opinion" nonsense, that convinced no one.

Personally, I am glad Bonifield was retained. He was not the villain of the piece. His naked honesty was a refreshing contrast to the subsequent CNN spin. Besides, the most important thing to take away from this first video was not his insight into Russia but his insight into the culture of CNN.

As inevitably happens in Big Media, when one outlet is attacked, the others rush to its defense. On Stelter's CNN Show *Reliable Sources*, the *Baltimore Sun*'s media critic, David Zurawik, dismissed me as a "propagandist." This was a frequent charge and a perverse one. We do nothing but allow our targets to reveal themselves in their own words.

The *Washington Post*'s response a day after the Bonifield video aired was purely Pavlovian. The article by Paul Farhi, "What the Latest James O'Keefe Video Leaves Out," said almost nothing about Bonifield's comments or the culture of CNN.[16] Instead, it challenged the right of the *Samizdat* to question the major media cartel, our collective *Pravda*.

Allow me to add a disclaimer here. Although my name has become something of a brand, there is no longer any such thing as a "James O'Keefe" video. We have assembled an excellent team of journalists, technicians, and producers at Project Veritas. They do the work. I get the credit and, by extension, the abuse. Farhi was sparing with the former and overly generous with the latter. Did you know, for instance, that I have a "criminal record" and that our work has been "criticized for intentionally deceptive editing"? In fact, Farhi managed to squeeze into the article every misstep, real or imagined, that I have made in my humble nine-year career without even mentioning the missteps CNN had made within the *previous month*, missteps that led to the termination of Kathy Griffin, Reza Aslan, and three high-profile journalists. Twitter user Janene @justsickoflies cut right through the obfuscation, tweeting at Farhi: "Haha Right, but publishing articles with no sources, or unnamed sources, are more credible then a mans words on video. Shut up & sit down."[17]

Farhi made a broadside attack on undercover journalism in general and our brand of it in particular. Although I introduced and explained the Bonifield video in much the same fashion as any news anchor would, Farhi trivialized my role, calling me a "kind of master of ceremonies." As Farhi saw things, we failed to identify our undercover reporter or to name Bonifield's specific assignment at CNN. Then, too, said Farhi, I did not "disclose that Bonifield is based in Atlanta."

Of course, we did not reveal the identity of our undercover. Who would? We did not explain Bonifield's role in detail. It was not relevant. Working as he did at CNN company headquarters in Atlanta, he was fully exposed to the larger company culture. But how was the viewer to know Bonifield worked in Atlanta? That was easy. I said so right up front.

In response to an email from a reader who accused Fahri of lying, Farhi said something with which I agree, namely that there is a difference between making an error and lying. Farhi likely just erred. That said, the reader apparently touched a nerve. Farhi ended his response with the decidedly uncivil, "Apologize or drop dead."[18] I kind of tipped this whole episode to the absurd when I used the occasion of a Steven Crowder podcast interview to urge listeners to ask Farhi why he wasn't issuing a retraction.

I then put out another direct appeal to Farhi asking for a retraction. He tweeted back, "Sorry to disappoint you, folks. There is NO retraction coming."[19] I suspected there would be, and I was right. Late on Sunday night, July 2, the *Washington Post* added a retraction above the online Farhi article. Yes, the editors admitted, I did say Bonifield worked in Atlanta. We promptly framed the article and put it prominently on our office's "Wall of Shame" alongside previous retractions from the *Washington Post* and other members of the cartel.

A day after the Bonifield video dropped, we answered the critics like Stelter who claimed that since Bonifield was not "involved in Russia or Trump coverage," his opinion did not much matter. The same could not be said for Van Jones. One of CNN's most prominent political commentators, Jones had appeared on CNN in the past attacking President Trump for his "Putin relationship." In a more honest moment, Jones told one of our undercover reporters, "The Russia thing is just a big nothing burger."[20] It was one of the rare times this former leftist radical found common cause with President Trump. He said this unprompted but, when exposed, he claimed his comments were taken out of context. They were not. He also slammed our piece as "edited right-wing propaganda video."[21] He was right about "video," wrong about everything else. We did not edit his remark at all. A Twitter user, @argmachinetv, aptly summed up Jones's criticism—"Liberal hocus pocus. Just say 'edited' and you can disregard very obvious remarks that amount to a full on confession."[22]

Despite Jones's response, reality was starting to set in. Our friends and even our enemies were beginning to see the contradictions discussed throughout this book. Why indeed was CNN calling ours an "edited" video? As @NotPaxDickinson put it, "Have you ever seen media religiously describe a video as 'edited video' when reporting on ANYONE other than @JamesOKeefeIII?"[23]

The Van Jones video set the world of internet memes on fire. By the end of that day, the term "nothing burger" entered the public lexicon. One of our favorite memes read, "Welcome to CNN, home of the nothing burger, can I take your order?" The meme replaced the face of the clerk from *All That*'s famed "Good Burger" sketch with that of Jones. @PatrioticCovfefe tweeted, "How does @VanJones68 like his #Nothingburgers served? On hidden camera and spread with fake news! #CNN you're toast." Christopsy666 tweeted, "Is it acceptable to call Grilled Cheese a "#nothingburger" now? Y'know because grilled cheese has no protein." @RhondaRoseFlora tweeted, "I'll have one #RussianNothingBurger with extra RATINGS, please.! @VanJones68 @CNN #FakeNews."[24]

The Jones nothing burger video made the top of the Drudge Report and, like the Bonifield video, was the number-one trending video on YouTube that day. President Trump even embedded clips of our videos on his Instagram account, which at the time had more than 7 million followers. Even I got in on the nothing burger fun, tweeting, "My staff at @Project_Veritas is getting hungry. I think I'll get them a big order of nothing burgers. #FakeNews @CNN @VanJones68."[25] The whole world was paying attention to our videos, and CNN was starting to bleed.

We, on the other hand, were just warming up. Jimmy Carr, associate producer for CNN's *New Day*, shared with one of our undercovers what the CNN people in New York thought about President Trump and the people who elected him. "On the inside," said Carr, "we all recognize he is a clown, that he is hilariously unqualified for this. He's really bad at this and that he does not have America's best interests. We recognize he's just fucking crazy."[26]

When asked whether CNN was impartial, he smirked, "in theory." The reality varied dramatically from the theory. According to Carr, "90 percent of us are on board with just the fact that he's crazy." As to how Trump got elected, that was not too hard to figure. Said Carr about the voters, "They're stupid as shit." To kick off the day, I tweeted, "ACTION ITEM FOR YOU ALL: Tweet this video to @ChrisCuomo, @clarissaward at @NewDay."[27]

At this point CNN went silent on Twitter: Brian Stelter wasn't tweeting; Chris Cuomo wasn't tweeting anything. This was unusual for Cuomo, who is usually extremely engaged with his audience. He made not a single mention of our video, even though tens of thousands of Twitter users were slamming him and the producer of his we caught on tape. Some samples:

@Calideplorable1: "One sided outrage has no place here. The #MSM dishes it out buy cannot be on the receiving side. @ChrisCuomo needs to get it real!!!!"[28]

@Jayne720: "Comment? Are you reporters or opinion propaganda pushers? @clarissaward @ChrisCuomo @NewDay @CNN #FridayFeeling."[29]

Ohio Deplorable @JennStitts: "@ChrisCuomo still waiting on you to publicly denounce your producer's hateful comment about @ KellyannePolls you only comment on Trumps."[30]

Ohio Deplorable was referring to one additional comment made by Cuomo's producer. Carr volunteered that Trump advisor Kellyanne Conway "looks like she got hit with a shovel." As it happens, on the very day we released this video, the media, with CNN in the lead, were savaging Trump for the sexist remarks he made about MSNBC host Mika Brzezinski.

For good measure, in the Jimmy Carr video, we compared a finished piece by Alisyn Camerota speaking to a panel of Trump supporters with the raw audio provided by one of the panelists in the room during the segment's production. The audio showed that CNN had selectively edited the segment to make the Trump voters look, as Carr might say, "stupid as shit."[31] It was just another day on the job at CNN. For her selective-editing stunt, Camerota received a ton of criticism on Twitter:

@S_L_J730: "Editing tape is never helpful either Alyson. Wow you've sunk to the bottom #AmericanPravda #FakeNews."[32]

Paul Joseph Watson (@PrisonPlanet): "CNN caught editing out poll watcher's eyewitness testimony of voter fraud to characterize him as a conspiracy theorist. @JamesOKeefeIII."[33]

@DeplorableShay: "Care to comment @brianstelter? @jaketapper? @ChrisCuomo? @AlisynCamerota? We the #StupidAsShit people want answers. #AmericanPravda."[34]

@Spone63: "@AlisynCamerota @ChrisCuomo oooppsie ship be sinkin' #JeffZucker @TimeWarnerFdn."[35]

@Wtrogers4: "How you work for an unethical company?! @Alisyn-Camerota @ChrisCuomo you're all jokes!"[36]

@lilium479: "It's on tape, You Lied to America, Alisyn. BREAK-ING: new #AmericanPravda @CNN video is out NOW. https://youtu.be/4dRGMME4VnM @AlisynCamerota."[37]

@mrstsw01: "You are so outed—it's all 'bout that check, 'bout that check, isn't it, Alisyn? You have sold your soul for a paycheck. #AmericanPravda."[38]

Soon thereafter, Camerota deleted her Twitter account altogether. Although she did not mention Project Veritas, the timing was too perfect. In her Dear John letter, "Why I'm breaking up with Twitter," she wrote, "You've become mean and verbally abusive. In fact, you gross me out. You're a cesspool of spleen-venting from people who think it's acceptable to insult other people in public and anonymously."[39]

I guess Twitter stopped being a "safe space" for her. As to why neither Cuomo nor Camerota were willing to mention Veritas by name, our sources informed us of a corporate edict that instructed them not to. Our effectiveness had become something of an inverse Gandhi: first they fight you, *then* they ignore you—then you win.

The beauty of this particular part of our exposé was that we were able to level the same accusation of "selective editing" at CNN that Jones threw at us. The difference, of course, was that our accusation was substantive. The proof can be found in the video of the Camerota panel discussion when compared to the audio captured by a participant. Jones's "nothing burger" comment, on the other hand, was uncut and fully in context. We played our American Pravda videos like chess pieces, and we were always one move ahead of the media.

As a case in point, Jeremy Peters of the *New York Times* said to me of Bonifield, "He's just a health producer." I retorted by bringing up Van Jones. Peters minimized the importance of Jones, implying that Jones was not a serious political journalist. When I brought up Jimmy Carr, Cuomo's producer, Peters said, "Well CNN is just . . . ," basically changing the subject and insinuating that CNN is ridiculous.

The Peters conversation exemplifies two irrational, if predictable, reactions to our interaction with CNN. For one, journalists are inclined to change the subject when cornered in an argument. For another, they will highlight the job position of the unwitting whistle-blower as if position somehow negated content. The "health producer" worked in Atlanta. That is headquarters. He interacted with the CEO. If the cleaning lady had stumbled on a CEO memo, it would still count.

We could not take our eyes off the computer screens that week or ears off our phones. Tweets, Facebook messages, and YouTube comments were all flooding in with their own creative input. Stefan Molyneux, a friend of mine, tweeted, "Why is every fake news media coffee fetcher and each feminist with a poetry blog @verified while @JamesOKeefeIII and @JulianAssange are not?"[40] Law and Order USA tweeted, "#ProjectVeritas undercover reporters are doing what journalists used to do. Finding the truth & sharing it: essential pillar of democracy."[41] Comments like these keep us going.

If June was a bad month for CNN, July 4, 2017, was a terrible, horrible, no good, very bad day. CNN producers had no one to blame for the mess but themselves. Weary of Trump's teasing and our revelations, they decided to take their frustrations out on one hapless individual citizen. The fellow, a redditor, claimed to have contributed to an amusing little internet video that superimposed the CNN logo on the head of a wrestling promoter that Trump had body-slammed ringside a decade earlier. Trump's attack, of course, was clearly a prank, as was the internet video.

CNN did not find it amusing. Its producers hunted down the redditor and threatened to ruin him unless he made the kind of public confession Soviet citizens were routinely forced to make during the Great Terror. Stranger still, CNN bragged about what it had done. "How CNN Found the Reddit User behind the Trump Wrestling GIF," read the headline of a story by Andrew Kaczynski, head of CNN's investigative unit, the KFile.[42] CNN had a certain leverage on the redditor. He had apparently posted some racist comments as well under his perfectly Reddit name, "HanAssholeSolo." If the redditor worked for anyone other than himself, exposure by CNN would cost him his job. He had little choice but to cooperate.

In addition to apologizing for his racist comments, HanAssholeSolo groveled before the media cartel that held his future in its collective grip. "The meme was created purely as satire, it was not meant to be a call to violence against CNN or any other news affiliation," he wrote, adding, "I have the highest respect for the journalist community and they put their lives on the line every day with the jobs that they do in reporting the news." CNN accepted the terms of the redditor's surrender but only conditionally. Kaczynski's response was chilling: "CNN reserves the right to publish his identity should any of that change."[43]

The internet, including many left-leaning libertarian blogs, exploded in outrage. "#CNNBlackmail" was the top trending Twitter topic the day the story went public. "A multi-billion dollar TV network blackmailing a private citizen into not making funny videos about it is not journalism, CNN," tweeted Julian Assange.[44] The generally anti-Trump conservative publication *National Review* called CNN's action "a disturbing new precedent for a major media outlet."[45] And scores of citizens joined in making videos of their own mimicking the wrestling video and mocking CNN.

Once again, the major media colluded to protect one of their own. On the very day #CNNBlackmail was trending, the *New York Times* posted *two* articles defending the embattled network, one focusing on the controversy, the second on CNN CEO Jeff Zucker. Like many of its media allies, the *Times* saw CNN's actions as defensible but worthy of discussion. Reporter Daniel Victor framed the debate around whether CNN was right to withhold the name of the redditor.[46] He did not question why the network used its ample resources to hunt the man down and coerce a Lubyanka-worthy confession. That issue scarcely surfaced.

Victor gave the final word to Kaczynski supporter Ben Smith, the editor in chief of BuzzFeed, citing a Smith tweet, "[Kaczynski] is among the most careful, transparent reporters on the *internet. He's* never operated with the bad faith of ppl attacking him today."[47] Smith could not have conceived a neater way of ingratiating himself to CNN and getting his name into the *New York Times*. As to the intimidated redditor and the "ppl" defending him, who cared?

In his article on Zucker, Michael Grynbaum brushed off the blackmail scandal with a petty caveat, namely that some media critics thought intimidating HanAssholeSolo into silence was "an unusual choice."[48] The article focused instead on the "digital war" being waged against CNN by Trump and his supporters. "My job is to remind everyone that they need to stay focused doing their job," Zucker told Grynbaum. Said Zucker of Trump, "He's trying to bully us, and we're not going to let him intimidate us. You can't lose your confidence and let that change the way you conduct yourselves."[49]

Our CNN videos are rather the first installment in a series through which we will continue to expose the moral corruption of the mainstream media. On this note, @realDonaldTrump tweeted: "I am extremely pleased to see that @CNN has finally been exposed as #FakeNews and garbage journalism. It's about time!"[50] I wrote out a response to him, "Guess what, Mr. President. We still have a whole lot more coming, both about @CNN and exposing the entire rotten #FakeNews Media Complex."[51]

That same day, the president also tweeted, "So they caught Fake News CNN cold, but what about NBC, CBS, & ABC? What about the failing @nytimes & @washingtonpost? They are all Fake News!"[52] We are way ahead of him. I promise you that Project Veritas will continue to expose the media complex for what it is, unabashed American Pravda. To the patriots who support us, I thank you. The assault against the complex will forever be an uphill one, but with *veritas* as our guide and an army of supporters as our inspiration, may the Overton Window be thrown wide open.

This takes us back to where we began. The people reading the *New York Times* on July 5 actually *believed* that CNN treated the cowed redditor appropriately, that CNN reporters focused on doing solid objective journalism, and that the price for doing that job was to be bullied "by the leader of the free world." Back in the day, the readers of *Pravda* would not have believed this nonsense for a minute.

The *New York Times* was in for a shock or two of its own. On October 10, 2017, we dropped part one of our American Pravda series on the *Times*. The unwitting star of this video was the "audience strategy editor," Nick Dudich. As Dudich told our undercover, he was responsible for choosing which videos go on Facebook, YouTube, and Instagram, among other social media. He claimed to be the *Times*'s "gatekeeper" for its video content. Boasted Dudich, "My imprint is on every video we do."[53]

Journalists, according to the *Times*'s handbook on journalistic ethics, "may not do anything that damages The Times's reputation for strict neutrality in reporting on politics and government."[54] Having worked on both the Obama and Hillary Clinton campaigns, Dudich had no intention of honoring that commitment. "I will be *objective*," he told our u/c with undisguised sarcasm before revealing his true intentions. "No, I'm not. That's why I'm here." In fact, Dudich returned to journalism following Clinton's defeat for the purpose of remaining politically active: "After the Clinton campaign, I'm like, 'No I need to get back into news and keep doing shit because, like, this isn't going to change.'"[55]

"Journalists have no place on the playing fields of politics," so claim the *Times* editors in their handbook. "Staff members are entitled to vote, but they must do nothing that might raise questions about their professional neutrality or that of The Times."[56] That chapter seems to have been overlooked in Dudich's orientation.

Like many of his colleagues, perhaps all, Dudich was no fan of President Trump. To the degree that his job allowed him, he hoped to make Trump's life difficult. "I'd target his businesses, his dumb fuck of a son, Donald Jr., and Eric," he explained. He argued that the way to force Trump out of office was to "ruin the Trump brand." The way to ruin the brand was to launch investigations into his various businesses. "He cares about his business more than he cares about being president," said Dudich. "He would resign." That simple.

In a bizarre digression, Dudich tried to convince the Project Veritas reporter that former FBI head James Comey was his godfather: "Well, the Comey hearing, I should have recused myself, but I'm not ever telling anybody there [at the *Times*] that I have a tie with that or else I don't know if they can keep me on." Before running with this angle, we did a careful background check. It turns out Dudich was fibbing. "He's not James Comey's godson," Dudich's father told us. "I don't even know James Comey." For all his dissembling, Dudich was indeed a gatekeeper at the *Times*. That fact should be worrisome to the bosses at "the paper of record." We had to wonder who else they let spread misinformation in their name.

The *Times* responded in its "Reader Center" the same day we posted the first video. The spokeswoman, Danielle Rhoades Ha, did not say much. In her retelling, Dudich was a "recent hire in a junior position." That said, he appeared to have "violated our ethical standards."[57] A review was under way.

While the *New York Times* was assessing Dudich's future, we posted the second in this American Pravda series.[58] In this video, Dudich revealed how he worked with his friends at Facebook to limit damage on stories unfavorable to Facebook. "We actually just did a video about Facebook negatively, and I chose to put it in a spot that I knew wouldn't do well," he told us.

To get more information on insider trading, social media style, one of our undercovers spoke with Earnest Pettie, the brand and diversity curation lead at YouTube. A friend and former coworker of Dudich's at Fusion ABC, Pettie honored the friendship by maximizing exposure for videos produced by the *Times*. Yes, blind algorithms drive the process, at least in theory, but there are features within a story, said Pettie, that can be "definitely optimized for news." Pettie's technique was pretty simple. He deemed stories from the *Times* "legitimate" to position them front and center on a news carousel.

As part of its mission statement, YouTube insists that "people—not gatekeepers—decide what's popular."[59] Gatekeeper Pettie does appear, however, to be putting his thumb on the popularity scale. Dudich did not share his optimization secrets with his bosses. A pragmatist, he just wanted "to make it look like what [I] do is harder than what it is." Here's hoping his new bosses appreciate his initiative.

After the second "American Pravda" video was released, the *Times* executive editor Dean Baquet decided he had seen enough. Weighing in during a live-streamed *Times* forum, he seemed far less upset about what Dudich said than by how we recorded him saying it. "For those of you who saw it," Baquet said of the video, "it was an undercover operation in which James O'Keefe, who I think is a despicable person who runs a despicable operation. He essentially tries to catch people from what he sees as the left-wing media saying inappropriate things."[60]

It pays to remember that when the undercover video of Mitt Romney saying 47 percent of Americans are dependent on the government fell into the hands of the *Times*, the editors did not call the recording of that video "despicable." No, they praised the video as "offering a rare glimpse of [Romney's] personal views."[61] When the *Times* published the content of the eleven-year-old *Access Hollywood* video, neither Baquet nor anyone else at the *Times* expressed any concern about how the tape was secured or whether it was even legal. From all appearances, the *Times*'s overriding concern in October 2016 was to derail the Trump candidacy.[62]

As it happens, California, where the video was recorded, is a two-party consent state. On the Access Hollywood tapes, neither Trump nor his conversation partner, Billy Bush, knew they were being recorded.[63] Florida, where Romney was recorded, is also a two-party consent state. Romney was clearly unaware he was being secretly recorded. A Politico headline, a day after the story broke, addressed the issue head on: "Mitt Recording May Have Been Illegal."[64] The editors at the *Times* apparently did not care whether either video was legally secured or not.

The media can be selective about which videos they share with the public. In 2008, the *Los Angeles Times* famously refused to release a video of Barack Obama speaking extemporaneously at a farewell dinner for Palestinian radical Rashid Khalidi. Citing a confidentiality agreement between source and reporter, the *Times* has argued that journalistic ethics prevented the video's release.[65] I wonder, however, whether those ethics would have withstood the pressure to share something like the *Access Hollywood* tape. I think not.

Three days after our first *New York Times* video dropped, the paper of record announced a new set of guidelines for its journalists' use of social media. We like to think we had something to do with this, especially since it dealt specifically with Dudich's bailiwick. NPR thought so as well. The headline on its coverage of this change read, "New York Times Changes Social Media Policy after Claims of Bias."[66]

The new guidelines are a study in damage control. "If our journalists are perceived as biased or if they engage in editorializing on social media," reads the introduction, "that can undercut the credibility of the entire newsroom."[67] You think? The posted guidelines seem sincere and make sense. If honored, they have the potential to at least change the perception of the *Times*, but they will not change any hearts in the newsroom.

Writing in the *New York Post*, Karol Markowicz cited Project Veritas's Dudich videos as a possible inspiration for the new guidelines. Just as usefully, she sniffed out the contradiction at the heart of such a halfhearted reform. "The problem for the Gray Lady is that it can't have it both ways," Markowicz wrote. "If its reporters and editors are going to be overwhelmingly liberal and anti-Trump, as they clearly are, it's a bit dishonest for the paper to insist they pretend otherwise."[68]

On Monday, October 17, Baquet appeared at another one of these stuffy journalistic forums, this one the Kalb Report at the National Press Club. The subject at hand was "the administration's threats to press freedom." As expected, Baquet served up some ominous guff about President Trump. It was in the Q&A session that one of the journalists in attendance surprised us and, I expect, Baquet as well by inquiring into the American Pravda videos. Specifically, he asked Baquet whether he considered what we do "investigative journalism." Good question.

Not surprisingly, Baquet denied us the status of "journalist." He repeated his previous slander that I was "despicable" and insisted that all I wanted to do was "hurt some institutions and get some clicks." He came down particularly hard on me for "jeopardizing that kid's career." Baquet used the word "kid" to describe Dudich several times, both in this appearance and in the earlier live stream conversation. For the record, Dudich was twenty-eight years old at the time our videos were recorded. When they initiated their Watergate investigation, Woodward was twenty-nine and Bernstein was twenty-eight. For that matter, I was twenty-five when we "hurt" that institution formerly known as ACORN, the astonishingly corrupt institution the *Times* ignored for decades.

A real journalist, Baquet insisted, "has to have in his or her heart a desire to make society better."[69] *No*, I wanted to shout, *a real journalist wants to pursue the truth and let the citizens use that truth to build a better society.* Without intending, Baquet fingered his institution's fatal flaw. If his journalists think as he does, they sort and shape the news to realize their collective vision of a better society.

Des Shoe, the London-based senior staff editor for the *Times,* boasts of doing just that. As she told one of our British undercovers in London, she and her colleagues set out to subvert the Trump candidacy: "I think one of the things that maybe journalists were thinking about is like, 'Oh, if we write about him, about how insanely crazy he is and how ludicrous his policies are,' then maybe people will read it and be like, 'Oh wow, we shouldn't vote for him.'"[70]

Yes, she actually said that. Unlike Dudich, whom Baquet dismissed as a "recent hire," Shoe is a senior-level employee who has been with the *Times* since January 2009. More troubling than her views on Trump, whom she called "an oblivious idiot," were her views on Vice President Mike Pence. Her contempt for Pence was not personal but ideological. "If you impeach [Trump], then Pence becomes president, Mike Pence, who's fucking horrible," she told our u/c. "I think maybe, possibly worse than Trump."

The reason why the generally benign and well-respected Pence was "horrible," Shoe explained, was because "he's extremely, extremely religious." As an example of the deforming effect of Christianity, Pence, according to Shoe, "at one point backed a bill that hinted at conversion therapy for gay people, which is like electrocution, stuff like that." Even the left-leaning Snopes could not swallow that one. In its "What's False" category, Snopes writes, "Pence never stated that he supported the use of electric shocks or 'gay conversion' therapy."[71]

Over the years, the *Times* has quietly conceived a marketing strategy around its very biases. The paper, admitted Shoe, "is widely understood to be liberal leaning." The catch, she noted, was that "our main stories are supposed to be objective." To write objectively was "very difficult in this day and age" because readers expected to have their biases confirmed, and the business model was "built on what the readers want."

Post-election, like all liberal audiences, *Times* readers have hungered for news stories that portray Trump in a negative light. "Speaking on, you know, for the *New York Times,*" said Shoe, "our subscriptions have skyrocketed since [the election]. I mean, they call it the Trump bump." This sentiment was echoed by Nick Dudich. He explained, "I mean honestly, Trump has driven us more business than anybody else. Anytime he says 'failing,' we add a boost of subscribers."

As the reader will recall, CNN's John Bonifield said much the same thing. "I think there are a lot of liberal viewers who want to see Trump really get scrutinized," he told our undercover reporter in Atlanta, "but I think if we had behaved that way with President Obama, I think our viewers would have been turned off." He added, "Trump is good for business right now."

On October 18, my cameraman and I waited outside the Brooklyn home of the *Times*'s deputy managing editor, Clifford Levy, to get an update on the employment status of Nick Dudich and Des Shoe. Dudich's name had been removed from the *Times*'s phone directory. For that matter, it had been removed from LinkedIn. As I see it, Dudich and Shoe had made the mistake of telling the truth about the real *New York Times* and were likely to be punished for their honesty.

An inauspicious middle-aged man, as gray as the Gray Lady, Levy left his home on schedule. I tried my polite best to get him to answer a few salient questions but could not even get a "no comment" out of him. I finally asked him if he agreed with Dean Baquet's assessment of me as a "sinner," but he would not bite on that either. He scurried off in silence, but with at least half a sense of how the thousands of people the *Times* has hounded, deserving or otherwise, must have felt.

The following day, we dropped still another video, this one with a fair-minded IT consultant who has worked with the *New York Times* for twenty years. Although not involved in shaping the paper's editorial product, Todd Gordon has had a wide-ranging exposure to the company's corporate culture. When the Project Veritas undercover asked him if he ever met a Trump supporter at the *Times*, Gordon did not have to think hard to come up with an answer: "Not one, not one. Everyone hates him. They hate him like the plague, dude."[72]

The hatred for Trump is so universal and so visceral at the *Times* that there is no way it cannot deform the news coverage. As Todd Gordon, told us, "I'm like, 'Beautiful day today,' and they're like, 'As good as it could be, fuck Trump.' Everywhere I go, everywhere I go, they're like, 'As good as it could be, but we're fucked.'" When asked if this hatred causes the *Times* to report unfairly on Trump, Gordon responded, "100 percent, 100 percent!"

Shoe described the current state of affairs as a "conundrum." By skewing left, the major media have been cultivating an increasingly left-leaning audience. To preserve their credibility, however, the major media still have to feign objectivity. The problem is that if they actually practiced objective journalism, they would alienate the audience their slanted news has attracted. As a result, America's mainstream publishers and editors are living as much a lie as the publishers and editors at *Pravda*. Truth takes a back seat to money, and objectivity takes a back seat to politics. From the editors who dictate the paper's coverage to the journalists who sway the public with their reporting, corruption is inescapable. Indeed, it is part of the business model. I have to sympathize with the publishers of *Pravda*. They were working with a gun to their heads. Their American counterparts have no such excuse.

A more fundamental difference between the American Pravda and the Soviet original, however, is in the mind-set of their respective audiences. The readers of the *New York Times* want and need to be lied to and not just about President Trump. Those lies sustain their worldview and feed their anger on any number of issues. *Pravda* readers were much more jaded. They may not have known the truth, but after decades of manufactured news, they knew a lie when they saw one.

We judged the *Times* exposé to be a success. In exposing the paper's unsustainable conundrum, we inspired the paper's executive editor to respond to "Despicable Me" and forced the *Times* to change its social media policy. By and large, the *Times*'s allies in the major media pretended not to notice, but there were exceptions. *Newsweek* chose to slice and dice us with an editorial that began, "James O'Keefe Wants You to Think That He's a Journalist." Dean Baquet could not have said it better himself. Like so many others in the print media whose enterprise is sinking, *Newsweek*'s Alexander Nazaryan clings to the identity of "journalist" like a life vest.

Twitter, of course, was alive with sophomoric scorn from the blue checkmark crowd. Tweeted Erin Gloria Ryan of the Daily Beast, "lol an IT contractor has about as much knowledge of how editorial sourcing works as your average journalist has about tech support."[73] Of course we were not talking editorial with Gordon but corporate culture. After twenty years on the job, he seemed to have a handle on it.

In the way of explanation, Twitter gives out a "blue verified badge" in the form of a checkmark to those sources "determined to be an account of public interest." Ryan—"Scarin Gloria Ryan" as she is known on Twitter—has 2,500 followers on Twitter and a blue checkmark. I have 350,000 followers and no checkmark. This is the way Twitter works.

Long gone was the urge to debate these people. This was, after all, mid-October in Westchester County. Walking through the streets of Mamaroneck, the air brisk, the trees alive in their reds and yellows and ambers, I could reflect on why we do what we do. The people who live here are the people who make New York work. They are the ones who fight New York's fires, police its streets, conduct its trains, drive its cabs, teach its children, move its garbage. They have a better sense of the way the world turns than the people who think they turn it.

"You're that investigative reporter guy! Drinks on me," said a local bartender I had not seen before. "I watch all your stuff!" said a young man in my gym. "Aren't you afraid that they're going to try to harm you?" said a third person and a fourth and a fifth. This last question has become a constant refrain among the people who follow our work. Now in my early thirties, I have begun to start considering what that all means.

At Project Veritas, we wake up every morning with the humble and profound realization that the whole system—media, legal, political—is lined up against us. As much as I enjoy the battle, I wish it were otherwise. No one likes to be called "despicable." TV stations continue to spike our stories. The major media try their best to ignore us, hoping we have not infiltrated their newsrooms. The blue checkmark crowd watches from a distance, waiting to catch us in a misstep. When we confront their people on the street, as we did with the *Times*'s Clifford Levy and Dean Baquet, they slither away in silence. The big media win by shining light on others. They lose when the light shines on them.

We are quiet too, but in a different way. The one regular sound you will hear from Project Veritas is that of our videos dropping with more and more frequency. In a media universe crowded with opinion and conjecture, we offer the unguarded words of those on whom we report and just enough commentary to put those words in context. The way forward for us is not to get covered by the media but to become the media, not to sit at their table but to host the table where others sit. As long as I have the privilege of being allowed to share the truth with the American people, we will stick to our guiding philosophy. We don't need a handbook to explain it. We just need three words. *Content is king.*

Acknowledgments

I'd like to thank my mother and father, Deborah and James O'Keefe Jr., who were there for me in the beginning, who were by my side when there was nothing in me "except the will which says . . . hold on." I'd like to thank my sister, Amanda, who in the face of difficult and untrue accusations reminded me of who I am.

To Don and Dana of California who taught me how to vacation and relax once in a while. For Megan who stood with me during this incredible journey and listened to and comforted me through sleepless nights. Her presence in my life has been a great source of strength.

Thank you to all the Project Veritas staff for your extraordinary efforts every day. To the best media team imaginable: Stephen Gordon, Nick Evangelista, and Marco Bruno. To Joe Halderman, Project Veritas's executive producer, who helped build out a dynamic production department and produce world class investigations.

Thanks to all of our attorneys. This includes Ben Barr and Steve Klein on the constitutional litigation front, who protect us against frivolous lawsuits. They are not just fighting for *Veritas*. They are fighting for the First Amendment rights of all Americans to express themselves freely in the face of resistance from the government and well-funded opponents. Thanks too to Mark Smith and Greg Zimmer, our General Counsel, Jason Torchinsky on IRS and FEC compliance, Paul Calli and Michael Madigan on criminal defense, and Leonard Leo for his excellent guidance in areas related to lawyers and the law.

Although I cannot name them all here, I owe a major thank you to our undercover journalists–Allison Maas for helping change the course of human history through her steadfast work inside Bob Creamer's office, Laura for getting the story at all costs, and Christian Hartsock for the irreplaceable loyalty and friendship he has given me for the last nine years. Thanks to Dan Sandini for caring so deeply about fighting alongside me since the beginning in Oregon.

A big thanks to Russell Verney, executive director of Project Veritas, for building out Project Veritas into both c3 and c4 nonprofit corporations, chief operations officer Will Keiper for helping take our operations to the next level, chief of staff Tony Catanese for helping build the new world-class Project Veritas headquarters, and office manager Jen Kiyak for years of loyalty and dedication helping run the office smoothly.

Thanks as well to Adam Guillette and Austin i.e., "MMM" and Brandon Patterson for your nights on the road and on airplanes meeting with our thousands of small donors, allowing us to be completely independent. Thanks to those supporters contributing a hundred dollars at a time, allowing us to remain truly independent. Thanks to Luke "Murddakh" Escarpeta for always being a good sport and Gio Lopez for always getting me where I need to go. To Fredy Mfuko for your hard work when it was just me and you in a production room. To Spencer Meads, thanks for your continued loyalty and recruitment efforts.

Thanks so much to my Board of Directors and advisors, including Matt Tyrmand, who has become one of my best friends talking through items for hours late at night; George Skakel, Colin Sharkey, Dr. Rick Richards, Paul Martino, Eric O'Keefe, Dr. Bob Shillman, Jim Young, and Larry Keith—for your continued advice and counsel on running a professional organization.

I'd like to thank present and past members of the Trump White House, including Hope Hicks, Kellyanne Conway and Dan Scavino Jr., as well as others for all the work they do. I'd like to personally thank President Donald Trump, as well as his sons Don Jr. and Eric Trump for their help supporting my stories and bringing them to the national spotlight. I'd also like to thank Sebastian Gorka for his kind words about me during the election.

I'd also like to thank the people who helped with the book itself: Alex Hoyt, who reminded me to write a second book, and to the whole

staff of St. Martin's Press. Special thanks to Adam Bellow for his guid-
ance helping me craft it. A big thank you to Tracey Guest, Joe Rinaldi,
Sarah Bonamino, Paul Hochman, Laura Clark, Kevin Reilly, and Alan
Bradshaw for all their work.

A very special thank you to my long-time friend Jack Cashill for all
of your advice and ideas throughout the process of writing this book.

As always, Andrew Breitbart—who taught me to walk toward the
fire, who taught that narrative is controlled by the media and "the
media is everything," and all of the folks at Breitbart.com, including
Steve Bannon, Alex Marlow, Joel Pollak, Matt Boyle, and Larry Solov.

For all of those who have helped me and supported my stories over
the years, in no particular order, thank you so much:

Sean Hannity and Lynda McLaughlin, for taking the risk to run
our "Rigging the Election" stories before any other TV network bit on
them. Sean has become a true friend and a believer in Project Veritas. Thank you for telling me nearly a decade ago not to read online
comments.

Rush Limbaugh and James "Bo Snerdly" Golden, for believing in
the work we do. Thank you, thank you, thank you.

The original modern muckraker Matt Drudge, who throws lighter
fluid on our stories.

Julian Assange and Wikileaks, who helped expose the rotten political complex during the 2016 election.

Tucker Carlson and Vince Coglianese, for being true allies at The
Daily Caller.

Michael Savage, for having me on his show regularly and speaking
truth directly to the people always.

Gavin McInnes, for your friendship, your continued support, and
your ability to make me laugh.

Alex Jones and Paul Joseph Watson, for unapologetically punching
through the media.

Michelle Malkin and Nick Short, for your great investigative work
and integrity.

Jim Hoft and Lucian Wintrich, for playing the media.

Stefan Molyneux, for the fantastic conversations we have on your
show.

Andrew Klavan, for your astute reading of the current political climate.

Tomi Lahren, for your help in gaining coverage when we broke our stories in October 2016.

Geraldo Rivera, for the example you set in investigative journalism.

J. Christian Adams, Hans Von Sponovsky and the Heritage Foundation for your support in the fight to expose voter fraud.

Liz Wheeler, OANN, and Charles Herring and Robert Herring, who took a chance on us when they aired an hour-long documentary series about Project Veritas investigating the *New York Times*.

Valerie Richardson and the *Washington Times* for covering us fairly in print.

Sheriff Arvin West, who was our guide near the Rio Grande River and spoke to the failures at the border that our Osama-border video illustrated.

Congressman Steven King for grilling elected officials, including Attorney General Eric Holder, after we received their voting ballots without proving our identity.

Congressman Pete Sessions, for holding field hearings on our Obamacare videos.

James Rosen, for his fair coverage on Bob Creamer and Democracy Partners.

Pat Caddell, for having the courage to bring our story up on television before anyone else.

Roger Stone, for beating the drum always, and loudly.

Mike Cernovich, for being a pulse in the alternative news media, and for your great citizen journalism reporting from the 2016 Republican and Democrat National Conventions.

The entire Reddit Army from "The_Donald" subreddit, for connecting the dots in the Democracy Partners story.

Ann McElhinney and Phelim McAleer, for their excellent work in challenging news narratives.

Jordan Peterson, for being a beacon in the fight for truth against the postmodern deconstructionists, for providing the intellectual foundation for what we do.

To Navy Seal Marcus Luttrell, for his statement at the RNC convention that "Your war is here." Marcus inspired me to write a first book and his words inspire us at Project Veritas daily.

To my many inspirations, including the legendary investigative reporters of the '70s at *The Chicago Sun Times* and *The Chicago Tribune,* Clarence Jones, Tom Wolfe, Nellie Bly, Upton Sinclair, and Mike Wallace, we at Veritas thank you deeply. Your example is a constant inspiration and guide for what we hope will be a renaissance of what you did.

Specifically, Pam Zekman, Zay Smith, William Crawford, and Robert Unger of *The Chicago Sun Times* for their legendary undercover reporting that became an inspiration and a teaching exercise for our undercover journalists.

To G. K. Chesterton and F. A. Hayek, the sources of my worldview, who have helped guide my judgment and helped sustain my integrity in the fight for truth.

To Saul Alinsky, his son Dave, and Ralph Benko of the Alinsky Institute. *Rules for Radicals* is profoundly misunderstood. *Tactics* means doing what you can with what you have and making the enemy live up to its own book of rules. The Alinsky framework showed me how to punch up and win.

To Aleksandr Solzhenitsyn, whose writings helped me understand human nature under a corrupt regime and who showed me that the line between good and evil runs "right through every human heart."

To David Daleiden, who became one of my heroes for his patient, years-long undercover project into Planned Parenthood in 2015, and who boldly faced the fire.

To certain patriotic members of the intelligence community—the "quiet professionals" whose names I cannot share, who gave their time and expertise in the service of building the skill-sets of our undercover journalist recruits.

And finally, to the salt of the earth, the citizenry, the people forgotten by the mainstream media, you hold our shared destiny in your hands. We are just getting started. We will never give up.

Notes

Meeting Citizen Trump

1. Joel Pollak, "The Vetting—Exclusive—Obama's Literary Agent in 1991 Booklet: 'Born in Kenya and Raised in Indonesia and Hawaii,'" Breitbart News, May 17, 2012, http://www.breitbart.com/big-government/2012/05/17/the-vetting-barack-obama-literary-agent-1991-born-in-kenya-raised-indonesia-hawaii/.
2. Madeleine Morgenstern, "Literary Agent Responds to 'Born in Kenya' Obama Bio: 'Nothing More Than a Fact Checking Error,'" The Blaze, May 17, 2012, http://www.theblaze.com/news/2012/05/17/obama-literary-agent-responds-to-born-in-kenya-bio-nothing-more-than-a-fact-checking-error/.
3. Emily Stewart, "Donald Trump Rode $5 Billion in Free Media to the White House," The Street, November 20, 2016, https://www.thestreet.com/story/13896916/1/donald-trump-rode-5-billion-in-free-media-to-the-white-house.html.
4. Victor Davis Hanson, "The Anti-Trump Bourbons: Learning and Forgetting Nothing in Time for 2020," American Greatness, August 14, 2017, https://amgreatness.com/2017/08/14/anti-trump-bourbons-learning-forgetting-nothing-time-2020/.
5. Edward S. Herman and Noam Chomsky, *Manufacturing Consent: The Political Economy of the Mass Media* (New York: Knopf Doubleday Publishing, 2002), 306.
6. Rachel Kurzius, "Maps: Looking at How D.C. Voted, Precinct by Precinct," November 29, 2016, http://dcist.com/2016/11/maps_looking_at_how_dc_voted_precin.php.
7. Angelo Codevilla, "The Rise of Political Correctness," *Claremont Review of Books*, November 8, 2016, http://www.claremont.org/crb/article/the-rise-of-political-correctness/.
8. Victor Davis Hanson, "Virtual Virtue," American Greatness, September 5, 2017, https://amgreatness.com/2017/09/05/virtual-virtue/.
9. George Orwell, *1984* (New York: Houghton Mifflin Harcourt, 1977), 76.
10. The Center for Medical Progress, Documentary Web Series, http://www.centerformedicalprogress.org/human-capital/documentary-web-series/.
11. Eliza Collins, "Hillary Clinton: Planned Parenthood Videos 'Disturbing,'" Politico, July 29, 2015, http://www.politico.com/story/2015/07/hillary-clinton-questions-planned-parenthood-videos-disturbing-120768.
12. Dan Diamond, "Take Two: Obama Talks ACA in Florida," Politico, October 20, 2016, http://www.politico.com/tipsheets/politico-pulse/2016/10/take-two-obama-talks-aca-in-florida-216969.

13. Planned Parenthood (@PPact), Twitter, April 23, 2016, 10:08 a.m., https://twitter
     .com/ppact/status/723921395214733315.

Defining the Veritas Journalist

1. Ken Auletta, "Bribe, Seduce, Lie, Steal: Anything to Get the Story," *More,* March
    1977, 14.
2. "Who's a Journalist?" Creators.com, July 19, 2013, https://www.creators.com/read
    /daily-editorials/07/13/who-s-a-journalist.
3. S. 987—Free Flow of Information Act of 2013, https://www.congress.gov/bill/113th
    -congress/senate-bill/987. See appendix for complete bill.
4. Walter Lippmann, *Liberty and the News* (New York: Harcourt, Brace and Howe,
    1920), 13.
5. Jeffrey Olen, *Ethics in Journalism* (Upper Saddle River, NJ: Prentice-Hall, 1988), 7.
6. James Ettema, "Trying to Stir Public Awareness," *IRE Journal,* July 1, 1989.
7. Nathan Russell, "An Introduction to the Overton Window of Political Possibilities,"
    January 4, 2006, Mackinac.org, https://www.mackinac.org/7504.
8. Michael Uhlmann, "Bring Back Institutional Jealousy," Liberty Law Forum, August
    20, 2015, http://www.libertylawsite.org/liberty-forum/bring-back-institutional-jeal
    ousy/.
9. Charles Murray, *By the People: Rebuilding Liberty without Permission* (New York:
    Crown Forum, 2015).
10. James Ettema and Theodore Lewis Gasser, *Custodians of Conscience: Investigative
     Journalism and Public Virtue* (New York: Columbia University Press, 1998), 69.
11. Tim Dickinson, "Michael Hastings, 'Rolling Stone' Contributor, Dead at 33," *Rolling
     Stone,* June 18, 2013, http://www.rollingstone.com/politics/news/michael-hastings
     -rolling-stone-contributor-dead-at-33-20130618.
12. "Couric Wins Walter Cronkite Award," CBSNews.com, March 10, 2009, https://
     www.cbsnews.com/news/couric-wins-walter-cronkite-award/.
13. Peter Hermann, "Meetings of Activists Planning to Disrupt Inauguration Were
     Infiltrated by Conservative Group," *Washington Post,* January 25, 2017, https://www
     .washingtonpost.com/local/public-safety/meetings-of-activists-planning-to-disrupt
     -inauguration-were-infiltrated-by-conservative-media-group/2017/01/24/b22128fe
     -e19a-11e6-ba11-63c4b4fb5a63_story.html?utm_term=.e27cae1cc464.
14. ABC World News with Diane Sawyer, March 9, 2011, https://archive.org/details
     /KGO_20110310_013000_ABC_World_News_With_Diane_Sawyer.
15. Brentin Mock, "James O'Keefe Hustles Voters into Backing ID Laws," CBSNews.
     com, May 31, 2012, https://www.cbsnews.com/news/james-okeefe-hustles-voters
     -into-backing-id-laws/.
16. John Philpot Curran Quotes, Ireland Calling, http://ireland-calling.com/john-phil
     pot-curran-quotes/.
17. Paul Farhi, "Is It Okay for James O'Keefe's 'Investigative Reporting' to Rely on
     Deception?" *Washington Post,* October 19, 2016, https://www.washingtonpost.com
     /lifestyle/style/is-it-okay-for-james-okeefes-investigative-reporting-to-rely-on-decep
     tion/2016/10/19/f32fd46a-962e-11e6-9b7c-57290af48a49_story.html?utm_term=
     .d822dbaf98d5.
18. Joe Miller, "The Stimulus Bill and ACORN," February 6, 2009, FactCheck.org,
     http://www.factcheck.org/2009/02/the-stimulus-bill-and-acorn/.
19. "Lila Rose on The Factor with Bill O'Reilly and Leslie Marshall," YouTube.com,
     April 7, 2011, https://www.youtube.com/watch?v=TZeS0hVs5Qk.

20. All videos accessible at ACORN investigation, Project Veritas, http://projectveritas.com/acorn/.

21. Ed Driscoll, "The Abu Ghraib of the Great Society—Andrew Breitbart on ACORN," PJ Media, October 19, 2009, https://pjmedia.com/eddriscoll/2009/10/19/abu-ghraib-of-the-great-society/.

22. Noel Sheppard, "Jon Stewart Mocks Media on ACORN Story: 'Where the Hell Were You?'" NewsBusters, September 16, 2009, https://www.newsbusters.org/blogs/nb/noel-sheppard/2009/09/16/jon-stewart-mocks-media-acorn-story-where-hell-were-you.

23. Ian Urbina, "Acorn on Brink of Bankruptcy, Officials Say," *New York Times,* March 19, 2010, http://www.nytimes.com/2010/03/20/us/politics/20acorn.html?mcubz=0.

24. Chris Rovzar, "Just How Heavily Edited Was the ACORN-Sting Video?" *New York,* April 2, 2010, http://nymag.com/daily/intelligencer/2010/04/just_how_heavily_edited_was_th.html.

25. "Report of the Attorney General on the Activities of ACORN in California," April 1, 2010, http://ag.ca.gov/cms_attachments/press/pdfs/n1888_acorn_report.pdf.

26. Dan Eggen, "Obama Says ACORN Should Be Investigated," *Washington Post,* September 21, 2009, http://www.washingtonpost.com/wp-dyn/content/article/2009/09/20/AR2009092002313.html.

27. Clark Hoyt, "The Acorn Sting Revisited," *New York Times,* March 20, 2010, http://www.nytimes.com/2010/03/21/opinion/21pubed.html?mcubz=3.

28. NPR Investigation, Project Veritas, http://projectveritas.com/npr-videos/.

29. Michael Gerson, "The NPR Video and Political Dirty Tricks," *Washington Post,* March 17, 2011, https://www.washingtonpost.com/opinions/the-npr-video-and-political-dirty-tricks/2011/03/17/ABbyMym_story.html?utm_term=.1640bb567ffe.

30. Mona Charen, "O'Keefe Not Deceptive," NationalReview.com, March 18, 2011, http://www.nationalreview.com/corner/262470/okeefe-not-deceptive-mona-charen.

31. American Pravda Part 3, Project Veritas, http://projectveritas.com/2017/06/30/american-pravda-part-3-cnn-selectively-edits-hates-trump-and-think-voters-are-stupid/.

32. Greg Marx, "O'Keefe Etc.," *Columbia Journalism Review,* February 5, 2010, http://archives.cjr.org/campaign_desk/okeefe_etc.php.

33. "Danziger Bridge Officers Sentenced: 7 to 12 Years for Shooters, Cop in Cover-Up Gets 3," nola.com, April 21, 2016, http://www.nola.com/crime/index.ssf/2016/04/danziger_bridge_officers_sente.html.

34. "O'Keefe Exonerated," Internet Scofflaw, May 29, 2010, https://internetscofflaw.com/2010/05/29/okeefe-exonerated/.

35. Settlement Agreement and Release, Project Veritas, http://projectveritas.com/wp-content/uploads/2016/05/OKeefeVeraACORNSettlement.pdf. Italics added.

36. "ABC News Settles $1.9B 'Pink Slime' Lawsuit with Beef Products," FoxBusiness.com, June 28, 2017, http://www.foxbusiness.com/markets/2017/06/28/abc-news-settles-1-9b-pink-slime-lawsuit-with-beef-products.html.

37. Michael Parrish and Donald Nauss, "NBC Admits It Rigged Crash, Settles GM Suit," *Los Angeles Times,* February 10, 1993, http://articles.latimes.com/1993-02-10/news/mn-1335_1_gm-pickup.

38. Sydney Ember, "Sarah Palin's Defamation Suit against the New York Times Is Dismissed," *New York Times,* August 29, 2017, https://www.nytimes.com/2017/08/29/business/media/sarah-palin-lawsuit-new-york-times.html?mcubz=0&_r=0.

39. Eriq Gardner, "HBO Suffers Setback in Coal Baron's Defamation Lawsuit over John Oliver Segment," *Hollywood Reporter,* August 10, 2017, http://www.hollywoodreporter.com/thr-esq/hbo-suffers-setback-coal-barons-defamation-lawsuit-john-oliver-segment-1028555 http://www.hollywoodreporter.com/thr-esq/hbo-suffers-setback-coal-barons-defamation-lawsuit-john-oliver-segment-1028555.

40. Sydney Ember, "Rolling Stone to Pay $1.65 Million to Fraternity over Discredited Rape Story," *New York Times,* June 13, 2017, https://www.nytimes.com/2017/06/13/business/media/rape-uva-rolling-stone-frat.html?mcubz=0.

41. Kristine Phillips, "James O'Keefe's Undercover Video Stings Damaged Liberal Icons. Can a New Lawsuit Take Him Down?" *Washington Post,* June 8, 2017, https://www.washingtonpost.com/news/the-fix/wp/2017/06/08/james-okeefes-undercover-video-stings-damaged-liberal-icons-can-a-new-lawsuit-take-him-down/?utm_term=.1a26d35d9a15.

42. League of Conservation Voters, letter to Judge Xavier Beccera, August 4, 2017, https://www.lcv.org/wp-content/uploads/2017/08/Confidential-Complaint_CLCV_LCV-8.4.17-final.pdf. Italics added.

43. Darryl Fears and Carol D. Leonnig, "Duo in ACORN Videos Say Effort Was Independent," *Washington Post,* September 18, 2009, http://www.washingtonpost.com/wp-dyn/content/article/2009/09/17/AR2009091704805.html?sid=ST2011020203536.

44. "ACORN Just About Buried in Criticism," Associated Press, September 19, 2009, http://www.denverpost.com/2009/09/19/acorn-just-about-buried-in-criticism/.

45. "Washington Post Admits to Bogus Quote," Human Events, September 29, 2009, http://humanevents.com/2009/09/29/washington-post-admits-to-bogus-quote/.

46. Campbell Robertson and Liz Robbins, "4 Arrested in Phone Tampering at Landrieu Office," *New York Times,* January 26, 2010, http://www.nytimes.com/2010/01/27/us/politics/27landrieu.html?mcubz=0.

47. Carol D. Leonnig and Garance Franke-Ruta, "ACORN Foe Charged in Alleged Plot to Wiretap Landrieu," *Washington Post,* January 27, 2010, http://www.pressreader.com/usa/the-washington-post/20100127/282690453327843.

48. Corrected version of "wiretap" article: Carol D. Leonnig and Garance Franke-Ruta, "James O'Keefe Charged in Alleged Phone Tampering of Senator Mary Landrieu's Office," *Washington Post,* January 27, 2010, http://www.washingtonpost.com/wp-dyn/content/article/2010/01/26/AR2010012604145.html.

Crossing Borders

1. Alexander Bolton, "Reid: Southern Border Is Secure," The Hill, July 15, 2014, http://thehill.com/homenews/senate/212328-reid-southern-border-is-secure.

2. Stephen Dinan, "Hillary Clinton Says U.S.-Mexico Border Is Now Secure," *Washington Times,* March 17, 2016, http://www.washingtontimes.com/news/2016/mar/17/hillary-clinton-says-us-mexico-border-secure/.

3. This conversation was recorded on video, available on request.

4. Patterico, "Destroyed by Court Order: The Footage of a Landrieu Staffer Admitting the Senator's Office Had No Problem with Their Phones," Hot Air, May 29, 2010, https://hotair.com/archives/2010/05/29/destroyed-by-court-order-the-footage-of-a-landrieu-staffer-admitting-the-senators-office-had-no-problem-with-their-phones/.

5. This conversation was not recorded live, but notes were made immediately afterward.

6. Clip of Cyber Security and Terrorism Threats, C-SPAN, September 10, 2014, https://www.c-span.org/video/?c4508145/mccain-okeefe.

7. This conversation was not recorded live, but notes were made immediately afterward.

8. Alexis de Tocqueville, *Democracy in America*, part 1 (New York: Library of America, 1984), 105.

9. Project Veritas recording.

10. Ibid.

11. Timaeus, "UPDATED x2: Was It Correct for Customs to Detain James O'Keefe?" *Daily Kos,* June 23, 2015, http://www.dailykos.com/story/2015/6/23/1395778/-Was-It-Correct-For-Customs-To-Detain-James-O-Keefe.

12. Jonathan Turley, "Controversial Filmmaker O'Keefe Detained at Border by Customs," Jonathan Turley.org, June 24, 2015, https://jonathanturley.org/2015/06/24/controversial-filmmaker-okeefe-detained-at-border-by-customs/.

13. Project Veritas recording.

14. Paul Farhi, "Is It Okay for James O'Keefe's 'Investigative Reporting' to Rely on Deception?" *Washington Post,* October 19, 2016, https://www.washingtonpost.com/lifestyle/style/is-it-okay-for-james-okeefes-investigative-reporting-to-rely-on-deception/2016/10/19/f32fd46a-962e-11e6-9b7c-57290af48a49_story.html?utm_term=.d25de6aef8a1.

15. George Orwell, "Politics and the English Language," *The Collected Essays, Journalism and Letters of George Orwell* (New York: Harcourt, Brace, Jovanovich, 1968), 127–40.

16. Jerry Markon, "Conservative Video-Maker James O'Keefe: Homeland Security Targeted Me, Asked Intrusive Questions," *Washington Post,* August 13, 2105, https://www.washingtonpost.com/news/federal-eye/wp/2015/08/13/conservative-video-maker-james-okeefe-homeland-security-targeted-me-asked-intrusive-questions/?utm_term=.94f9d21a4c05.

17. Hugh Handeyside and Esha Bhandari, "Warrantless Border Searches of Smartphones Are Skyrocketing. We're Suing to Stop Them," ACLU, https://www.aclu.org/blog/privacy-technology/privacy-borders-and-checkpoints/warrantless-border-searches-smartphones-are.

Honoring a Tradition—The History of Journalism and Its Demise

1. Undercover Reporting, Deception for Journalism's Sake: A Database, NYU, http://dlib.nyu.edu/undercover/.

2. Theodore Roosevelt, speech, Washington, DC, April 14, 2006, http://izquotes.com/quote/393284.

3. Orrin Grey, "10 Days in a Madhouse: Nellie Bly's Living Nightmare," The Lineup, August 22, 2016, https://the-line-up.com/nellie-bly.

4. "James Aucoin, *The Evolution of American Journalism* (Columbia, Missouri: University of Missouri Press, 2005), 28–29.

5. Marthe Jocelyn, "*Scribbling Women": True Tales from Astonishing Lives* (Toronto: Tundra Books, 2011), 105.

6. William Mullen and George Bliss, "Poll Judge Violations Condoned in Election Office," *Chicago Tribune,* September 12, 1972, http://archives.chicagotribune.com/1972/09/12/page/2/article/poll-judge-violations-condoned-in-election-office.

7. "Willowbrook: The Last Great Disgrace," Geraldo, http://geraldo.com/page/willowbrook.

8. *Time* / Light Box, Erica Fahr Campbell, http://time.com/3808808/first-photo-electric-chair-execution/.

9. "Award-Winning Trib Reporter Bill Mullen Retires; Helped Uncover Voter Fraud," Crain's Chicago Business, February 10, 2012, http://www.chicagobusiness.com/article/20120210/BLOGS03/120219999/award-winning-trib-reporter-bill-mullen-retires-helped-uncover-voter-fraud.

10. Brooke Kroeger, *Undercover Reporting: The Truth about Deception* (Evanston, IL: Northwestern University Press, 2012), 73.

11. Michael Miner, "To Investigate and Advocate," *Chicago Reader,* July 15, 2010.
12. Jack Fuller, *News Values: Ideas for an Information Age* (Chicago: University of Chicago Press, 1997), 47.
13. "On the Media," WNYC, March 18, 2011, http://www.wnyc.org/story/133116-james -okeefe/.
14. Howard Kurtz, "NPR's Polarizing Shake-Up: Vivian Schiller Resigns over O'Keefe Video," Daily Beast, March 9, 2011, http://www.thedailybeast.com/nprs-polarizing -shake-up-vivian-schiller-resigns-over-okeefe-video.
15. Ben Shapiro (@benshapiro), Twitter, February 5, 2016, 8:03 a.m., https://twitter.com /benshapiro/status/695638866993115136?lang=en.

Swilling Chardonnay

1. Bob Steele, "Deception/Hidden Cameras Checklist," Poynter, July 5, 2002, https:// www.poynter.org/2002/deceptionhidden-cameras-checklist/744/.
2. Robert J. Casey, *Most Interesting People* (Indianapolis: Bobbs-Merrill Co., 1947), 78.
3. Philip Meyer, "Tricks of the Trade," Nieman Reports, http://niemanreports.org/arti cles/tricks-of-the-trade/.
4. Greg Marx, "The Ethics of Undercover Journalism," *Columbia Journalism Review,* February 4, 2010, http://archives.cjr.org/campaign_desk/the_ethics_of_undercover _journalism.php.
5. Andrew Jones, "Holder: 'No Proof Our Elections Are Marred' in Voter Fraud," Raw Story, March 13, 2012, https://www.rawstory.com/2012/03/holder-no-proof-our-ele ctions-are-marred-in-voter-fraud/amp/.
6. "To Catch a Journalist," Project Veritas, October 27, 2011, https://projectveritas .com/2011/10/27/to-catch-a-journalist-new-york-times-jay-rosen-clay-shirky/.
7. "About Us," Arthur L. Carter Journalism Institute at NYU, https://journalism.nyu .edu/about-us/.

Practicing Magic

1. David Samuels, "The Aspiring Novelist Who Became Obama's Foreign Policy Guru," *New York Times,* May 5, 2016, https://www.nytimes.com/2016/05/08/magazine/the -aspiring-novelist-who-became-obamas-foreign-policy-guru.html?_r=2.
2. Saul Alinsky, *Rules for Radicals: A Practical Primer for Realistic Radicals* (New York: Vintage Books, 1989), 126.
3. Stephen Gordon, "Undercover Common Core Video: Executive Says 'I hate kids, it's all about the money,'" Project Veritas, January 12, 2016, http://projectveritas .com/2016/01/12/undercover-common-core-video-executive-says-i-hate-kids-its-all -about-the-money/.
4. Laura Loomer, "Caught on Camera: Teachers Union Officials Advise Fraud to Cover Up Child Abuse," Project Veritas, June 7, 2016, http://projectveritas.com/2016/06/07 /caught-on-camera-teachers-union-officials-advise-fraud-to-cover-up-child-abuse/.
5. "Textbook Publisher Sacked Employee in O'Keefe Sting Video on Common Core," TPM, January 12, 2016, http://talkingpointsmemo.com/livewire/houghton-mifflin -harcourt-james-o-keefe-common-core.
6. Hezi Aris, "Yonkers Public School District Drop Charges of Misconduct against Yonkers Federation of Teachers President Pat Puleo," *Yonkers Tribune,* April 6, 2017, http://www.yonkerstribune.com/2017/04/yonkers-public-school-district-drop -charges-of-misconduct-against-yonkers-federation-of-teachers-president-pat-puleo -by-hezi-aris.

7. Bob Bowdon, writer and director, *The Cartel*, 2009, http://thecartelmovie.com.
8. Although the quote is often attributed to Jefferson, there is no documentation of the same.
9. James O'Keefe, *Breakthrough: Our Guerilla War to Expose Fraud and Save Democracy* (New York: Simon and Schuster, 2013), 210–18.
10. Kevin Sheehan and Carl Campanile, "Garner's Kid on Sharpton: 'He's All About the Money,'" *New York Post*, February 24, 2015, http://nypost.com/2015/02/24/eric-garners-daughter-on-al-sharpton-hes-all-about-the-money/.
11. "Undercover: Middle School Health Teacher Caught on Camera Offering Cocaine," Project Veritas, June 18, 2016, http://projectveritas.com/2016/06/18/undercover-middle-school-health-teacher-caught-on-camera-offering-cocaine/.
12. Ibid.
13. Alinsky, *Rules for Radicals*, 127.
14. *Glengarry Glen Ross*, dir. James Foley, 1992.
15. Hannah Parry, "Middle School Health Teacher Caught on Hidden Camera Offering Cocaine to Undercover Reporters and Boasting His Job Had Taught Him How to Avoid Getting Caught," *Daily Mail*, June 15, 2016, http://www.dailymail.co.uk/news/article-3643351/New-Jersey-middle-school-teacher-caught-camera-offering-cocaine-undercover-reporters.html.
16. Kala Kachmar and Alex Gecan, "Howell Teacher on Leave after Reported Drug Video," app.com, June 16, 2016, http://www.app.com/story/news/education/2016/06/16/howell-teacher-placed-leave-after-purportedly-offering-drugs-video/85986192/.
17. Alex Gecan, "Howell Cops Investigating Teacher, Hidden Camera 'Stunt,'" *USA Today*, June 17, 2016, https://www.usatoday.com/story/news/crime/jersey-mayhem/2016/06/17/howell-cops-investigating-teacher-hidden-camera-stunt/86029634/.
18. "Howell Happenings," Facebook, https://www.facebook.com/jack.cashill/posts/10212449065727793?notif_t=feedback_reaction_generic&notif_id=1489063352291772.

Meeting Candidate Trump

1. "High-Level Clinton Campaign Staff Caught on Video Knowingly Breaking the Law," Project Veritas, September 1, 2015, https://www.projectveritasaction.com/video/high-level-clinton-campaign-staff-caught-on-video-knowingly-breaking-the-law/.

Recognizing Propaganda

1. F. A., Hayek, *The Road to Serfdom* (New York: Routledge Classic, 2001), 164.
2. Edward Bernays, *Propaganda* (Brooklyn: Ig Publishing, 2005), 16.
3. Tim Hains, "MSNBC's Brzezinski: Trump Thinks He Can 'Control Exactly What People Think,' But That's 'Our Job.'" RealClearPolitics, February 22, 2017, https://www.realclearpolitics.com/video/2017/02/22/msnbcs_brzezinski_trump_thinks_he_can_control_exactly_what_people_think_but_thats_our_job.html.
4. Ibid.
5. Elihu Katz, *Personal Influence: The Part Played by People in the Flow of Mass Communications* (New York: Routledge, 2017), 3.
6. Hayek, *Road to Serfdom*, 166.
7. "Podesta Emails Showed Facebook Colluded with Clinton, Assange Reminds," Reuters, September 27, 2017, https://www.rt.com/usa/404971-assange-facebook-podesta-collusion/.

8. Will Rahn, "The Unbearable Smugness of the Press," CBS News, November 10, 2016, http://www.cbsnews.com/news/commentary-the-unbearable-smugness-of-the -press-presidential-election-2016/.

9. Hayek, p. 166.

10. Aleksandr Solzhenitsyn, "A World Split Apart," June 8, 1978, American Rhetoric, http://www.americanrhetoric.com/speeches/alexandersolzhenitsynharvard.htm.

11. Ibid.

12. David Ernst, "Donald Trump Is the First President to Turn Postmodernism against Itself," The Federalist, January 23, 2017, http://thefederalist.com/2017/01/23/donald -trump-first-president-turn-postmodernism/.

13. Hayek, p. 157.

14. Sophie Tatum, "Trump: NFL Owners Should Fire Players Who Protest the National Anthem," CNN, September 23, 2017, http://www.cnn.com/2017/09/22/politics/don ald-trump-alabama-nfl/index.html.

15. Michael McCarthy, "Why Didn't TV Networks Show Angry, Booing NFL Fans Sun- day or Monday?" *Sporting News,* September 28, 2017, http://www.sportingnews .com/nfl/news/nfl-tv-networks-deliberately-avoided-booing-fans-cbs-nbc-fox-espn -monday-night-football/wp37jk7eoiha1p7ktogwfftzs.

16. Hayek, p. 157.

17. Solzhenitsyn, "A World Split Apart."

Meeting Alan Schulkin

1. Laura Loomer, "NYC Democratic Election Commissioner 'I Think There Is a Lot of Voter Fraud,'" October 1, 2016, http://projectveritas.com/video/hidden-camera-nyc -democratic-election-commissioner-i-think-there-is-a-lot-of-voter-fraud/.

2. Gregory Mango, "Elections Official Caught on Video Blasting de Blasio's ID Pro- gram," *New York Post,* October 11, 2016, http://nypost.com/2016/10/11/elections -official-caught-on-video-blasting-de-blasios-id-program/.

3. Rich Calder and Carl Campanile, "De Blasio Demands Resignation of Elections Official Who Blasted ID Program," *New York Post,* October 14, 2016, http://nypost .com/2016/10/14/de-blasio-demands-resignation-of-elections-official-who-blasted -id-program/.

4. Despite the press, as of June 2017, Schulkin is still listed as a commissioner. http:// vote.nyc.ny.us/html/about/management.shtml.

5. Erin Durkin, "NYC Elections Commissioner Alan Schulkin Keeps Post until City Council Confirms Replacement," New York *Daily News,* January 3, 2017, http:// www.nydailynews.com/news/politics/nyc-elections-boss-post-city-oks-replacement -article-1.2933426. Italics added.

6. John Fund and Hans von Spakovsky, *Who's Counting? How Fraudsters and Bureau- crats Put Your Vote at Risk* (New York: Encounter Books, 2012), 48.

7. Ibid.

8. Ibid., 49–50.

9. B. Drummond Ayres, "St. Louis Sees Specter of Vote Fraud," *New York Times,* March 4, 2001, http://www.nytimes.com/2001/03/04/us/st-louis-sees-specter-of-vote -fraud.html?mcubz=0.

Channeling Chicago

1. The conversations that follow can be seen in the "Rigging the Election" series. Video I, October 17, 2016, https://www.projectveritasaction.com/2016/10/17/rigging

-the-election-video-i-clinton-campaign-and-dnc-incite-violence-at-trump-rallies/. Video II, October 18, 2016, https://www.projectveritasaction.com/2016/10/18/rig ging-the-election-video-ii-mass-voter-fraud/. Video III, October 26, 2016, https:// www.projectveritasaction.com/2016/10/26/rigging-the-election-video-iii-creamer -confirms-hillary-clinton-involvement/. Video IV, October 27, 2016, https://www .projectveritasaction.com/2016/10/26/rigging-the-election-video-iii-creamer-con firms-hillary-clinton-involvement/.

2. Project Veritas recording.

Going Deep

1. Allison Maass, "You Can't Make Fun of Terrorists at the U. of Minnesota," Campus-Reform, March 3, 2015 https://www.campusreform.org/?ID=6329.
2. Project Veritas recording.
3. Project Veritas recording.
4. Monica Davey and Julie Bosman, "Donald Trump's Rally in Chicago Canceled after Violent Scuffles," *New York Times,* March 11, 2016, https://www.nytimes.com /2016/03/12/us/trump-rally-in-chicago-canceled-after-violent-scuffles.html?_r=0.
5. Ibid.
6. Project Veritas recording.
7. Jacob Gershman, "DNC Cuts Ties with 'Donald Ducks,'" *Wall Street Journal,* September 8, 2016, https://blogs.wsj.com/law/2016/09/08/dnc-cuts-ties-with-donald-ducks/.
8. Project Veritas recording.
9. Democracy Partners, http://www.democracypartners.com.
10. "Congresswoman's Husband Pleads Guilty to Two Felonies," *USA Today,* August 31, 2005, https://usatoday30.usatoday.com/news/washington/2005-08-31-congress woman-husband_x.htm.

Pulling Back the Curtain

1. "Barbara Jordan's Vision of Immigration Reform," NumbersUSA, October 7, 2015, https://www.numbersusa.com/resource-article/barbara-jordans-vision-immigration -reform.
2. WikiLeaks, https://wikileaks.org/podesta-emails/emailid/3833.
3. Project Veritas recording.

Counting Down

1. Aaron Adelson, "69-Year-Old Woman Allegedly Punched in Face by Trump Supporter outside NC Rally," WLOS, updated May 9, 2017, http://wlos.com/news /local/69-year-old-woman-punched-in-face-outside-rally-by-trump-supporter.
2. Ibid.

Always Be Closing

1. Project Veritas recording.
2. Natalie Shutler, "Cesar Vargas Is New York's First Openly Undocumented Lawyer," Vice.com, November 14, 2016, https://www.vice.com/en_us/article/5gqda3/cesar-var gas-is-new-yorks-first-openly-undocumented-lawyer-v23n8.
3. Project Veritas recording.
4. Project Veritas recording.
5. Project Veritas recording.

Banned from Twitter

1. Project Veritas recording.
2. Zeke Miller, "Democratic Senate Campaign Catches Conservative Infiltrator," *Time*, August 7, 2016, http://time.com/4456711/democratic-senate-campaign-catches-con servative-infiltrator/.
3. Project Veritas recording.
4. Lacey Rose and Marisa Guthrie, "Bill Bush Breaks His Silence on Trump, the 'Access Hollywood' Tape, NBC, and a Comeback Plan," *Hollywood Reporter*, May 21, 2017, http://www.hollywoodreporter.com/features/billy-bush-breaks-his-silence-trump -access-hollywood-tape-nbc-a-comeback-plan-1005744.
5. "Caught on Camera: Clinton Staffer Says I Could 'Grab [Her] Ass' and Not Get Fired; Ripping Up Ballots Is 'Fine,'" Project Veritas, October 12, 2016, http://daily caller.com/2016/10/12/hidden-cam-clinton-staffer-brags-i-could-grab-coworkers -ass-and-not-get-fired-video/.
6. #Grabthembytheass!, Twitter, October 12, 2016, https://twitter.com/hashtag/grab thembytheass.
7. Original was deleted, captured on reddit.com, https://www.reddit.com/r/KotakuIn Action/comments/57fvy5/to_reactive_twitter_account_james_okeefe_forced/.
8. James O'Keefe, Twitter, October 12, 2016, https://twitter.com/jamesokeefeiii/status /786263324036136960.
9. Abby Ohlheiser, "Just How Offensive Did Milo Yiannopoulos Have to Be to Get Banned from Twitter?" *Washington Post*, July 21, 2016, https://www.washington post.com/news/the-intersect/wp/2016/07/21/what-it-takes-to-get-banned-from -twitter/?utm_term=.f85600098c0f.
10. Jim Hoft, "Breaking: James O'Keefe Is Locked Out of Twitter," Gateway Pundit, October 12, 2016, http://www.thegatewaypundit.com/2016/10/breaking-james-oke efe-locked-twitter-posting-videos-exposing-corruption-video/.
11. MYBOYSPLAYBALL TWITTERFEED, October 14, 2016, http://myboysplayball .com/2012/10/30/and-the-bullet-takes-aim/.
12. Real Jack, Twitter, October 12, 2016, https://twitter.com/RealJack.
13. Frank Flag, Twitter, October 15, 2016, https://twitter.com/rightlyaligned/status /787155913123606529.
14. Garbage Kekistani, Twitter, October 13, 2016, https://twitter.com/Kekistani_Proud /status/786637198057676800.
15. Guy Benson, Twitter, October 12, 2016, https://twitter.com/guypbenson/status /786417248629993473.
16. "CLASSY: Kathy Griffin Tweet about Sarah Palin from 2009 Shows She's Been Attacking Kids for Years," Twitchy.com, June 4, 2017, http://twitchy.com/samj -3930/2017/06/04/classy-kathy-griffin-tweet-about-sarah-palin-from-2009-shows -shes-been-attacking-kids-for-years/.
17. Alex Pfeiffer, "Twitter Forces O'Keefe to Delete Tweet Critical of Hillary Staffer in Order to Get Account Back," *Daily Caller*, October 13, 2016, http://dailycaller .com/2016/10/13/twitter-forces-okeefe-to-delete-tweet-critical-of-hillary-staffer-in -order-to-get-account-back/.
18. About Twitter, https://about.twitter.com/company.

Closing Up Shop

1. Wikipedia, https://en.wikipedia.org/wiki/Cut-out (espionage).

2. Chris Kahn, "Clinton Leads by 7 Points as Trump Faces Grope Claims," Reuters, October 14, 2017, http://www.reuters.com/article/us-usa-election-poll-idUSKBN12E2CS.
3. Joe Schoffstall, "David Brock Offers Money for New Dirt on Donald Trump," *Washington Free Beacon*, September 15, 2016, http://freebeacon.com/politics/david-brock-offers-money-new-dirt-donald-trump/.
4. Alex Seitz-Wald, "Democratic Super PAC to Pay for Dirt on Donald Trump," NBC News, September 15, 2016, http://www.nbcnews.com/politics/2016-election/democratic-super-pac-pay-trump-dirt-n648591.

Spiking the News

1. This call was put on speaker and recorded on video.

Breaking Through

1. James O'Keefe, Twitter, October 16, 2016, https://twitter.com/JamesOKeefeIII.
2. Gavin McInnes, Twitter, October 17, 2016, https://twitter.com/Gavin_McInnes.
3. Ethan Porter, "Drudge Has Lost His Touch," *Columbia Journalism Review*, September 2009, http://archives.cjr.org/feature/drudge_has_lost_his_touch.php.
4. "Post Sex Story about Clinton Gets the Spike," *Washington Times*, March 25, 1994.
5. Michael Isikoff, *Uncovering Clinton: A Reporter's Story* (New York: Three Rivers Press, 2000).
6. "History of University of Virginia on the Web," University of Virginia, http://www.virginia.edu/virginia/archive/webstats.html.
7. Edward S. Herman and Noam Chomsky, *Manufacturing Consent: The Political Economy of the Mass Media* (New York: Knopf Doubleday Publishing, 2002), 19.
8. James O'Keefe, Twitter, October 17, 2016, https://twitter.com/jamesokeefeiii/status/788140510749814786.
9. Jake Tapper, Twitter, October 17, 2016, https://twitter.com/search?q=Jake%20Tapper&src=typd.
10. James O'Keefe, Twitter, October 17, 2016, https://twitter.com/JamesOKeefeIII/status/788151933278322688.
11. Brit Hume, Twitter, October 17, 2016, https://twitter.com/brithume/status/788143729383055360?lang=en.
12. Brit Hume, Twitter, October 17, 2016, https://twitter.com/brithume/status/788162054016249856?lang=eu.
13. James O'Keefe, Twitter, October 17, 2016, https://twitter.com/i/web/status/788173578399313920.
14. James O'Keefe, Twitter, October 17, 2016, https://twitter.com/JamesOKeefeIII/status/821141663347277824.
15. Bret Baier, Twitter, October 17, 2016, https://twitter.com/search?q=Bret%20Baier&src=typd.
16. James O'Keefe, Twitter, October 17, 2016, https://twitter.com/jamesokeefeiii/status/788214349408108545?lang=en.
17. Charlie Kirk, Twitter, October 17, 2016, https://twitter.com/charliekirk11/status/788207283981291520.
18. "Make No Mistake: Leftists Are to Blame for Anarchy at Trump Rallies," *The Rush Limbaugh Show*, March 14, 2016, https://www.rushlimbaugh.com/daily/2016/03/14/make_no_mistake_leftists_are_to_blame_for_anarchy_at_trump_rallies/.

19. *Anderson Cooper 360,* October 18, 2017, https://archive.org/details/CNNW_20 161019_040000_Anderson_Cooper_360.

Weaponized Autism

1. Jacob Silverman, "Is Charles Johnson a Digital Darth Vader?" Politico, December 11, 2014, http://www.politico.com/magazine/story/2014/12/charles-johnson-a-digital -darth-vader-113522.
2. Welcome to /r/IAmA, https://www.reddit.com/r/IAmA/wiki/pages/.
3. 00Spartacus, "Hi, I'm James O'Keefe. Ask me anything!" reddit.com, https://www .reddit.com/r/The_Donald/comments/57jd2p/hi_im_james_okeefe_ask_me_any thing/.
4. Ibid.
5. James O'Keefe, Twitter, October 10, 2016, https://twitter.com/jamesokeefeiii/status /785573385308962818?lang=en.
6. Cybork91, Twitter, October 10, 2016, https://twitter.com/search?q=Cybork91&src =typd.
7. James O'Keefe, Twitter, October 10, 2016, https://twitter.com/jamesokeefeiii/status /785586566710304769?lang=en.
8. Melissa Gott, Twitter, September 28, 2016, https://twitter.com/MelissaGottNC/sta tus/781263168773431296.
9. James O'Keefe, Twitter, September 28, 2016, https://twitter.com/jamesokeefeiii /status/781263804948774912?lang=en.
10. Project Veritas Action, "Major Hillary Donor Inside Dem Fundraiser: Blacks Are "Seriously F°°°ed in The Head," YouTube, November 2, 2016, https://www.youtube .com/watch?v=j1L1gNUPbTw.
11. Thomas Friedman, "Online and Scared," *New York Times,* January 11, 2017, https:// www.nytimes.com/2017/01/11/opinion/online-and-scared.html?mcubz=3&_r=0. Friedman had used this phrase as early as 2009 on *Meet the Press.*
12. Anonymous, 4chan, October 27, 2016, https://archive.4plebs.org/pol/thread/94792 066/.
13. PrinceCamelton, "TONIGHT: James O'Keefe, award winning journalist and writer, will be joining us for AMA at 7:30 PM EDT!!" reddit.com, https://www.reddit .com/r/The_Donald/comments/57izps/tonight_james_okeefe_award_winning _journalist_and/.
14. "Hi, I'm James O'Keefe. Ask me anything!" Reddit.com, https://www.reddit.com/r /The_Donald/comments/57jd2p/hi_im_james_okeefe_ask_me_anything/ (all four citations).
15. "Rigging the Election" series. Video I, October 17, 2016, https://www.projectveritas action.com/2016/10/17/rigging-the-election-video-i-clinton-campaign-and-dnc-in cite-violence-at-trump-rallies/.
16. Reddit.com, https://www.reddit.com/r/The_Donald/comments/589pa4/zulema_rod riguez_the_female_riot_activist_in_the/d8ymyp2/.
17. Thomas Kennedy, "Donald Trump's Cuban-American Problem," *Huffington Post,* October 4, 2016, http://archive.is/FPhIw#selection-3097.193-3097.199.
18. Reddit.com, https://www.reddit.com/r/The_Donald/comments/589pa4/zulema_rod riguez_the_female_riot_activist_in_the/d8ymyp2/.
19. Reddit.com, https://www.reddit.com/r/The_Donald/comments/589pa4/zulema_rod riguez_the_female_riot_activist_in_the/.
20. WikiLeaks, https://wikileaks.org/dnc-emails/emailid/12012.

21. Reddit.com, https://www.reddit.com/r/The_Donald/comments/58f9kx/i_just_disco vered_more_proof_verifying_statements/.

22. Reddit.com, https://www.reddit.com/r/The_Donald/comments/5809hx/i_found_pr oof_that_the_hillary_campaign_had_the/?limit=500.

23. Reddit.com, https://www.reddit.com/r/The_Donald/comments/589pa4/zulema_rod riguez_the_female_riot_activist_in_the/d8ymyp2/.

24. WikiLeaks, https://wikileaks.org/dnc-emails/emailid/3934.

25. Reddit.com, https://www.reddit.com/r/The_Donald/comments/5809hx/i_found_pr oof_that_the_hillary_campaign_had_the/?limit=500.

26. Reddit.com, https://www.reddit.com/r/The_Donald/comments/5809hx/i_found_ proof_that_the_hillary_campaign_had_the/?limit=500.

27. Blake Neff, "Activist Who Took Credit for Violent Chicago Protests Was on Hillary's Payroll," *Daily Caller,* October 8, 2016, http://dailycaller.com/2016/10/18/activist -who-took-credit-for-violent-chicago-protests-was-on-hillarys-payroll/.

28. Colorado-living, Hi, I'm James O'Keefe. Ask me anything! https://www.reddit.com /r/The_Donald/comments/57jd2p/hi_im_james_okeefe_ask_me_anything/.

29. Rebrn.com, http://rebrn.com/re/the-fired-robert-creamer-was-a-wh-regular-frequen tly-visiting-ob-2902980/.

30. James O'Keefe, Twitter, October 20, 2016, https://twitter.com/jamesokeefeiii/status /789164209711882240?lang=en.

Going Viral in Vegas

1. Alan Rappeport, "Right-Wing Video Suggests D.N.C. Contractors Schemed to Incite Chaos at Donald Trump Rallies," *New York Times,* October 19, 2016, https://www .nytimes.com/2016/10/20/us/politics/dnc-video-trump-rallies.html?_r=0.

2. Wayne Dupree, "CNN Labels O'Keefe a 'Criminal, Convicted Criminal'; Crowd Responds!" waynedupree.com, October 18, 2016, http://waynedupree.com/cnn -labels-okeefe-a-criminal-convicted-criminal-crowd-responds/.

3. The Center for Medical Progress, http://www.centerformedicalprogress.org/2015/08 /intact-fetal-cadavers-at-20-weeks-just-a-matter-of-line-items-at-planned-parent hood-tx-mega-center-abortion-docs-can-make-it-happen/.

4. Adam Raymond, "James O'Keefe's Latest Videos Cost Two Dem Operatives Their Jobs," *New York,* October 19, 2016, http://nymag.com/daily/intelligencer/2016/10 /james-okeefes-latest-costs-two-dem-operatives-their-jobs.html.

5. Susan Crabtree, "Earnest Dodges on Dem Operative Visits to White House," *Washington Examiner,* October 19. 2016, http://www.washingtonexaminer.com/earnest -dodges-on-dem-operative-visits-to-white-house/article/2605006.

6. James O'Keefe, Twitter, October 19, 2016, https://twitter.com/jamesokeefeiii/status /788898459067613184?lang=bg.

7. Dave Weigel, "Scott Walker, Other Republicans Tread Lightly on O'Keefe Video Sting," *Washington Post,* October 19, 2016, https://www.washingtonpost.com/news /post-politics/wp/2016/10/19/scott-walker-other-republicans-tread-lightly-on-okeefe -video-sting/?utm_term=.1392fc9fc98c.

8. James O'Keefe, Twitter, October 19, 2016, https://twitter.com/jamesokeefeiii/status /788755564302065664?lang=en.

9. David Weigel, Twitter, October 19, 2016, https://twitter.com/daveweigel/status/78 8761437464330241.

10. Eugene Kim, "The Washington Post Plans to Add $100 million in Annual Revenue by Selling Software," *Business Insider,* June 28, 2016, http://www.businessinsider .com/washington-post-cms-revenue-plans-2016-6.

11. James O'Keefe, Twitter, October 19, 2016, https://twitter.com/jamesokeefeiii/status
/788765697786519552?lang=en.
12. "Full Transcript: Third 2016 Presidential Debate," Politico, October 20, 2016,
http://www.politico.com/story/2016/10/full-transcript-third-2016-presidential
-debate-230063.
13. James O'Keefe, Twitter, October 19, 2016, https://twitter.com/jamesokeefeiii/status
/788921688658317313?lang=he.
14. Best Post Debate Clip Ever, YouTube.com, October 20, 2016, https://www.youtube
.com/watch?v=IlyT8wMSZgU.
15. John Wagner, "Clinton Chides Trump as Her Plane Prepares to Leave Las Vegas,"
Washington Post, October 20, 2010, https://www.washingtonpost.com/news
/post-politics/wp/2016/10/20/clinton-chides-trump-as-her-plane-prepares-to-leave
-vegas/?utm_term=.73d2e4349c6d.
16. Steve Eder and Jonathan Martin, "Videos Put Democrats on Defensive about Dirty
Tricks," *New York Times,* October 20, 2016, https://www.nytimes.com/2016/10/21
/us/politics/video-dnc-trump-rallies.html.
17. "Ex-SEAL Marcus Luttrell's Entire GOP Convention Speech," CNN, July 19, 2016,
http://www.cnn.com/videos/politics/2016/07/19/rnc-convention-marcus-luttrell
-navy-seal-veteran-entire-speech.cnn.

Anticipating Hillary

1. Robert Channick, "Sinclair to Buy WGN Owner Tribune Media for $3.9 Billion Plus
Debt," *Chicago Tribune,* May 8, 2017, http://www.chicagotribune.com/business/ct
-sinclair-acquires-tribune-media-0509-biz-20170508-story.html.
2. Marie Brenner, "The Man Who Knew Too Much," *Vanity Fair,* May 1996, http://
www.vanityfair.com/magazine/1996/05/wigand199605.
3. Eric Roth and Michael Mann, *The Insider,* shooting script, http://www.dailyscript
.com/scripts/the-insider_shooting.html.
4. Clarence Jones, *They're Going to Murder You: My Life at the News Front,* rev. 1st
ed., 74–75, ebook.
5. Ibid., 24.
6. Recorded conversation. Name withheld to protect the truth-teller.

Fleeing Philly

1. Project Veritas recording.
2. John Fund, "Holder's Black Panther Stonewall," *Wall Street Journal,* August 20,
2009, https://www.wsj.com/news/articles/SB10001424052970203550604574361071
968458430.
3. Michael Memoli and Christi Parsons, "Obama Tells Trump to 'Stop Whining,'"
Los Angeles Times, October 9, 2016, https://www.pressreader.com/usa/los-angeles
-times/20161019/281513635683082.
4. Darren Samuelsohn, "A Guide to Donald Trump's 'Rigged' Election," Politico, October 25, 2016, http://www.politico.com/story/2016/10/donald-trump-rigged-election
-guide-230302.
5. Miriam Hill, Andrew Seidman, and John Duchneskie, "In 59 Philadelphia Voting Divisions, Mitt Romney Got Zero Votes," Philly.com, November 12, 2012,
http://www.philly.com/philly/news/politics/20121112_In_59_Philadelphia_voting
_wards__Mitt_Romney_got_zero_votes.html.

6. James O'Keefe, Twitter, November 7, 2016, https://twitter.com/jamesokeefeiii/status/795754874227060737.
7. MacGordon, Twitter, November 7, 2016, https://twitter.com/JimmyXJames/status/795758186552659968.
8. Jeremy Stahl, "James O'Keefe Stalks Van of Voters, Alleges Fraud, Is Himself Possibly Breaking Law," *Slate*, November 8, 2016, http://www.slate.com/blogs/the_slatest/2016/11/08/james_o_keefe_creepily_stalks_pastor_s_bus_alleges_improper_behavior.html.
9. John Fund and Hans von Spakovsky, *Who's Counting? How Fraudsters and Bureaucrats Put Your Vote at Risk* (New York: Encounter Books, 2012), 52.
10. Jeremy Stahl, "James O'Keefe Stalks Van of Voters, Alleges Fraud, Is Himself Possibly Breaking Law," *Slate*, November 8, 2016, http://www.slate.com/blogs/the_slatest/2016/11/08/james_o_keefe_creepily_stalks_pastor_s_bus_alleges_improper_behavior.html.
11. Brendan Gauthier, "James O'Keefe Is Spending Election Day Following Vans around Philadelphia," *Salon*, November 8, 2016, http://www.salon.com/2016/11/08/james-okeefe-is-spending-election-day-following-vans-around-philadelphia/.
12. Matt Shuham, "James O'Keefe Spends Election Day Stalking Vans of Voters around Philly," TPM, November 8, 2016, http://talkingpointsmemo.com/livewire/james-o-keefe-following-philadelphia-voter-buses.
13. Brad Reed, "James O'Keefe Films Himself Committing Voter Intimidation by Stalking a Church Van Bringing People to Polls," Raw Story, November 8, 2016, http://www.rawstory.com/2016/11/james-okeefe-films-himself-committing-voter-intimidation-by-stalking-a-church-van-bringing-people-to-polls/.
14. Stahl, *Slate*.
15. Dan Merica, "Pastor Who Endorsed Perry Accused of Breaking Tax Rule," CNN, October 12, 2011, http://religion.blogs.cnn.com/2011/10/12/pastor-who-endorsed-perry-accused-of-breaking-tax-rule/.
16. Josh Hicks, "Political Pastors Openly Defying IRS Rules on Candidate Endorsements," *Washington Post*, November 4, 2014, https://www.washingtonpost.com/news/federal-eye/wp/2014/11/04/political-pastors-defying-irs-rules-on-candidate-endorsements/?utm_term=.6abb1d095d44.
17. "As 2016 Presidential Campaign Gets Under Way, IRS Should Act to Enforce Non-Profit 'No-Politicking' Rule," Americans United for Separation of Church and State, March 26, 2015, https://www.au.org/media/press-releases/as-2016-presidential-campaign-gets-under-way-irs-should-act-to-enforce-non.
18. YouTube.com, https://www.youtube.com/watch?v=-zV2GdctaKU.
19. ACLU, Twitter, November 8, 2017, https://twitter.com/ACLU/status/796080341685510144.
20. FAQs about trends on Twitter, https://support.twitter.com/articles/101125.

Making History

1. Bre Payton, "Watch These Talking Heads Predict a 'Landslide' Clinton Victory," Federalist.com, November 9, 2016, http://thefederalist.com/2016/11/09/watch-the-media-predict-landslide-victory-for-clinton/.
2. *The Circus: Inside the Biggest Story on Earth*, Showtime, Kevin Vargas producer, 2016, http://www.sho.com/the-circus-inside-the-greatest-political-show-on-earth.
3. Jonathan Haidt, *The Righteous Mind: Why Good People Are Divided by Politics and Religion* (New York: Vintage Books, 2013), 86.

Targeting the Media

1. Mark Hensch, "Poll: More Trust Trump WH Than Political Media," The Hill, April 28, 2017, http://thehill.com/homenews/administration/331034-poll-more-trust-trump-wh-than-political-media.
2. "Social Network Advertising Revenue from 2014 to 2017 (in Billion U.S. Dollars)," statista.com, https://www.statista.com/statistics/271406/advertising-revenue-of-social-networks-worldwide/.
3. Thomas Friedman, "Online and Scared," New York Times, January 11, 2017, https://www.nytimes.com/2017/01/11/opinion/online-and-scared.html?mcubz=0&_r=0.
4. Jack Shafer, "Trump Is Now Assigning the News," Politico, January 25, 2017, http://www.politico.com/magazine/story/2017/01/trump-is-now-assigning-the-news-214690.
5. Jennifer Schuessler, "Yes, He Thought Trump Would Win. No, He Didn't Use Hard Data," New York Times, November 9, 2016, https://www.nytimes.com/2016/11/10/arts/yes-he-thought-trump-would-win-no-he-didnt-use-hard-data.html?mcubz=0.
6. Jonathan Martin, "Donald Trump Was Essentially a Third-Party Candidate on a G.O.P. Ticket," New York Times, November 9, 2016, https://www.nytimes.com/2016/11/10/us/politics/donald-trump-gop.html?mcubz=0.
7. Rebecca Savransky, "Tom Hanks Mocks Trump Supporters in 'SNL' Skit," The Hill, October 23, 2016, http://thehill.com/blogs/in-the-know/in-the-know/302375-tom-hanks-plays-trump-supporter-in-saturday-night-live-skit.
8. Will Rahn, "The Unbearable Smugness of the Press," CBS News, November 10, 2016, http://www.cbsnews.com/news/commentary-the-unbearable-smugness-of-the-press-presidential-election-2016/.
9. Gerry Smith, "War Between Trump, Media Seen Escalating with Presidency's Power," Bloomberg.com, November 10, 2016, https://www.bloomberg.com/news/articles/2016-11-10/war-between-trump-media-seen-escalating-with-presidency-s-power.
10. Nicholas Evangelista, "American Pravda: CNN Part 1, Russia Narrative Is All about 'Ratings,'" Project Veritas, June 27, 2017, http://projectveritas.com/2017/06/27/american-pravda-cnn-part-1-russia-narrative-is-all-about-ratings/.
11. Nicholas Kristof, "Lies in the Guise of News in the Trump Era," New York Times, November 12, 2016, https://www.nytimes.com/2016/11/13/opinion/sunday/lies-in-the-guise-of-news-in-the-trump-era.html?mcubz=0&_r=0.
12. Michael Grynbaum, "Trump Strategist Stephen Bannon Says Media Should 'Keep Its Mouth Shut,'" New York Times, January 26, 2017, https://www.nytimes.com/2017/01/26/business/media/stephen-bannon-trump-news-media.html?mcubz=0.
13. Derek Hunter, "The Media Honestly Doesn't Get It," Townhall, January 29, 2017, https://townhall.com/columnists/derekhunter/2017/01/29/the-media-honestly-doesnt-get-it-n2277978.
14. John Schwartz (@john_schwartz), Twitter, November 10, 2016, 10:48 a.m., https://twitter.com/john_schwartz/status/796786641289486338.
15. Dinesh D'Souza (@DineshDSouza), Twitter, May 16, 2017, 3:47 p.m., https://twitter.com/DineshDSouza/status/864613246413787137.
16. Joe Concha, "New York Times Launches Major Ad Campaign: 'The Truth,'" The Hill, February 23, 2017, http://thehill.com/media/320787-new-york-times-launches-major-ad-campaign-the-truth.
17. Robert Kraychik, "Watch CNN's Latest Self-Promotional Ad," Daily Wire, June 7, 2017, http://www.dailywire.com/news/17292/watch-cnns-latest-self-promotional-ad-robert-kraychik.

18. Donald J. Trump (@realDonaldTrump), Twitter.com, February 17, 2017, 1:48 p.m., https://twitter.com/realdonaldtrump/status/832708293516632065?lang=enhttps://twitter.com/realdonaldtrump/status/832708293516632065?lang=en.

Manufacturing Consent

1. Edward S. Herman and Noam Chomsky, *Manufacturing Consent: The Political Economy of the Mass Media* (New York: Knopf Doubleday Publishing, 2002), 2.
2. Ibid., 19.
3. Memorandum of Points and Authorities in Support of Motions to Dismiss by the Project Veritas Defendants, in the United States District Court for the District of Columbia, July 28, 2017.
4. "COMPANY NEWS; Food Lion Stock Falls after Report," *New York Times,* November 7, 1992, http://www.nytimes.com/1992/11/07/business/company-news-food-lion-stock-falls-after-report.html.
5. Jean McNair, "ABC Food Lion Verdict Reversed," *Washington Post,* October 21, 1999, http://www.washingtonpost.com/wp-srv/aponline/19991021/aponline032848_000.htm.
6. Joan Biskupic and Howard Kurtz, "'48 Hours' Wins 11th-Hour Case to Show Undercover Videotape," *Washington Post,* February 10, 1994, https://www.washingtonpost.com/archive/politics/1994/02/10/48-hours-wins-11th-hour-case-to-show-undercover-videotape/06f56302-e2e2-4e5f-b62b-6078f80f3b91/?utm_term=.d0e34b72bd0e.
7. Aly Nielsen, "Nets Protect Their Own: Ignore ABC Defamation Settlement with Beef Company," Newsbusters, July 5, 2017, http://www.newsbusters.org/blogs/business/aly-nielsen/2017/07/05/nets-protect-their-own-ignore-abc-defamation-settlement-beef.
8. Kristine Phillips, "James O'Keefe's Undercover Video Stings Damaged Liberal Icons. Can a New Lawsuit Take Him Down?" *Washington Post,* June 8, 2017, https://www.washingtonpost.com/news/the-fix/wp/2017/06/08/james-okeefes-undercover-video-stings-damaged-liberal-icons-can-a-new-lawsuit-take-him-down/?utm_term=.3e11c11f4ad1.
9. *Project Veritas Action Fund v. Conley,* Law360, https://www.law360.com/cases/56d9fe9a4f4e7e28ba000001.
10. *Glik v. Cuniffe,* FindLaw, http://caselaw.findlaw.com/us-1st-circuit/1578557.html.
11. Editorial Board, "The Success of the Voter Fraud Myth," *New York Times,* September 19, 2016, https://www.nytimes.com/2016/09/20/opinion/the-success-of-the-voter-fraud-myth.html?_r=0.
12. Steve Klein, "Project Veritas Action v. Conley: Undercover Newsgathering and the First Amendment," Federalist Society, March 2, 2016, http://www.fed-soc.org/blog/detail/project-veritas-action-v-conley-undercover-newsgathering-and-the-first-amendment.

Freezing the "Anti-Fascist" Fascists

1. Sarah Jaffe, "DisruptJ20 Plans Resistance from Day One," The Progressive, January 19, 2017, http://progressive.org/multimedia/legba-carrefour/.
2. Mark Segrave, "Comet Ping Pong Case Moved to Federal Court," NBCWashington.com, http://www.nbcwashington.com/news/local/Man-Who-Fired-Shots-in-Comet-Ping-Pong-Expected-in-Court-406223705.html.
3. "Part I: Undercover Investigation Exposes Groups Plotting Criminal Activity at Trump Inauguration," YouTube.com, https://www.youtube.com/watch?v=MHZSfhd1X_8.

Disrupting the Disruption

1. "Part II: NEW Investigation Uncovers Plot to Chain the Trains & Shut Down DC During Inauguration," YouTube.com, https://www.youtube.com/watch?v=xIjbkYLI 1nY.
2. Ibid.
3. Ibid.
4. "Over-the-Top Anti-Trump Protesters Intimidate and Harass Young Female Journalist," YouTube.com, January 31, 2017, https://www.youtube.com/watch?v=68i0b d2BIKk.
5. Kerry Picket, "Netroots Nation Attendees Ambush Breitbart," *Washington Times,* June 17, 2011, http://www.washingtontimes.com/blog/watercooler/2011/jun/17/pick et-video-netroots-nation-attendees-ambush-brei/.
6. Project Veritas recording.
7. "DisruptJ20 Releases Statement on Project Veritas Video," January 16, 2017, http://www.disruptj20.org/media/vertas/.
8. Steven Nelson, "Anti-Trump DisruptJ20 Activists Scale Back Inauguration Blockade Plans," January 17, 2017, usnews.com, https://www.usnews.com/news /articles/2017-01-17/anti-trump-disruptj20-activists-scale-back-inauguration-block ade-plans.
9. Andrea Noble, "Police: Arrested Activist Featured in Project Veritas Inauguration Video," *Washington Times,* January 20, 2017, http://www.washingtontimes.com /news/2017/jan/20/police-arrested-activist-scott-ryan-charney-featur/.
10. Peter Hermann, "Meetings of Activists Planning to Disrupt Inauguration Were Infiltrated by Conservative Group," *Washington Post,* January 25, 2017, https://www .washingtonpost.com/local/public-safety/meetings-of-activists-planning-to-disrupt -inauguration-were-infiltrated-by-conservative-media-group/2017/01/24/b22128fe -e19a-11e6-ba11-63c4b4fb5a63_story.html?utm_term=.806d5c58a7e5.

Backtracking in Wisconsin

1. Jason Stein and Patrick Marley, "Attorney General May Investigate Secret Video," *Milwaukee Journal Sentinel,* October 20 2016, http://www.jconline.com/story /news/politics/elections/2016/10/20/attorney-general-examining-secret-video/9247 5526/.
2. Patrick Marley, "Wisconsin DOJ: James O'Keefe's Project Veritas Tape Did Not Show Election Law Violations," *Milwaukee Journal Sentinel,* April 25, 2017, http:// www.jsonline.com/story/news/politics/2017/04/25/wisconsin-doj-james-okeefes -project-veritas-tape-did-not-show-election-law-violations/100885192/.
3. Ibid.
4. "O'Keefe Confronts WI AG's Unfounded Attack on PVA," YouTube, April 27, 2017, https://www.youtube.com/watch?v=7BlgTGK_mtI.
5. Patrick Marley, "Conservative James O'Keefe Threatens to Investigate Attorney General Brad Schimel over Video Flap," *Milwaukee Journal Sentinel,* April 27, 2017, http://www.jsonline.com/story/news/politics/2017/04/27/conservative-james-ok eefe-threatens-investigate-wisconsin-attorney-general-brad-schimel-over-video-flap /100968610/.
6. James O'Keefe, Twitter, April 27, 2017, https://twitter.com/Lauren_Nann/status/85 7648595268448256.
7. Lauren Nann, Twitter, April 27, 2017, https://twitter.com/Lauren_Nann/status/85 7648595268448256.

8. Matthew Jacobs, Twitter, April 27, 2017, April 27, 2017, https://twitter.com/Lauren_Nann/status/857648595268448256 https://twitter.com/jamesokeefeiii/status/857648238308052992.

9. Andrew Beckett, "Schimel Defends Decision to Drop Investigation of Activist Video," WRN, April 27, 2017, http://www.wrn.com/2017/04/schimel-defends-decision-to-drop-investigation-of-activist-video/.

10. "Sen. Mike Ellis (R-WI) Investigation," Project Veritas, http://projectveritas.com/senator-mike-ellis-investigation/.

11. Patrick Marley, "Wisconsin Attorney General Brad Schimel Contradicts Self, Says Voter Fraud Probe Is Open," *Milwaukee Journal Sentinel,* April 28, 2017, http://www.jsonline.com/story/news/politics/2017/04/28/wisconsin-attorney-general-brad-schimel-schimel-contradicts-office-says-voter-fraud-probe-open/101034286/.

12. James O'Keefe, Twitter, April 28, 2017, https://twitter.com/jamesokeefeiii/status/858023397426683904?lang=ca.

13. Ernst-Ulrich Franzen, "What Game Is Schimel Playing?" *Milwaukee Journal Sentinel,* April 28, 2017, http://www.jsonline.com/story/opinion/blogs/real-time/2017/04/28/what-game-schimel-playing/101046352/.

Editing the News

1. Nicholas Kristof, "Lies in the Guise of News in the Trump Era," *New York Times,* November 12, 2016, https://www.nytimes.com/2016/11/13/opinion/sunday/lies-in-the-guise-of-news-in-the-trump-era.html?_r=0.

2. David Bauder, "Jon Stewart's Satirical Barbs Draw Viewers, Emmy Notice," Associated Press, August 4, 2003, http://the.honoluluadvertiser.com/article/2003/Aug/04/il/il05a.html.

3. Eric Alterman, "The Real 'Fake News,'" *Nation,* May 7, 2007, https://www.thenation.com/article/real-fake-news/.

4. Christopher Hitchens, "The Lies of Michael Moore," *Slate,* June 21, 2004, http://www.slate.com/articles/news_and_politics/fighting_words/2004/06/unfairenheit_911.html.

5. Stephanie Soechtig and Katie Couric, *Under the Gun,* 2016, http://underthegunmovie.com.

6. Stephen Gutowski, "Audio Shows Katie Couric Documentary Deceptively Edited Interview with Pro-Gun Activists," *Washington Free Beacon,* May 25, 2016, http://freebeacon.com/issues/audio-shows-katie-couric-gun-documentary-deceptively-edited-interview-pro-gun-activists/.

7. Katie Rogers, "Audio of Katie Couric Interview Shows Editing Slant in Gun Documentary, Site Claims," *New York Times,* May 25, 2016, https://www.nytimes.com/2016/05/26/business/media/audio-of-couric-interview-shows-editing-slant-in-documentary-site-claims.html.

8. Mureen Ballezza and Kate Zernike, "Memos on Bush Are Fake but Accurate, Typist Says," *New York Times,* September 15, 2004.

9. Jonathan Last, "What Blogs Have Wrought," *Weekly Standard,* September 27, 2004, http://www.weeklystandard.com/article/5857.

10. Greg Miller and Greg Jaffe, "Trump Revealed Highly Classified Information to Russian Foreign Minister and Ambassador," *Washington Post,* May 15, 2017, https://www.washingtonpost.com/world/national-security/trump-revealed-highly-classified-information-to-russian-foreign-minister-and-ambassador/2017/05/15/530c172a-3960-11e7-9e48-c4f199710b69_story.html?utm_term=.c788dcbe00f7.

11. Daniel Greenfield, "The Anonymous Sources of Washington Post and CNN Fake News," FrontPage Mag, May 18, 2017, http://www.frontpagemag.com/fpm/266714 /anonymous-sources-washington-post-and-cnn-fake-daniel-greenfield.

12. Andrew Ferguson, "The Kiss-Up That Wasn't," *Weekly Standard,* June 26, 2017, http://www.weeklystandard.com/the-kiss-up-that-wasnt/article/2008488.

Attacking Fox

1. Thomas Patterson, "News Coverage of Donald Trump's First 100 Days," Shoren-stein Center, May 18, 2007, https://shorensteincenter.org/news-coverage-donald -trumps-first-100-days/?utm_source=POLITICO.EU&utm_campaign=ab6d83 0a9d-EMAIL_CAMPAIGN_2017_05_19&utm_medium=email&utm_term =0_10959edeb5-ab6d830a9d-189799085.

2. Peter Drivas, "Obama Hits Fox News: They're 'Entirely Devoted to Attacking My Administration'—Fox News Responds," *Huffington Post,* June 16, 2009, http://www .huffingtonpost.com/2009/06/16/obama-hits-fox-news-theyr_n_216574.html.

3. Jann Wenner, "Obama in Command: The Rolling Stone Interview," *Rolling Stone,* October 14, 2010, http://www.rollingstone.com/politics/news/obama-in-command -br-the-rolling-stone-interview-20100928.

4. "Soros Gives $1 million to Media Matters," Politico, October 20, 2010, http://www .politico.com/blogs/onmedia/1010/Soros_gives_1_million_to_Media_Matters.html.

5. Ann Marimow, "A Rare Peek into a Justice Department Leak Probe," *Washing-ton Post,* May 19, 2013, http://www.washingtonpost.com/local/a-rare-peek-into-a -justice-department-leak-probe/2013/05/19/0bc473de-be5e-11e2-97d4-a479289 a31f9_story.html?tid=pm_pop.

6. Jann Wenner, "The Day After: Obama on His Legacy, Trump's Win and the Path Forward," *Rolling Stone,* November 29, 2016, http://www.rollingstone.com/politics /features/obama-on-his-legacy-trumps-win-and-the-path-forward-w452527.

7. Sharyl Attkisson, *The Smear: How Shady Political Operatives and Fake News Con-trol What You See, What You Think, and How You Vote* (New York: HarperCollins, 2017), 69.

8. Emily Steel and Michael Schmidt, "Bill O'Reilly Thrives at Fox News, Even as Harassment Settlements Add Up," *New York Times,* April 1, 2017, https://www.ny times.com/2017/04/01/business/media/bill-oreilly-sexual-harassment-fox-news.html.

9. Emily Steel and Michael Schmidt, "Bill O'Reilly Is Forced Out at FoxNews," *New York Times,* April 19, 2017, https://www.nytimes.com/2017/04/19/business/media /bill-oreilly-fox-news-allegations.html?action=click&contentCollection=Media&mo dule=RelatedCoverage&region=EndOfArticle&pgtype=article.

10. "Debbie Schlussel Accuses Sean Hannity of Sexual Harassment," *Pat Camp-bell Podcast,* April 21, 2017, https://art19.com/shows/pat-campbell-podcast/epi sodes/6a6aad9e-7c69-489d-8731-5273d1ee23ee.

11. Corky Siemaszko, "Sean Hannity Denies Right-Wing Blogger's Sex Harassment Claim," NBC News, April 24, 2017, https://www.nbcnews.com/news/us-news/sean -hannity-denies-right-wing-blogger-s-sex-harassment-claim-n750211.

12. Mandy Mayfield, "Liberal Watchdog Group Defends Promotion of Sean Hannity Boycott," *Washington Examiner,* May 27, 2017, http://www.washingtonexaminer .com/liberal-watchdog-group-defends-promotion-of-sean-hannity-boycott/article /2624339.

13. Joe Concha, "Hannity on Attempted Advertiser Boycott: 'Nobody Tells Me What to Say on My Show,'" The Hill, May 24, 2017, http://thehill.com/homenews/media /335054-hannity-nobody-tells-me-what-to-say-on-my-show.

14. Michael Nunez, "Former Facebook Workers: We Routinely Suppressed Conserva-tive News," Gizmodo, May 9, 2016, http://gizmodo.com/former-facebook-workers-we-routinely-suppressed-conser-1775461006.

15. Tom Warren, "Read Google CEO's Email to Staff about Engineer's Inflammatory Memo," The Verge, August 8, 2017, https://www.theverge.com/2017/8/8/16111724/google-sundar-pichai-employee-memo-diversity.

16. David Streifeld, "'The Internet Is Broken': @ev Is Trying to Salvage It," New York Times, May 17, 2017, https://www.nytimes.com/2017/05/20/technology/evan-williams-.

American Pravda

1. Callum Borchers, "CNN's President Has Fired a Warning Shot at Donald Trump," Washington Post, January 19, 2017, https://www.washingtonpost.com/news/the-fix/wp/2017/01/19/cnns-president-has-fired-a-warning-shot-at-donald-trump/?utm_term=.c5079e8e90c5.

2. YouTube, January 19, 2017, https://www.youtube.com/watch?v=HhoVnxYe6sQ.

3. Thomas Patterson, "News Coverage of Donald Trump's First 100 Days," Shorenstein Center, May 18, 2007.

4. Herman Wong, "CNN Cuts Ties with Kathy Griffin amid Controversy over Come-dian's Gruesome Anti-Trump Photo," Washington Post, May 31, 2017, https://www.washingtonpost.com/news/arts-and-entertainment/wp/2017/05/30/kathy-griffin-apologizes-for-severed-donald-trump-head-photo-after-backlash/?utm_term=.1e977d3a8db4.

5. Avi Seik, "Reza Aslan Becomes the Second CNN Personality Dumped after Attack-ing Trump," Washington Post, June 10, 2017, https://www.washingtonpost.com/news/arts-and-entertainment/wp/2017/06/10/reza-aslan-becomes-the-second-cnn-personality-dumped-after-attacking-trump/?utm_term=.9232d52f544c.

6. Michael Grynbaum, "3 CNN Journalists Resign after Retracted Story on Trump Ally," New York Times, June 26, 2017, https://www.nytimes.com/2017/06/26/business/3-cnn-journalists-resign-after-retracted-story-on-trump-ally.html?mcubz=0.

7. James O'Keefe, Twitter, June 26, 2017, https://twitter.com/jamesokeefeiii/status/879492066593656832?lang=en.

8. Paul Lee, Twitter, June 27, 2017, https://twitter.com/PaulLee85/status/879712053950169088.

9. Nicholas Evangelista, "American Pravda: CNN Part 1, Russia Narrative Is All About 'Ratings,'" Project Veritas, June 27, 2017, http://projectveritas.com/2017/06/27/american-pravda-cnn-part-1-russia-narrative-is-all-about-ratings/.

10. A. J. Katz, "April 2017 Ratings: CNN Scores with Younger Viewers," Adweek, May 2, 2017, http://www.adweek.com/tvnewser/april-2017-ratings-adults-25-54-are-flocking-to-cnn-across-total-day/328260.

11. Donald J. Trump (@realDonaldTrump), Twitter.com, June 27, 2017, 5:30 a.m., https://twitter.com/realDonaldTrump/status/879678356450676736?ref_src=twsrc%5Etfw&ref_url=http%3A%2F%2Fwww.politifact.com%2Ftruth-o-meter%2Farticle%2F2017%2Fjun%2F29%2Fwhite-house-plugs-anti-cnn-video-undercover-group%2F.

12. Eddie Scarry, "Sarah Sanders: CNN a 'Disgrace' to Journalism," Washington Exam-iner, June 27, 2017, http://www.washingtonexaminer.com/sarah-sanders-cnn-a-disgrace-to-journalism/article/2627242.

13. Brian Stelter, Twitter, Jue 27, 2017, https://twitter.com/brianstelter/status/879752371588485122?lang=en.

14. James O'Keefe, Twitter, June 27, 2017, https://twitter.com/jamesokeefeiii/status/879 753000302108674?lang=en.

15. Brian Stelter, Twitter, June 27, 2017, https://twitter.com/brianstelter/status/8797524 81516945409?lang=en.

16. Paul Farhi, "What the Latest James O'Keefe Video Leaves Out," *Washington Post,* June 28, 2017, https://www.washingtonpost.com/lifestyle/style/what-you-dont-see-in -okeefe-video-may-be-as-important-as-what-you-do/2017/06/28/dcb67446-5b7c -11e7-a9f6-7c3296387341_story.html?utm_term=.674bb2944360.

17. Janene, Twitter, June 28, 2017, https://twitter.com/justsickoflies.

18. J. Christian Adams, "Civility: *Washington Post* Reporter Tells Fact-Checking James O'Keefe Fan to 'Drop Dead,'" PJ Media, June 29, 2017, https://pjmedia.com /jchristianadams/2017/06/29/civility-washington-post-reporter-tells-fact-checking -james-okeefe-fan-to-drop-dead/.

19. Paul Fahri, Twitter, June 28, 2017, https://twitter.com/farhip/status/8801990034675 46624?lang=en.

20. "American Pravda: CNN Part 2," YouTube.com, https://www.youtube.com/watch ?v=l2G360HrSAs.

21. Lisa de Moraes, "Van Jones Slams 'Edited Right Wing Propaganda,'" Deadline, June 29, 2017, http://deadline.com/2017/06/van-jones-slams-right-wing-video-james-oke efe-donald-trump-russia-nothing-burger-1202122399/.

22. Old McDonalds, Twitter.com, https://twitter.com/argmachinetv?lang=en.

23. Not Pax Dickinson, Twitter, June 28, 2017, https://twitter.com/NotPaxDickinson /status/880165030951571456 (account suspended at this time).

24. WikiLeaks FF, Twitter.com, https://twitter.com/rhondaroseflora?lang=en.

25. James O'Keefe, Twitter, June 28, 2017, https://twitter.com/jamesokeefeiii/status /880118120979079168.

26. Nicholas Evangelista, "American Pravda Part 3: CNN Selectively Edits, Hates Trump, and Think Voters Are Stupid," Project Veritas, June 30, 2017, http://project veritas.com/2017/06/30/american-pravda-part-3-cnn-selectively-edits-hates-trump -and-think-voters-are-stupid/.

27. James O'Keefe, Twitter, June 28, 2017, https://twitter.com/JamesOKeefeIII/status /880756674696445952.

28. Cali Deplorable, Twitter.com, https://twitter.com/calideplorable1.

29. Jayne720, Twitter.com, https://twitter.com/search?q=%40Jayne720&src=typd.

30. Jenn Stitts, Twitter.com, https://twitter.com/search?q=Jenn%20Stitts&src=typd.

31. James O'Keefe, Twitter, June 28, 2017, https://twitter.com/JamesOKeefeIII/status /880756674696445952.

32. Jensen MAGAISMEGA, Twitter, July 1, 2017, https://twitter.com/S_L_J730/status /881220576039378944.

33. Paul Joseph Watson, Twitter, June 30, 2017, https://twitter.com/PrisonPlanet/status /880779002348273664.

34. Deplorable Shay, Twitter.com, June 30, 2017, https://twitter.com/DeplorableShay /status/880848101086515201.

35. Anthony Spano, June 30, 2017, https://twitter.com/Spone63/status/88080918364 1292800.

36. William Rogers, Twitter, June 30, 2017, https://twitter.com/Wtrogers4/status/88081 0449888985092.

37. John Giglio, Twitter, June 30, 2017, https://twitter.com/lilium479/status/88077261 6151281665.

38. Linda Whidby, June 30, 2017, https://twitter.com/mrstsw01/status/880768842267 578368.

39. Alisyn Camerota, "Why I'm Breaking Up with Twitter," CNN.com, July 12, 2017, http://www.cnn.com/2017/07/11/opinions/dear-twitter-were-done-camerota-opin ion/index.html.

40. Stefan Molyneux, Twitter, June 29, 2017, https://twitter.com/stefanmolyneux/status /880508666645970944.

41. Law and Order USA, Twitter.com, https://twitter.com/search?src=typd&q=Law%20 and%20Order%20USA.

42. Andrew Kaczynski, "How CNN Found the Reddit User behind the Trump Wres- tling GIF," CNN Politics, July 5, 2017, http://www.cnn.com/2017/07/04/politics/kfile -reddit-user-trump-tweet/index.html.

43. Ibid.

44. Julian Assange, Twitter, July 4, 2017, https://twitter.com/julianassange/status/88244 0859370868737?lang=en.

45. Joe Simonson, "CNN Threatens a Trump Troll," *National Review,* July 5, 2017, Read more at: http://www.nationalreview.com/article/449235/cnn-vs-reddit-user-trump -wrestling-meme.

46. Daniel Victor, "CNN Story about Source of Trump Wrestling Video Draws Back- lash," *New York Times,* July 5, 2017, https://www.nytimes.com/2017/07/05/business /media/cnn-trump-tweet.html?mcubz=0.

47. Ben Smith, Twitter.com, July 5, 2017, https://twitter.com/buzzfeedben/status/8825 90713472368642.

48. Michael Grynbaum, "CNN Story about Source of Trump Wrestling Video Draws Backlash," *New York Times,* July 5, 2017, https://www.nytimes.com/2017/07/05/busi ness/media/cnn-trump-tweet.html?mcubz=0.

49. Ibid.

50. Donald J. Trump, Twitter, July 1, 2017, https://twitter.com/realdonaldtrump/status /881138485905772549?lang=en.

51. James O'Keefe, Twitter, July 1, 207, https://twitter.com/jamesokeefeiii/status/881164 916920659973?lang=en.

52. Donald J. Trump, Twitter, June 27, 2017, https://twitter.com/realdonaldtrump/status /879682547235651584?lang=en.

53. "American Pravda, NYT: Slanting the News and a Bizarre Comey Connection," Proj- ect Veritas, October 10, 2017, https://breaking.projectveritas.com/NYTimes1.html.

54. "Ethical Journalism, a Handbook of Values and Practices for the News and Editorial Departments," *New York Times,* September 2004, #6.

55. "American Pravda, NYT: Slanting the News and a Bizarre Comey Connection," Proj- ect Veritas, October 10, 2017, https://breaking.projectveritas.com/NYTimes1.html.

56. "Ethical Journalism," #62.

57. "The Times Responds to Project Veritas Video," *New York Times,* October 10, 2017, https://www.nytimes.com/2017/10/10/reader-center/project-veritas-video.html.

58. "American Pravda, NYT Part II: Exploiting Social Media and Manipulating the News," Project Veritas, October 12, 2017, https://breaking.projectveritas.com/NY Times2.html.

59. "Our Values," YouTube.com, https://www.youtube.com/yt/impactlab/about/.

60. "Covering the Trump White House | TimesTalks," YouTube.com, September 12, 2017, https://www.youtube.com/watch?v=73KabgPLIf0.

61. Michael Shear and Michael Barbaro, "In Video Clip, Romney Calls 47% 'Depen- dent' and Feeling Entitled," *New York Times,* September 17, 2012, https://thecaucus .blogs.nytimes.com/2012/09/17/romney-faults-those-dependent-on-government/? _r=0.

62. Alexander Burns, Maggie Haberman, and Jonathan Martin, "Donald Trump Apology Caps Day of Outrage over Lewd Tape," *New York Times,* October 7, 2016, https://www.nytimes.com/2016/10/08/us/politics/donald-trump-women.html?action =click&contentCollection=U.S.&module=RelatedCoverage&region=EndOfArticle &pgtype=article.

63. Marisa Guthrie, "Donald Trump, 'Access Hollywood' and 'The Apprentice': The Legal Issues Behind the Tapes," *Hollywood Reporter,* October 9, 2016, http://www .hollywoodreporter.com/thr-esq/donald-trump-access-hollywood-apprentice-93 6660.

64. Tony Romm, "Mitt Recording May Have Been Illegal," Politico, September 18, 2012, https://breaking.projectveritas.com/NYTimesResponse.html.

65. James Rainey, "The Truth behind the 'Khalidi Video' and Why It's Not for Sale," *Los Angeles Times,* September 21, 2012, http://articles.latimes.com/2012/sep/21/news /la-pn-khalidi-video-not-for-sale-20120921.

66. "New York Times Changes Social Media Policy after Claims of Bias," NPR, October 19, 2017, http://www.wbur.org/hereandnow/2017/10/19/new-york-times-social -media-trump.

67. "The Times Issues Social Media Guidelines for the Newsroom," *New York Times,* October 13, 2017, https://www.nytimes.com/2017/10/13/reader-center/social-media -guidelines.html?_r=0.

68. Karol Markowicz, "The Times' New Policy to Hide Reporters' Bias," *New York Post,* October 15, 2017, http://nypost.com/2017/10/15/the-times-new-policy-to-hide -reporters-bias/.

69. The Kalb Report: Guardians of the Fourth Estate, YouTube.com, October 16, 2017, https://www.youtube.com/watch?v=-VzXvexiDZw.

70. "Senior Homepage Editor Reveals Biased Political Agenda at New York Times," Project Veritas, October 17, https://breaking.projectveritas.com/NYTimes3.html.

71. "Shock Treatment," Snopes.com, http://www.snopes.com/mike-pence-supported -gay-conversion-therapy/.

72. "American Pravda, NYT Part IV," October 19, 2017, Project Veritas, http://project veritas.com/2017/10/19/american-pravda-nyt-part-iv-new-york-times-company-cul ture-revealed-everyone-hates-trump/.

73. Erin Gloria Ryan, Twitter, October 19, 2017, https://twitter.com/morninggloria /status/921015968939298816.

Index